IN SEARCH
St Walstan

East Anglia's Enduring Legend

Carol Twinch

FIRST EDITION 1995

Front cover by The Boardroom Design Studio
based on a stained glass window at the Church of St. Mary, Kenninghall, Norfolk
by permission of Kings of Norwich.

Published by Media Associates, Norwich, Norfolk

Printed and bound by The Lavenham Press, Lavenham, Suffolk

ISBN 0 9521499 1 5

CONTENTS

LIST OF ILLUSTRATIONS

A copy of the **1864 leaflet** poking fun at the Monk's Pilgrimage led by 'Father' Ignatius. This is reproduced from a copy taken by the author of an original held in the Norfolk Local Studies Library, Norwich, which is believed to have been destroyed in the fire of 1994. (Norfolk Studies Library)   *116*

1989 pilgrimage: The Bishop of Norwich addresses pilgrims in May, 1989, whose pilgrimage from Taverham to Bawburgh was in celebration of British Food & Farming Year. (Betty Martins)   *124*

AND **The Rongaian Church of St. Walstan** was built in the 1950s in the form of a solid stone cruciform edifice said to remind the settlers of their Scottish origins. (Peter and Margot Markham)

The modern **Worship Centre** at Bowthorpe (top) is built alongside the ruins of the ancient Church of **St. Michael** (below).   *128*

St. Andrew's at Walberswick is the last of three churches to have been built in the parish. Beside it can still be seen the ruins of the second church which was the site for 'Seynt Walsteneys Wyndown'. (Byron E. Bellows)   *136*

AND **Taverham's village sign**, carved by Harry Carter, was presented by members of the Women's Institute in 1970, and uses the Medieval representation of Walstan at Barnham Broom as the model.

The only known Medieval wall painting depicting St. Walstan is at **St. Andrew's, Cavenham**. Although it was discovered in 1967, it remained unidentified for almost twenty years.   *140*

An early 20th-century carving at **Gaywood**, Norfolk, which is unique in that a dog has been placed at the feet of St. Walstan and he carries a staff and bible.   *142*

A modern representation of St. Walstan, this at **Great Ryburgh**, Norfolk, is one of only two which use the spade as his specific emblem instead of the traditional scythe. (Betty Martins)   *144*

The panels of St. Blida and St. Walstan now at the Church of St. Mary Magdalene, Norwich, are the only known example of the two saints in the same location.   *153*

The sign for Easton College portrays Walstan's last journey and incorporates the essence of the region's farming activities. (Easton College)   *162*

In 1981 a **carved figure of St. Walstan** was dedicated at Bawburgh in memory of Miss Margaret Young. It now stands in the north-east section of the nave – the old entrance to the Shrine Chapel.   *IBC*

Except where otherwise stated, the photographs are the copyright of the author.

INTRODUCTION

*T*HERE IS, in Norfolk, a site of religious pilgrimage even older than that at Walsingham. It is not as famous or renowned as Walsingham, but the story of St. Walstan of Bawburgh, Confessor, has nonetheless offered spiritual encouragement and inspiration to countless pilgrims for nearly one thousand years. From its beginnings in the last days of Anglo Saxon England, the legend of St. Walstan survived to enjoy the heydays of Medieval pilgrimages. In spite of its desecration by Henry VIII – and it fared little better under the Cromwellian scourge of the churches – the cult endured, living on through the bloody and treacherous reign of Mary I to become established, with the Church of England, under Elizabeth I. On and on, through the sixteenth, seventeenth and eighteenth centuries, the story of Walstan thrived and drew generations of pilgrims to the Holy Well of Bawburgh. And now – most relevantly – in modern times, when the basic concepts of Christianity are questioned, and the world appears stricken by turmoil and human crisis, this most humble of saints is still celebrated in religious services which have united Catholic, Protestant and Non-Conformist in prayer.

The most recent milestone in this long history took place in 1988, when Archdeacon Antony Foottit suggested that St. Walstan, by way of his traditional association with agriculture and farm workers, be adopted as Patron Saint of British Food & Farming Year, due to take place during 1989. The seeds of inquisitiveness were thus sown for a new generation of pilgrims, such recognition being endorsed by Norwich Diocesan Board of Social Responsibility which nominated 1989 to be 'St. Walstan's Year'. At Bowthorpe, in January of that year, a Prayer Cell was dedicated in the name of St. Walstan.

It was as Editor of the *Bawburgh News* that in 1989 I supervised the publication of *Walstan of Bawburgh*, though it was really little more than an extended village guide. Re-reading it only a year later, errors of fact and obvious omissions jumped off the pages. After all, when it came down to it, how much did we really know about St. Walstan? In over nine hundred years, just two primary sources had emerged from the writings of narrators, historians and hagiographers down the centuries: one was the *Sanctilogium*, a manuscript in Latin by the fourteenth-century monk, John of Tynemouth; the second an 'English Life', an intriguing copy of 'an ancient triptych', made in 1658. These two lives, the Latin and the English, were the basis for the Walstan legend which has persisted for over nine centuries.

Since *Walstan of Bawburgh*, I have moved from Norfolk back to my native Suffolk, but during the fifteen years that my husband and I lived and farmed in Bawburgh my file on 'St. W' had grown fat. What was to be done with it all? The *Bawburgh News* was a means of recording much of it, but that was a community magazine, not a newsletter for Walstanians.

Nothing was decided until a visit to the Church of the Assumption of the Blessed Virgin Mary in Bury St. Edmunds, in search of, not St. Walstan, but Edmund, King and Martyr. Coming as I do from Hoxne, the story of England's former Patron Saint was as familiar as that of St. Walstan, and there were new discoveries being made at Hoxne in that connection. Yet it was there, in the very heart of Edmundsbury, that I chanced upon a Chapel dedicated to St. Walstan. Did this mean that those historians who had waved Walstan aside as 'local' and 'without substance' were wrong? A fuller investigation into the legend of St. Walstan was, then, clearly unavoidable.

The most accessible place to start the new search was with Carl Horstman's 1901 edition of the sixteenth-century compendium of saints' lives, *Nova Legenda Anglie*, where a footnote immediately threw into confusion one of the accepted primary sources, namely the *Sanctilogium*. Then there was a reference to another fourteenth-century attempt to collect the lives of English saints, extant as MS. Lansdowne 436, which had in it forty-seven lives, one of them *Wlstanus*. Furthermore, this second MS was unknown to the fourteenth-century monk, John of Tynemouth, the original author of the *Sanctilogium*, on which the *Nova Legenda Anglie* was based, and who is traditionally Walstan's first biographer. It remained to be seen whether MS Landsdowne could add to the Walstan legend, or whether a mistake had been made with the name, a phenomenon by no means restricted to the twentieth century. Perhaps there were two Walstans; certainly there was more than one Wulfstan, a name often confused with Walstan.

A year after finding the Bury Chapel, it was with no small measure of amateur enthusiasm that I was admitted to Lambeth Palace Library to see for myself the sixteenth-century copy of an ancient triptych which contained the English Life. Inevitably, this document raised more intrigue than it solved, while later discoveries of a Medieval wall painting of St. Walstan in West Suffolk, and a rood screen representation in Essex, took the search beyond its previously accepted boundaries.

In Search of St. Walstan does not set out to prove or disprove any of the versions of his life, of which there are at least forty, since they differ but marginally in their text. Some contain interesting details which seem to derive purely from the imagination of the writer, while others vary only slightly from the Latin or English Lives. Whether or not the stories are merely interpretive, symbolic, opinion, or pure fantasy, hardly matters. What does matter is how and when the legend of Walstan was established and why it grew and flourished to such an extent that by the thirteenth century, there were six Chantry Priests in attendance at the Norfolk Shrine. The question of why St. Walstan continues to be talked and written about now, almost at the end of the twentieth century, also needs to be addressed, since it could reasonably be argued that to take such matters seriously in today's world is at least naive.

Such whys and wherefores are fascinating to anyone with even a passing interest in local or church history, but an observer could be forgiven for thinking that there is a limit to the amount of digging which can be done around a well-worn and ancient legend which derives from a small village. There is usually, in such cases, an exhaustable amount of material. In regard to St. Walstan, and the absorbing history of Bawburgh village, this is simply not so. An infinite, daunting trail of forgotten history lay before the chronicler in search of St. Walstan, East Anglia's Patron Saint of Farm Workers. In order that this book might finally be 'finished', and so published, only a portion of the available material is contained here and it is no exaggeration to say that the surface is still only scratched. One day, a new book will emerge, from another author, to throw a different – and more academic – light on the story of St. Walstan and this search will be considered as the spadework. There will be some criticism of the lack of footnotes, but all sources are indexed fully in the bibliography and quotes are attributed in context.

A survey (Appendix I), carried out principally by the current editor of *Bawburgh News*, Betty Martins, results in a comprehensive gazetteer of representations of St. Walstan and St. Blida in East Anglia, and logs for the first time several dedications made this century. It also brings together the iconography of St. Walstan found in churches of differing denominations in the spirit of ecumenicalism which is itself a feature of the Bawburgh legend. Where possible, each example of the East Anglian imagery has been verified by either Betty or the author and investigations are continuing into a claim that an effigy of Walstan can be found atop All Saints Church, Gresford, in Clwyd.

In addition to Betty, I would like to thank the following for their help and advice:

Dr. David Rollason, University of Durham; Melanie Barber, Lambeth Palace Library; Rosemary CE Hayes, The Royal Commission on Historical Manuscripts; Dr. Martin Kauffmann, Bodleian Library; Dr. W.J. Blair, Oxford University; Dr. Mark Nicholls, Department of Manuscripts and University Archives, Cambridge University Library; Dr. Paul Bibire, Department of Anglo Saxon, Norse and Celtic, University of Cambridge;

Margaret Smith, Reading County Library; Clive Paine; J. Conway and Miss
J.M. Backhouse, British Library; Mrs. Margaret Osborne, Bishop's House,
Northampton; Mrs. Elsie Berwick (for the story of St. James); Mrs. Dora
Cowton, St. John's Cathedral; Mr. Christopher Hohler, Oslo; Richard
Butler-Stoney; Mrs. E.M. Stilgoe (Round Tower Churches Society); Dennis
King, Kings of Norwich; Miss Miriam Gill (for details of the Cavenham
wall painting); Dr. David Park, Courtauld Institute of Art; Br. Francis, S.A.,
Catholic Central Library; Rev. Dr. E.C. Brooks; Robert Halliday; Ernest
Gage, and Merle Tidey.

Thanks also to Margot and Peter Markham of Great Melton, who visited
the Church of St. Walstan in Rongai, Kenya, in 1985 and who made available
the description of the African community and photograph (page 128).

Appreciation is especially due to the ladies of Woodbridge Library,
who patiently filled in the appropriate forms in order to comb the libraries
of Britain for obscure and elderly books on the lives of the saints; also
library staff at Bury St. Edmunds, Lowestoft, Ipswich and Norwich Record
Offices.

Grateful thanks are extended to Dr. Rollason, Betty Martins and Clive
Paine who kindly read part or all of the book, prior to publication, and who
gave advice or additional information. However, any mistakes, uncertainties
or inaccuracies which occur belong solely to the author.

In conclusion, my thanks are due to my husband, Christopher, who
proof-read the book and who accompanied me on numerous excursions into
the East Anglian countryside and beyond in search of St. Walstan.

CT
1994

Chapter One
THE LEGEND

'... Whoever of you does not renounce all that he has cannot be
my disciple.' Luke, Chapter 14:33

The following is the popular legend of St. Walstan of Bawburgh. Some
forty or fifty different 'lives' of Walstan have evolved into the twentieth
century, but the common elements of this version are taken chiefly
from the two accepted 'Primary' lives of St. Walstan. The first is the
Latin Life, published in the 1516 *Nova Legenda Anglie* (NLA) and
re-published in 1901; the second is an English copy of 'an ancient
triptych', written in 1658 and known as the Lambeth (or English) Life.
A translation of the Latin Life, by Dr. David Rollason, is given in
Appendix VII and appears in print for the first time.

Footnotes indicating which elements derive from which source
were considered intrusive; references and sources for the various parts
of the legend, therefore, are discussed throughout the book. This
account makes no attempt to rule on what might, or might not, be true.

IN 975 AD Walstan was born in the village of Bawburgh, in the county
of Norfolk, the son of Benedict and Blida. The family was a rich and
honourable one with close family ties to the Kings of Wessex and maternal
kinship with the Anglo Saxon King, Ethelred II, and his son, Edmund
Ironside. From the good example of his parents, the young Walstan learned
the meaning of the Scriptures, studying hard in his father's library but
always returning to the difficult text of Luke, Chapter 14, verse 33.

At the age of seven, he took instruction from Bishop Theodred of
Elmham and with the assistance of Aelred, the Parish Priest, he was to
make his first Communion during the Bishop's canonical visition to
Bawburgh. On this auspicious occasion, Benedict and Blida, with their
entire household, were present in the church, together with a number of
villagers and Church dignitaries. A Low Mass was said at an early hour by
the Bishop and, at his wish, Walstan served at the altar. At the moment
when the Host was held aloft, a white dove was seen by all present hovering
over the head of Walstan, though he seemed entirely unconscious of
anything but the holy act in which he was engaged.

In the afternoon of the same day he received the Sacrament of Confirmation. Later, as the shadows were lengthening, the Bishop went to the Church of St. Mary to pray and, in the dim light within, noticed a figure kneeling on the floor beside the altar. At first he thought it was a vision, then he recognised the figure as that of Walstan – his hands uplifted and his eyes raised to the holy Rood that hung from the sanctuary arch. He was praying aloud:

'I thank Thee, most Holy One, for feeding me with the Food of Angels this day, and for sending forth the Sevenfold Gifts of the Holy Spirit into my heart that I may become a valiant soldier of the Cross. And I would become more, dear Lord.'

A voice was heard to ask:

'What wouldst thou, dear Child?'

Walstan answered:

'I would fain give Thee, dear Lord, my heart and soul, and renounce all for love of Thee.'

And again the voice was heard, this time saying:

'But thou mayest become a king, and wear a golden crown.'

But Walstan renounced such an earthly crown, asking instead for an imperishable one, an eternal one, in Heaven.

The voice spoke again:

'Dear Child, I accept thy renunciation. Thou shalt share the Crown of Thorns with Me, and thy reward shall be eternal.'

At this, Walstan appeared to collapse. The Bishop, thinking the boy had fainted, stepped forward. Realising that he had been overheard, Walstan was afraid that the Bishop would tell his parents, who would then try to stop him from his vow of renunciation. But the Bishop reassured him, saying that Benedict and Blida had confided to him that they had already been told of this in a dream inspired by God.

Walstan then openly vowed to devote his life to God, in humility, and anonymity, renouncing the material security of his home and the ties of patrimony.

Shortly after his thirteenth birthday, Walstan told his parents that it was time for him to leave their house. Although unwilling to let him go, Benedict and Blida knew that their son was bound to fulfil his destiny and promise to God and duly consented.

Walstan left Benedict's house and took to the road. He hadn't gone far when he met two poor men, to whom he gave his rich garments. He then went northwards, clad only in the simplest of clothes, with no outward sign of his father's wealth. The path took him through a dense forest which led eventually to Taverham, where he rested. A farmer named Nalga saw him and, being in need of a labourer, offered Walstan a job as his farm worker.

Walstan readily agreed and very quickly gained a reputation for hard work and piety. At Taverham, he developed an affinity with the poor and was charitable in the extreme, giving his food and clothing to those less fortunate than himself.

Often he would carry out his work barefoot, having given even his shoes to the poor and needy. The farmer's wife, seeing him always meagrely clad and barefoot, one day gave him a pair of shoes, together with extra provisions for that morning's work in the field. Walstan had been at work only a short time when he saw two poor men go by, one of them barefoot. He gave them his food and his shoes. When Nalga heard of this he was angry and his wife berated Walstan for his ungrateful action. But Walstan told her that the man had been sent providentially by God to prove whether he, Walstan, loved God better than himself, adding 'I shod Christ in the poor man, though he did not crave'.

The woman sneered at this and ordered him to take a cart into the forest and fetch a load of briars, then to tread the thorns well down with his unshod feet. By a miracle, Walstan appeared to be treading on rose leaves; the thorns, soft as petals, emitted a sweet perfume. Seeing this, Nalga and his wife fell at Walstan's feet and begged forgiveness.

Over the years, Walstan became known, and loved, for his charity and for the dutiful way in which he went about his daily tasks. He maintained his vow of celibacy though never chose to enter a religious Order. As a signal of his approval, God allowed miracles to occur where Walstan was present. Animals were brought to him to be healed and people too claimed to have been cured through his prayers and ministrations. The seed corn miraculously increased in the basket he carried and whatever he did God blessed, since everything prospered and developed under his labours. Still he continued to live in poverty, keeping his royal identity a secret and giving away the wages that he earned.

Nalga and his wife – having no children of their own – grew to love Walstan, often entreating him to accept gifts, or extra food. After some years, Nalga urged Walstan to become his heir and accept their house as his own. But Walstan always refused such presents, and suggestions of earthly wealth, refusing too their offer of kinship. True to his oath of self-denial and absolute devotion to God, he continued an unbroken and faithful service to the farm for nearly thirty years. Then, Nalga's persistence was rewarded by Walstan agreeing to accept two bull calves of a certain cow, and a small waggon. This, he explained, he did not for covetousness' sake, but to fulfil God's will, an angel having commanded him to do so.

At the start of hay-making in May, 1016, Walstan was mowing with another labourer, when an angel appeared and said to him, 'Brother Walstan, on the third day after this thou shalt peaceably depart this life to enter Paradise'. Walstan immediately put down his scythe and left the field in search of the parish priest, from whom he received the holy sacraments. The next day, being Saturday, he stopped work at midday, saying that he was not allowed to work until the Monday. Then there could be heard the sound of heavenly bells ringing and an indescribable music of celestial trumpets. His comrade neither saw nor heard the heavenly music but Walstan told him, 'If you wish to believe, set your foot on mine with devout sentiments and intentions, when you shall see the heavens opened and the angels ringing heavenly bells to the glory and praise of the Undivided Trinity'. The man, doing as he was told, was immediately favoured with the celestial sights and sounds.

On that same Saturday afternoon, Nalga travelled to Norwich market where, to his amazement, he heard a proclamation that anyone knowing the whereabouts of Walstan, son of Blida and a relation of the East Anglian King, Ethelred, should tell the authorities. Nalga learned that the Danes were forcibly taking over East Anglia and Canute, son of Sweyn, intended to be the new king and overlord. Ethelred had fled to Normandy and his son, Edmund, was exhausted by constant war and without an adult heir. The proclamation gave a warning that whoever sheltered the man named Walstan of Bawburgh must deliver him up immediately, on pain of confiscation of goods and death in the case of non-compliance. Alarmed, Nalga rushed back to Taverham and confronted his servant.

'What shall I say,' he asked, 'when you tell me you are heir to the Kingdom and I risk all by harbouring you?'

Walstan answered that he should tell the truth and that he was his servant. He then told Nalga that an angel had appeared to him in a vision and foretold of his death the following Monday, adding 'I beseech you therefore to desire the priest to come to me when I shall be at work on the morning of that day, that I am to receive the Holy Sacrament of the Altar and take counsel of that holy man, so to be delivered from all the works of darkness'.

On the 30th May, the priest attended Walstan as directed in the field where he was at work, mowing the hay. He worked with his scythe until the morning ended, then he ceased, for the hour had come. The priest prepared for the ablution but there was no time to fetch the required water. Walstan prayed and immediately a spring appeared at his knee as he knelt in prayer and preparation for the Blessed Sacrament. He then told the assembled company that after his death they were to put his body on the waggon and yoke to it the two white calves. No one should direct them, but they should go wherever God pleased. He then beseeched God that every labourer who had any infirmity in his own body, or any distemper among his cattle, should obtain his desire of healing, provided he came out of devotion and reverence. A voice from heaven granted his wish, saying 'Oh holy Walstan, that which you have asked is granted. Come from your labour to rest'. With that, Walstan died and from his mouth proceeded a white dove that flew upwards and vanished in a bright cloud.

As directed, Nalga and the people of Taverham laid the body on the waggon and secured it to the two white oxen. They followed the procession along the bank of the River Wensum and through the wood. Reaching the deepest part of the river, the oxen and waggon passed over the water as if it were solid ground, and those who followed were enabled to pass miraculously along the tracks made dry where the wheels had gone. The oxen went on to Costessey Wood, then again stopped to rest. Where they stood a second spring occurred and flowed with clear water.

The gathering, with increased numbers, continued to process behind the oxen along some low land, and then across a wide tract of marsh and mire, until they came to Bawburgh, near to the where the land rises away from the bank of the River Yare. There they paused and instantly a third spring began to flow with miraculous water. The oxen then mounted the short, steep hill to the Church and entered with the cart through an opening in the north wall, which angels had come to open. The wall closed behind them and the oxen stopped, refusing to go any further. They remained there until the third afternoon, when the Bishop Aelfgar of Elmham came with priors and monks to officiate at the burial of Walstan.

The Bishop, knowing something of Walstan's childhood, listened attentively to Nalga, and the local people, who told of the many wonders God had enabled Walstan to perform in life, and he made diligent inquiries as to their truth. Then, being satisfied, he allowed the remains to be venerated as the relics of a saint and sent notice to that effect to all the churches in the neighbourhood.

The body was enshrined in a Chapel forming a half transept on the north side of Bawburgh Church. With the Bishop's blessing, and by popular consent, the site became a place of pilgrimage. Through Walstan's intercession, God bestowed miracles of healing on man and beast and those who sought the healing properties of the Well water were rewarded by miraculous cure.

In 1047 the enhanced Church and Shrine Chapel was re-dedicated by Aethelmar, Bishop of Elmham, to Saint Mary and Saint Walstan.

~ • ~

ST WALSTAN.

Born at Bawburgh. Died at Taverham,
May 30th 1016.

Chapter Two
BENEDICT AND BLIDA

*'Sanctus Walstanus Deo acceptus, australi in parte Maioris
Britannie in villa de Bawburg oriundus, ex stirpe regia, patre
scilicet Benedicto, matre vero Blida nomine, preclaram duxit
originem.' Nova Legenda Anglie, 1516
[St. Walstan, a man acceptable to God, was born in the southern
part of Great Britain in the villa of Bawburgh. He derived his
parentage of distinguished royal stock, his father being called
Benedict, his mother Blida.]*

THERE is no definitive Life of St. Walstan and no proof that he or his
Royal parents ever existed. Were it to be otherwise, it would be easy to
set out, clearly and with authoritative conviction, such a life. The words
'legend' and 'cult' would be insufficient description, and we could refer to
Walstan with the same confidence as, say, St. Felix of Dunwich, or
England's early Patron Saint, King Edmund, about whom a prodigious
amount has been written. Although Walstan is not alone among the saints in
having few biographical credentials, it has to be admitted that his origins are
obscured by a total lack of contemporary documentation, and the search for
literal or reliable truth is thus hindered. The search, then, must be not so
much for written evidence that a humble farmworker left Bawburgh in 988
AD to go and work on a farm in Taverham, but rather to examine the
legend itself, and ask what it was about this Norfolk Saint that inspired the
beginnings of a prolonged cult and which ensured its survival for almost
one thousand years. When did an ancient and anonymous chronicler first
commit the legend to manuscript, thereby bestowing on Walstan, Benedict,
and Blida the gift of immortality?

It is logical to begin by examining the claim that Walstan's parents
were Benedict (often called Saint and occasionally King), and Blida, said to
be a Royal Princess and Saint in her own right. How do these two come to
be named and why?

BENEDICT

Some coincidence surrounds the use of the name Benedict (which in Latin
means 'blessed'). Occasionally Walstan's father is referred to as King
Benedict, which he almost certainly was not, the name written variously as

Benet, or Bennet. Apart from the single mention of him as being the husband of Blida and father of Walstan – in both the Latin and English lives – nothing of any substance can be said about him. To Walstan's first biographer, likely to have been a cleric as lay chroniclers were something of a rarity in the eleventh century, the name of Benedict would have been familiar, and one which would have come easily to mind. (Attwater gives twelve saints named Benedict, including Benedict Biscop (628-689), commonly called Benet, while the Ramsgate Monks' *Book of Saints* has twenty-two Benedicts.)

However, any writer who seriously named St. Benedict (c.480-c.550) as Walstan's father was no good at mathematics. If we accept such a suggestion, Blida must qualify as the Patron Saint of the Impossible since her husband would have been over four hundred years old at the time of their son's birth!

If we are seeking more coincidence, and one likely to appeal to an eleventh-century writer with political ambitions, the two reigning Popes in 975 and 1016 were both named Benedict. For what it is worth, Benedict VII (974-984) was Pope at the time of Walstan's birth, and Benedict VIII (1012-1024) was Pope at the time of his death. There would seem to be no significance in that *S. Benedictus Abbass* appears on the same screen as Walstan at North Burlingham (although one Thomas Benet is among the donors for the screen), or that briars, a feature of Walstan's legend, are among the various specific emblems of St. Benedict. It must also be pure chance that St. Benedict, author of the Rule which bears his name, is Patron Saint of Italian Farmers, just as Walstan is named Patron Saint of Farmers in East Anglia.

A suitable option to being either a saint or a king is that Walstan's father was indeed a Christian man named Benedict (or Benet), who lived or came to live in Bawburgh, but about whom little is known. It is more than possible that there was such a learned and devoutly Christian man of high Saxon birth living in the village at the time and there is no harm in using such an example to be parent of Walstan. If he were a landowner, he might have been the patron of the Shrine, or possibly the Church itself. Often, when churches were originally built they were sponsored by a landowner who settled land on it in order that the priest might supplement his tithe income by farming. The writer David Rollason tells us that hagiographical texts relating to the Anglo Saxon period often show the saints as defenders of the rights of landowners, or others with a claim to land. Very often, ownership of land was intimately linked with ownership of relics and gave churches clear opportunities to acquire new lands. At Brandon in Norfolk, for example, St. Etheldreda is said to have defended property by afflicting the nobleman who unjustly seized the lands with an inability to eat or drink. The unfortunate thief, and his family, perished in due course. Only when the man's brother returned the land to the community was St. Etheldreda satisfied and allowed the rest of the family to end their days less dramatically.

ST. BLIDA

The origins of Saint, or Princess, Blida are marginally less ethereal than those of Benedict and it is through her that Walstan is traditionally said to claim kinship to the last of the East Anglian Kings, Edmund Ironside, son of Ethelred the Unready. Nothing has so far been discovered which throws any light onto this assertion but, another in a succession of coincidences, both Ethelred, and the newly ennobled King Edmund Ironside, died in the same year as did Walstan, i.e. 1016. In fact, Blida is only royal by implication, in that Walstan derived his parentage of 'distinguished royal stock' (the NLA) and was 'a Kings sonne' (Lambeth Life).

In *Suffolk and Norfolk*, M.R. James dismisses Blida as a mythical personage and suggests she is a mistake for St. Bride, although there are few churches in Norfolk where an image of St. Bride survives. Given what *The Oxford Dictionary of Saints* has to say about St. Bride, who is more properly entitled Brigid or Bridget, such confusion is unlikely. As befits an Irish Saint there is much folklore surrounding this Abbess of Kildare, whose feast day is a transformation of a Pagan festival to Brigantia, the Celtic Goddess of fertility. St. Bride is not without agricultural connections (a barn, a red cow and a pan of milk are numbered among her specific emblems), and her miracles follow the theme of multiplication of food, which include the changing of her bath water into beer to slake the thirst of visiting clergy!

Taking M.R. James' suggestion of a confusion of names further, an unsubstantiated St. Brida/Beda had a certain following at Westhall in Suffolk, but again there are few parallels to be drawn. Stories of Medieval worship to a saint who assisted housemaids to find things they had lost are associated with Westhall, but the saint is commonly held to be St. Sitha (Zita or Citha) who is featured on the Church screen and whose cult has a certain authenticity. Nothing, therefore, is to be found at Westhall which could be linked to St. Blida.

There is no reason why Blida should not have been what she is commonly held to be, namely a member of Ethelred II's household or, indeed, his family. As he had two wives, his list of in-laws was potentially large. It is going too far to suggest she might have been a queen, either by succession or marriage. If there was any firm historical evidence for a Queen or Princess Blida it is fairly certain that an Anglo Saxon scholar would long since have identified her, although if we are looking for a Wolston with royal connections, it is possible to work back from Ethelred II to Ethelred I (865-71) to find Wolston (or Wulstan), Earl of Wiltshire. This Wolston was married to St. Alburga (d. 810), half-sister to the

Wessex King, Egbert. In her widowhood, Alburga founded Wilton Abbey, near Salisbury, where she took the veil.

This, and other such legends, serve to show that it was the practice, in the ninth and tenth centuries, for the Church to both credit saints with royal blood and to endow royalty with sainthood. In Blida's case, her Anglo Saxon blood would, if combined with a Christian sainthood, stand as an example to lesser, impressionable mortals. Wholesale conversion of the Saxons to Christianity had not happened overnight and the new religion had only succeeded after being sanctioned by the kings and lords whose authority ruled the lives of the people. Many kings, and most of the East Anglians who were slain in battle, were sainted, notably Edgar, Sigebert, Ethelbert and Edmund. Even a certain Edwold of Cerue, reputedly St. Edmund's brother, lived a hermit's life, surviving only on a diet of bread and water. He nevertheless managed to work many miracles in his lifetime and in death was endowed with confessorship.

If we are to believe that Blida and Benedict were related to the cowardly Ethelred the Unready (Unready meaning 'unwise', rather than 'not ready') we must also think they were associated with Ethelred's older half-brother, Edward the Martyr (975-8), who succeeded to the throne in the year of Walstan's birth. This martyrdom of a legitimate and reigning King of England was developed into a cult by Ethelred himself who, in a Charter of 1001 called him Saint and Martyr. Some years later he ordered the observance of Edward's feastdate and his inclusion in the Church Calendar.

According Blida a royal saintliness was, though, as far as the scribes were prepared to go, since none of them bothered to give her any sort of life other than statements of marriage and motherhood. Nothing survives in folklore which might justify her as a saint (and neither the Latin nor English Life make such a claim), and no *legenda* exists. There is no mention, either, of any children other than Walstan, and no known feast date to show that she might have been included in any Church Calendar. Indeed, she rarely appears in reference books as anything other than St. Walstan's mother except when Roeder ascribes to her the patronage of motherhood. Only at Cawston in Norfolk is the word 'Blida' to be found on a tiny fragment of Medieval glass, thus making it impossible to dismiss entirely the possibility of a cult to St. Blida.

In his *History of Norfolk*, Blomefield refers to '... the Chapel of St. Blide of Martham' (1479), and to a bequest from Richard Fuller of Norwich, tanner, who gave 10s. to the Church at Martham '... where St. Blide lyeth' (1522), thereby providing some evidence that a Chapel in Martham church was once dedicated to St. Blida. The present Church of St. Mary's was rebuilt in 1377 and it is not known if the Chapel dedication belonged also to the original building.

Blomefield does not refer to the legend of St. Walstan in the Martham entry and under Bawburgh he simply repeats the name Blida as being Walstan's mother, minus any royal or saintly title.

Bryant says there was 'probably' a Chapel on the south aisle dedicated to St. Blide, Blida or Blythe, who was buried there and said to be the wife of Benedict. A manuscript in the British Museum (cited but not named by Bryant) says that Blida's Chapel is mentioned in 1479 and 1506.

Although in 1917 M.R. James wrote '... the name Blida occurs on the Worstead screen (1512) as that of a donor's wife', the screen itself was subjected to over-enthusiastic Victorian restoration, and both the donor and his wife have come in for differing interpretations of their names. (See also Appendix I, Worstead.) It is likely that James took the Worstead reference from Husenbeth, whose identification of Blida is invariably unsubstantiated, and who often suggested Blida in consideration of previously unidentified female saints.

Since no mention is made of Benedict or Blida at the end of the legend, when the oxen bring Walstan home to Bawburgh, we must assume that the household had left the area, or been driven from Bawburgh to a safer place. It would be understandable if they had moved, since the final years of the tenth century were turbulent and dangerous enough for ordinary people, but even more so for any family of political or social importance.

During the first ten years of the eleventh century, while Walstan worked on the Taverham farm, the Danes had continued to ransack East Anglia. In 1004, King Sweyn had sailed up the River Yare to burn and pillage Norwich and Thetford, and in 1012 the Archbishop of Canterbury was killed by Danes during a drunken feast in Greenwich. Ethelred, having fled to Normandy, died in 1016, leaving the throne to his son, Edmund Ironside, a young man already worn out by constant war. Sweyn was a formidable enemy, and a determined one. By December, only six months after Walstan's own death, Edmund Ironside was also dead and Sweyn's son, Canute, had become King of all England and overlord of East Anglia.

The question might idly be asked as to whether either of Walstan's parents heard the same proclamation about Walstan as did Nalga, at Norwich market. Did they know where their son was in 1016? Taverham is only a few miles north of Bawburgh and there would have been travellers who passed from one village to another, carrying local gossip with them. But, no doubt if they did connect their son with the talk of a Holy Man on Nalga's farm, they preferred to honour his wish for secrecy as well as fearing the consequences for them all if his whereabouts were disclaimed. (The name 'Nalga' does not appear in either the English or Latin Life.)

However, even if there is no account of what happened to Benedict and Blida, the legend portrays such anxiety as they and Nalga, whether real or imagined, would have felt in the spring of 1016. Although Canute was converted to Christianity, even sending English missionaries to his heathen subjects in Denmark, he was nevertheless a conquering force, as was shown quite soon after Edmund Ironside's death when his infant sons were dispatched to Poland and his brother hunted down and killed.

Can we here detect a chronicler who used his pen to illustrate, rather than to record history? Is this one of the first examples whereby Walstan was used to touch and influence the lives of ordinary men and women? It is likely that when the story came to be rewritten, probably in the earliest years of Anglo-Norman England, Walstan was given a defiant link with the old Anglo Saxon royalty, the legend already acknowledging the interests of the Danish regime in naming his father as Benedict (Canute became Patron of the Benedictine Order and founded St. Benet's Abbey). Might there also have been yet more judicious acknowledgement when the reign of Canute began to crumble and Edward the Confessor, a surviving son of Ethelred II by his second wife, returned from Normany to claim the throne in 1042?

Some discrepancy exists in regard to Blida's burial date and Walstan's birth, since one chronicler gives her death as occurring 'late 11th century'. Having given birth in 975, she would certainly have been a great age by the end of the next century and such discrepancies aid the theory that St. Blide and Blida, mother of Walstan, had separate identities.

Why Blida should have been honoured as a saint in Martham can only be speculated upon, and it has been suggested that her Marian-like example was honoured by the inmates of a thirteenth-century Cistercian nunnery. Inconveniently for such a conjecture, the nunnery was founded at Marham, in 1249, not Martham, where there is also an absence of any named relic to Blida.

So, without an extensive search of all remaining historical manuscripts, which might reveal nothing at all on the subject, the life of St. Blida must, for now, remain shrouded in mystery and doubt. Apart from the known references to her in Medieval wills and bequests (and no doubt there are others which have not yet come to light), only two pieces of evidence for her cult survive to the present day: one is at Cawston, where the fragment of glass clearly bears the name 'Blida'; another is in the Church of St. Mary Magdalene, Norwich, where she is portrayed on a panel which once belonged to a Medieval screen. She is also named as a figure on the accompanying font, but not until this century and purely, it seems, on the authority of Husenbeth, who also identified the panel. On the screen she is depicted holding a book (probably a bible) and a quill (sometimes called a palm), next to St. Walstan.

The claim that St. Blida was represented at Babingley in North Norfolk must add a little to the thought that Blida was not the mother of St. Walstan but a saint in her own right. Even if the Babingley claim is thought a little spurious, it does gain a place in Keyser's *List of Buildings Having Mural Decorations* (1883).

Although M.R. James refers to a female figure bearing the name of Blida as being in the north-east chancel window at North Tuddenham, this is taken to be heresay, since no such figure can be traced. Just as there is now no relic of Blida at Martham, there is no evidence either that she was honoured as a saint at Bawburgh. In *Suffolk and Norfolk*, James also says that Blida appears on two screens, but only names that at St. James'; in the same volume Blida is indexed at Horsham, but at Horsham devotion to St. Faith is prevalent.

To establish the merits of Benedict and Blida beyond what has been discussed here is not profitable, and cannot add to our search for Norfolk's most enduring legend. We are anyway in the hands of biographers who, down the ages, have exercised the gift of creative writing, or at least did not fully understand plagiarism, or who were swayed by political motive.

CHRISTIAN SYMBOLISM

Before turning to Walstan himself some of the familiar Christian symbolisms and folklore, which are apparent in most versions of his life, should be referred to, notably the recurrence of the number three. There are, for example, three wells; saints were always needing water for all sorts of reasons, usually where no water existed. Janet and Colin Bord give several examples, including St. Torranan (or Ternan) who prayed for a spring to quench his thirst on Benbecula, Outer Hebrides. Similarly, St. Alban and St. Frideswide prayed for water in an area where there was none. St. Walstan first prayed for water when the Taverham priest needed it for the Last Rites.

Walstan's death vision lasted for three days, as did his final stop in Bawburgh church before burial, and shortly before he died he directed his companion that if he, too, wanted to see the gate of heaven open, he should place his foot over Walstan's own. Thorns get a mention in a miraculous context, while there is also a reference to a pentecostal dove escaping from Walstan's mouth at his death. (The dove is a symbol of the Holy Ghost, one third of the indivisable Holy Trinity.) Similarly, a dove is seen at the Service of Confirmation in Bawburgh Church, a 'fact' which does not appear in either 'primary' life and must be described as an example of wishful thinking on the part of the author. There is also mention of the miracle of the proliferation of food, similar to the parables of the New Testament; the story of how the cart bearing Walstan's body passed over the River Wensum, opening up dry paths for the procession to tread, is reminiscent of Christ's ability to walk on water and vaguely similar to the taming of the Red Sea.

The story of the final journey, with three resting places, is not unlike that of St. Cuthbert, whose body was moved after his death and on the three occasions that the procession stopped, a well appeared.

While the character of Benedict has some parallel with that of Joseph, Blida bears comparison with Mary, the Mother of Christ, and there is no mention of children other than Walstan. Many legends of the saints, including that of St. Walstan, have been identified as no more than a thin disguise for the Holy Family.

Walstan himself bears some similarity to St. Francis of Assisi (1180-1226) who also renounced his inheritance, was obsessed with giving away his clothing and whose cult embraces an affection for animals. When such themes are seen repeatedly in hagiography, it does nothing to offend the notion that we are looking at well-intentioned, if pious, liturgical fiction, albeit in St. Walstan's case likely to have been woven round real people and events.

Saintly links with a prevailing Royal House are too numerous to list, above those already cited, but that is no reason to suppose that Benedict and Blida were not, in truth, members of a prominent and Christian family, who had a son named Walstan. While it would be unreasonable to give implicit belief in the detail of the legend, it is equally so to sceptically dismiss it and other such lives as having no historical base. The search for St. Walstan continues, and while safe proof of his life may never be found, we turn instead to the discernible evidence of the generations of men and women who feature in the nine hundred-year-old history of this cult. They sought less for the truth of the legend than for the all-important reason for it, namely a search for God through the example of a mortal man. The fact of such popular veneration qualifies Walstan to be named Saint as surely as Bishop Aelfgar's declaration in 1016. Even the sceptical nineteenth-century Bollandist Monk, Hippolyte Delehaye, wrote of such legends:

> *'It is impossible for the people's mind to be strongly impressed by some great event or by some powerful personality without their feelings finding expression in stories in which popular fancy is given full play. To say that legend has flourished luxuriantly in the neighbourhood of shrines is simply to underline the importance of the* cultus *of saints in the life of people. Legend is a homage that the Christian community pays to its patron saints. As such, one cannot ignore it.'*

~ • ~

Chapter Three

WALSTAN, SAINT AND PATRON

Here in England through the ages,
While the Christian years went by,
Saints, confessors, martyrs, sages,
Strong to live and strong to die,
Wrote their names upon the pages
Of God's blessed company.
    C.A. Allington, Hymns Ancient & Modern No. 574

WALSTAN, we are given to understand, was a man of unbelievable piety, an example of perfect humility, and a pure earthly illustration of the true art of charity and Godliness. He was a man beyond human reproach, although, unlike some other saints, he was given no human imperfection to conquer, other than the possession of wealth. Poor Walstan! The emphasis on his humility, highly applauded as an example to follow, has invariably resulted in his portrayal as a grim-faced and rather miserable wretch. Life as a saint looks to have been a pretty harrowing business, the God-given honour of presiding over so many miracles, and the high esteem in which he was held by the good people of Taverham, only adding to the burden. Medieval artists were expected to portray these beatific and rather pained expressions as part of their task of illustration, in order to impress an illiterate audience with due gravity and sanctity. However, whereas other saints were often endowed with a beatific smile, to indicate that earthly travail was but a step towards eventual paradise, Walstan, then and now, is more often than not portrayed as positively downtrodden, definitely mournful, and somewhat 'put upon'.

For the detail of Walstan's boyhood we are in the hands of just one writer, Walter J. Piper. In 1915, Mr. Piper described himself as being well acquainted with Bawburgh and Taverham, having gone to some lengths to glean items of folklore and tradition concerning St. Walstan, particularly certain 'missing links' in Walstan's early life which he thought had been overlooked or considered unworthy of mention by others. It is this intrepid collector who tells of Walstan's instruction by the Bishop of Elmham, about the Confirmation Service, and of the heavenly dreams granted to Benedict and Blida. Posterity can only regret that the source for this information remained a secret which Mr. Piper took with him to the grave.

Mr. Piper was among those who think that the messengers searching for Walstan in Norwich market were not Danish saboteurs, but rather a band of Anglo Saxon followers. The news was grim; Ethelred the Unready had fled to Normany, while his son, the brave Edmund Ironside, was failing in his strength and had only infant children to succeed him. Might a band of Norfolk and Suffolk landowners not have looked to Walstan, who was 'on the spot', to take the Anglo Saxon throne?

Whether or not the child Walstan was sent to Bishop Theodred at Elmham, and whatever the truth of his formative years, he is said to have been instructed in the Christian faith, and to have been a gentle and hard-working soul, whose charity endeared him to all those he met. Even in the self-inflicted and dire poverty of his mature years, he found the means to assist the poor by giving them his own clothes and food. It is precisely because of his life of heroic virtue that Walstan is named 'Confessor'.

CONFESSORSHIP

The cult of the Confessors – those who spent their lives in quiet piety and self-denial, and who died peacefully – does not extend back as far as does the devotion to martyrs but is no less valid. Confessorship seems to have been a substitute for martrydom and the process of canonization did not begun until the papacy of Alexander II (1159-81). But, until the seventeenth century, when Pope Urban VIII reserved his exclusive right of canonization, a Bishop could still proclaim a confessor to be a saint. The fact that Walstan, or Blida for that matter, was not formally canonized in Rome is no barrier to sainthood. Fewer saints than might be imagined were ever given the Papal blessing. Popular veneration and approval by a Bishop (in Walstan's case Bishop Aethelmar of Elmham) would have been enough in those times. Although members of the same Church, embracing all of Western Christendom, it was a long way from the local Parish Priest to the Pope in Rome, not just geographically but in attitudes and education. Then, and now, Churches everywhere are made up of several levels of relevance and importance.

However, only acceptance by the Pope himself could make any cult a universal one and is the reason why so many, including Walstan's, are described as 'local'. Without going through the vast *Acta Apostolicae Sedis* archive (an account of the acts of the Pope and the Papal *Curia* for each year) it is not possible to say whether the case for Walstan was ever submitted to a pre-Reformation Pope. Before 1234, when Pope Gregory IX assumed some control over canonization, there was no real definition of a saint. Such designation had, until then, been the province of the Bishop, frequently as the result of popular devotion. In some cases this went rather too far and resulted in saints who never existed. Roeder, for example, tells us that the French St. Decimil was honoured as a Roman martyr, and a *legenda* composed, after the discovery of his tombstone. Only later was the 'tomb' found to be part of a Roman milestone erected to direct the legions marching into Gaul!

If a search for a link between Norfolk and the Papacy was to be instigated one place to start would be with Pandulp (d. 1226), who was Papal Legate and Bishop of Norwich. Pandulp first visited England in 1211 as the nuncio of Innocent III. He was consecrated to the See of Norwich in Rome in 1222, but died four years later and was buried in Norwich Cathedral.

PATRON SAINT

In the light of the fact that, until the Industrial Revolution, agriculture formed the basis for all society, and therefore affected the life of every citizen, Walstan ranks as a rarity among his kind, namely that of patron saints for agricultural workers, often extended to include farming in general with harmless interchange of 'farming' and 'agriculture'. *The Oxford Dictionary of Saints* remarks that '... his cult is interesting as an example of veneration by humble folk of one who shared the same round of agricultural pursuits as themselves and had attained sanctity in doing so'.

It is puzzling indeed why so little intercession was craved by the tillers of the soil – or perhaps not. The provision of food, the basic requirement for survival, was so fundamental that farming might have been too commonplace an occupation upon which to exalt a saint. On the other hand, the importance of farming to members of the early Church is woven into the Christian Calendar, as instanced by Plough Sunday, Rogation Sunday and Lammas. The English, or Anglo Saxon, invaders who replaced Roman domination brought with them a culture deeply embedded in agriculture and allegiance to ancestral gods. They even named the month of May *Thrimilci* in honour of the cow, a fact worth noting in view of Walstan's specific emblem.

Walstan's chosen way of life was not in any way elevated, or apart from everyday life, as might reasonably be expected in a saint whose legend has lasted for so long. Yet it is his very power of intervention with God which would seem to be chiefly responsible for acknowledging Walstan's devotion to farm work. Given the oppression of the Anglo Saxon villein class, and their lack of political say, it is astounding that the cult ever got off the ground at all, a consideration which suggests that there was already a cult of a similar nature in existence prior to 1016.

Taking the archaeological evidence of, amongst other artefacts, Pagan and Saxon brooches found recently in Bawburgh, it is certain that the area has been the site of cultural activity since long before 1016. So far, we have assumed that the legend originated in the eleventh century. No doubt the particular legend of St. Walstan did begin then, but Man has lived in, and visited, Bawburgh since before 800 BC. Among the archaeological sites and monuments on record are Bronze Age barrows, prehistoric flints, handtools from the late Palaeolithic age, and Neolithic shafts and flints.

There is overwhelming evidence, too, that Bawburgh was once the site of a Roman villa of second- or third-century date. As well as a Roman bronze bell, and coins dated 330 and 350 AD, a first-century Colchester-derivative brooch has been found, together with a rare Roman brooch of a type of which only nine others are known. During 1947 and 1971 the site of a Roman cremation cemetery was excavated, compounding the theory that the Romans, followed by the English, practised the worship, social habits, and conventions of their age in the village of Bawburgh. Significantly, sacred wells are commonly to be found in the vicinity of Roman cemeteries.

These numerous ancient local sites lend further support to the belief that the foundations of what became the legend of St. Walstan were laid down before the final years of Anglo Saxon England; the raising of a Christian saint might just be the continuance of a long-standing reverence for the area. The new Christian religion wisely employed the existing and hallowed site, conveniently situated at a point where the river is easily bridged and where, no doubt, the Anglo Saxon invaders found an ideal place to cultivate their crops and graze their cattle.

The *Victoria County History of Norfolk* voiced the belief that '….. [St. Walstan's] remarkable legend records powers possessed by him which might be attributed to some pagan divinity than to a Christian saint'.

It might be supposed that the opportunities of the saints for heavenly intercession, in favour of those still on earth, might have been more frequently invoked by the peasantry. Life was harsh and unremitting for those who worked on the land at the beginning of the eleventh century and such days off as there were remained restricted to Sundays and Holy Days. The latter, in the early Middle Ages, still owed much to superstition, especially in the villages. Many saints' days replaced older festival dates and were borrowed from the Pagan Calendar. Holy Days were often no more than established Pagan or pre-Pagan celebrations. (Bede, for instance, writes that the old Pagan year began on the 25th December.) For Christian purposes, they were 'borrowed' or reformed, and as such were likely to owe their existence to agrarian origin. Although many academicians refute the influence of old festival dates being utilised by new Calendars, history shows that it has always been difficult for legislators to change a popular celebration date, especially if it meant the loss of a holiday. Early Church leaders found it easier and more effective to adapt such dates than to erase them, no better illustration being the Papal envoy, Mellitus. Following the arrival in England of the first Benedictine monk (St. Augustine, in 597), Gregory the Great sent a second envoy, Mellitus (d. 624) with instructions that Augustine should not destroy the temples of the Saxons, only their idols. The temples, he commanded, should be converted into churches and their feasts taken over and directed to Christian purposes.

Almost half a century later, Canute forbade allegiance to heathen or Pagan gods, many of them legacies of ancient and time-honoured worship of springs and rivers. It comes as no surprise to learn that all East Anglian liturgical books were destroyed by the Danish invaders, and that no early Calendars survive.

It is plausible, then, that there was a Holy Man of Bawburgh – Walstan – whose loyal following there, and at Taverham and Costessey, wanted to raise him up into the new Christian hierarchy. Perhaps he was royal, as well as holy, and perhaps his family were landowners, but in any event, the manner of his life and death justified the belief that his soul had gone straight to heaven. His life could well have been spent in the service of farming and when it came to assigning his feastdate the Elmham Bishops would prudently have used a pre-Christian festival date connected with some aspect of agriculture. It was a feature of Christianity that feastdates were not, as in Heathenism, the birthday, but instead the anniversary of death, and therefore the beginning of everlasting life. Thus it is credible that the legend owes a debt not only to ecclesiastical expediency but to a one-time Roman, Pagan or Saxon god of agriculture or, at the very least, a Maytime celebration of some antiquity.

The Church's subsequent encouragement of the concept of intercession – a sympathetic voice in God's ear – confirmed Walstan as patron of farming and farm workers, and proved to be the chief reason for the strong popular support which the legend subsequently enjoyed. Who better to persuade God towards mercy for the men and beasts of agriculture than 'one of their own' whose sympathy with the worshipper would be wholehearted and readily available for those places and causes which had been dear to them in life? In the Latin Life, Walstan's dying prayer is for workmen and their brute animals, and he was at his own labours only a short time before he died. For his final journey home he relied on two bulls, yoked to a cart, which were left to follow the divine will. That the 30th May survived to become an occasion for pilgrimage, the ultimate Holy Day, is a tribute to the early keepers of the Shrine. If it was their intention to gain, or keep, an extra day off in the year for farm workers, this too met with local success. If, as seems likely, the intent was particularly to honour those who worked on the land, and who had charge of the farm animals, posterity has rewarded them equally.

If there were other farming saints, either in East Anglia or elsewhere, their fame has not stood the test of time. It was only in 1961 that Pope John XXIII officially confirmed St. Benedict as patron saint of Italian farmers and farm workers, on the grounds that the Benedictine monks were responsible for the cultivation of so much waste land across Europe. A year earlier, the same Pope formally proclaimed Isidore the Farmer to be patron of farm labourers and country dwellers of Spain. St. Walstan remains unique among English saints as having been popularly adopted patron of farm workers. Taking the cue from the legend ('The next day, being Saturday, he stopped work at midday, saying that he was not allowed to work until the Monday'), at least one commentator credits Walstan as wholly responsible for the long-held tradition that the farm workers' week stops at lunch time on Saturday. Where nowadays farm labourers do work on a Saturday, they qualify for overtime rates, so perhaps Walstan can be regarded as a heavenly trades union leader!

A CONFUSION OF NAMES

Not every chronicler of the legend of St. Walsan has been entirely sure how to spell the name of their hero. As often as not, two or more alternatives (such as Wolstan, Wolston, Wulfstan and Wulstan) appear in the same book, even the same paragraph. The similarity in names between Walstan and Wulfstan, Bishop of Worcester (c.1008-1095) and last of the Anglo Saxon saints, has occasionally been the cause of error.

There seems little significance in the name of Walstan; it is fairly uncommon now, but according to Walter Rye the name was popular in East Anglia well into the fifteenth century. Eric Partridge, in the 1951 edition of *A Dictionary of Traditional First Names*, lists Walstan as an obsolete, or obsolescent, name. While St. Christopher translates as 'Christ-bearer', or St. Agnes as 'lamb', we can find no similar clues to the origins of the name, and therefore to the origins of the legend. Paul Bibire, at the University of Cambridge, suggests the problem could be that several originally distinct forms fall together to give rise to the modern 'wal', 'tan' or 'ton'. However, some Anglo Saxon derivatives can be applied, such as *weall* (wall or corner stone), and *waelle* (well of water). While Walstan translates as 'wall-stone', Wulfstan is roughly 'Wolf-stone'; the switching of the 'u' for 'o' could be the cause of confusion down the ages.

Since accuracy and consistency were not concepts widely adhered to in early literature, and not every chronicler's handwriting was decipherable, it is easy to imagine how different spellings of the same name arrived. Many fifteenth-, sixteenth- and seventeenth-century works were copied or translated from earlier manuscripts, resulting in a number of variants in general spelling and interpretation. Matters were not helped by the use of 'f' for 's' in later English scripts and, as hagiography gradually became popular through increased literacy, mistakes were made but not corrected. Medieval Englishmen wrote their native tongue phonetically and were content to spell accordingly. The famous Abbot Samson, head of the Abbey at Bury St. Edmunds, could speak English, French and Latin, but insisted on preaching in English and always in the dialect of Norfolk, where he was born and bred. If a Norfolk accent could be identified in a written version of the legend of St. Walstan it would be entertaining at the very least!

To illustrate other and partially contemporary use of the name, it is interesting to note that not long after the Norman Conquest, another centre of Medieval pilgrimage, Bromholm Abbey, was founded by the first of the Paston family to settle in Norfolk. Wolstan Paston (alternatively spelt Walstan and Wulstan) is said by Arthur Mee to have come from France soon after the Battle of Hastings. This Wolston had a son, also named Wolston. Yet another Paston descendant of the same name turns up in the sixteenth century, when Wolston, youngest son of Sir Thomas Paston, is recorded as having entered the religious life under the name of Augustine Beeston.

During the research for this book it became clear that even now Walstan is not immune from mistake or confusion with other similarly named saints or from uncertain spelling, especially as vowels are commonly missing on Latin manuscripts. It is also apparent that over the years the intricacies of Latin grammar were not approached with a universal degree of competence. In the NLA, for example, the normal use of Latin declension results in *Walstanus, Walstane, Walstanum,* etc., which led to unsafe copy. The use of the final 'e', merely the masculine vocative of a second-declension noun, is retained as the proper noun by some writers, e.g. Roscarrock and Bale.

As recently as 1985, Mortlock & Roberts refer to 'Walston' and 'Walstan' in the same volume and almost inevitably, wise and estimable librarians identified Walstan as Bishop Wulfstan of Worcester. It seems that where a reference is bereft of vowels, Wul(f)stan is assumed to be the most likely candidate due solely to his greater fame. Such an assumption is likely to mislead those in search of St. Walstan, a problem highlighted by an invocation to '*Sancte Wlstane*' in a fifteenth-century liturgy extant in the Bodleian Library.

The manuscript, which dates from the second quarter of the fifteenth century and is listed under the Benedictine Abbeys of Wymondham and Tynemouth, invokes '*Sancte Wlstane*' between St. Edmund and St. Hugo;

if it could be proved to be 'Walstan', it is another step towards thinking that the Order had a special regard for St. Walstan. Inmates of the early Benedictine houses were pioneers in the practice of farming, often draining marshes and felling trees to improve and increase agricultural land, and thus were likely to champion a rural saint. However, while there is currently no proof that this '*Wlstane*' is to be interpreted as Walstan (since 'W' by itself is generally emended as 'Wu' or 'Vu') it does at least offer the potential for comparison with other litanies from, say, St. Albans.

The Rev. F.G. Holweck, in *A Biographical Dictionary of the Saints*, lists Walstan with both a's, but gives Bishop Wulfstan as 'Wulstan', with Wolstan and Wulfstan as alternatives. It is fairly certain that more than one historian over the years has mistaken St. Walstan for the above-named Bishop Wulfstan of Worcester, or any of the other Wulstans, namely: Wulfstan, Archbishop of York (d. 956); Wulfstan the Cantor (c. 996); Wulfstan II, Bishop of London and Worcester, afterwards Archbishop of York (d. 1023).

Charles Keyser, in his *List of Buildings Having Mural Decorations* (1883) names '*Wlstan*' as one of the paintings formerly on the north wall of the choir at Ely Cathedral. Although indexed by Keyser as Bishop Wolston, and said to be a Bishop of Ely, the painting is now destroyed and there are no specific details regarding '*Wlstan*' of Ely. However, in the *Liber Eliensis*, a twelfth-century history and chronicle of Ely Abbey, he is named '*Ulstan*', Archbishop of York (d. 1023), and is therefore better identified as Wulstan II, who also held the see of Worcester.

In the eighteenth century, Alban Butler missed out an 'f' to entitle the Bishop 'Wulstan'. Since Butler's *Lives* became for many years the definitive source for the Bawburgh legend this alone accounts for many subsequent errors. Apart from the fact that Wulfstan chose to be celibate (Butler tells us that Wulfstan 'perceiving himself somewhat touched with wanton love on seeing a woman dance, withdrew into a thicket hard by, and, lying prostrate, bewailed his fault before God'), there are no similarities – other than the name – between the two saints. (With some satisfaction, Butler gives assurance that the good Bishop was endowed with the gift of watchfulness over his senses and thus relieved of further temptation.) It is worth noting, also, that the Bishop worked closely with Lanfranc, the Norman Archbishop, on the matter of clerical celibacy.

Undeniably, Wulfstan is better known than Walstan, but the former's well-documented life is such that the two are distinguished from each other with ease, initially by comparing feast dates: Wulfstan's rarely deviates from the 19th January, while the 30th May (or the 28th December in some early Calendars) is accepted as belonging to Walstan. Bishop Wulfstan is undoubtedly an important personage, and has a certain status in the religious and political bridge between the Anglo Saxon and Anglo-Norman hierarchy – and thus not unconnected with our legend – but he is not to be confused with Walstan of Bawburgh.

If, however, the name of Walstan was invented (or changed) at any point and for whatever reason, it is not impossible that an Anglo-Norman writer might have used the name in the Bishop's honour, such as Benedict of Bawburgh might have been named for an influential namesake or patron. Certainly we must be glad that those early scribes did not change the name of Walstan to that of Colman; *The Oxford Dictionary of Saints* deplores the fact that over 300 saints of that name exist in Irish martyrology alone!

~ • ~

Chapter Four

THE SEARCH FOR WITNESS

*'Walstan, local Saint of Norfolk, almost unknown elsewhere, is
not mentioned in any known liturgical document, but there is
plenty of evidence for an unofficial cult of some importance.'*
The Oxford Dictionary of Saints

A T this point, it is reasonable to ask what formal documentation exists
for the legend of St. Walstan, other than hearsay evidence that the cult
flourished at Bawburgh throughout the early Middle Ages. Since the
Ramsgate Monks describe the cult as 'Approved', rather than 'Popular',
and credit it as being undisputed, it can be assumed that there is some
tangible proof that Walstan was celebrated as a Saint in Bawburgh.

As we now know, it is not possible to attribute the legend to any one
pen, since most early-English documents which constitute the beginnings of
organised religion have either perished or are incomplete. As likely as not,
the earliest account was composed at the instigation of either Bishop
Aelfgar or Aethelmar, and would have been written in Latin, the prevailing
language of public worship and formal Church business. Whether or not
that account was by an eye witness will never be known.

In the early days of Walstan's 'canonization' by Bishop Aethelmar, it
was customary for such news to be circulated to neighbouring churches.
But, as the Elmham See was moved to Thetford in 1075 and removed to
Norwich by Bishop Herbert Losinga in 1094, any document which might
have been part of the Elmham manuscripts has long since turned to dust. As
well, towards the end of the thirteenth century, relations between the
growing city of Norwich and the Benedictine Priory plunged to a new low.
Hostilities finally broke out between the two in 1272, when a mob set fire to
the Church of St. Ethelbert. For three days the Priory was plundered of
valuables, while books and sacred documents were burned; if a record of
the Bawburgh Shrine had been put there by the Papal nuncio, Pandulp, or if
Bishop's authorisation confirming Walstan's confessorship was there, it
went up in flames.

It is highly probable that a prevailing tenth- or eleventh-century Bishop
of Elmham would have ordered that a legend (Latin *legenda*, 'something to
be read') be written which would then be read publicly on St. Walstan's
feast day, at Bawburgh Church, in accordance with prevailing custom.

A copy of this might have been lodged in the Priory cartulary, since the Sacrist records show that the rents from Bawburgh during the thirteenth century were among the four highest from outside the city. Various additions and subtractions to the text of such a document would be made as time went on, especially during the reign of Walstan's supposed relative, Edward the Confessor (1042-1066) when links between the Old English Church and the Papacy were strengthened. This is illustrated by the use of such words as the Latin *sotulares* (shoes) and *carecta* (cart) which occur in the 1516 NLA, and were first recorded in the thirteenth century, as pointed out by Dr Rollason.

THE NORMAN INVASION

However, the ink was hardly dry when the original legend of St. Walstan faced the first test of its survival. In 1066, nearly twenty years after Bishop Aethelmar dedicated the Bawburgh Church to Saints Mary and Walstan, the shrine at Bawburgh became part of the first reformation of the English Church, carried out by the Italian monk, Lanfranc, at the instigation of William the Conquerer.

It is likely that if a Bishop's *legenda* was missing, the first official record would have come after the Norman Conquest when Lanfranc began his reformation of the English Church. The Invasion had brought with it a demand for documentation made necessary by the new rule of law. In order to regulate the Church Lanfranc's minions were sent to gather information at its source and their brief would have been similar to those conducting the Domesday Survey, namely to gather what records were available, whether verbal or written, from each diocese. If, during the latter half of the eleventh century, the legend of St. Walstan was only scant, such an omission would have been rectified by the meticulous Normans who were suspicious of the Anglo Saxon saints and demanded reliable information about the numerous cults before sanctioning their continued existence.

Reformer though he was, Lanfranc maintained a respect for custom, or rather, vested interest, although a good case for the continuance of any shrine would still have been required. Far from discouraging the legend, Lanfranc would have lent it credence.

Even the somewhat discreditable Herfast, sent by Lanfranc as Bishop of East Anglia, was eventually persuaded to move his attention from dice to church matters. However, when he eventually got down to diocesan business, he did so somewhat belatedly and dispensed with local shrines less efficiently than other Norman Bishops, leaving East Anglian folklore the richer. Therefore, with the sanction of the Normans, Walstan's stature as Patron of Agriculture grew stronger, and the Shrine became a site of pilgrimage which was to last for the next five hundred years.

Once in the written archives of the new rulers, the Bawburgh legend could begin its hold on posterity. The fact of St. Walstan's survival into the twelfth century is taken as proof that the legend passed Norman scrutiny and was thus formally acknowledged. Shrines that were not, suffered despoliation from which they seldom recovered. Happily, the invaders were relatively kind about those which remained. Rather than viewing them as subversive they philosophically reviewed the likelihood of a shrine's potential revenue. Where final approval was granted, Norman money was often used to develop a shrine to the point where it could command a better income as a centre for pilgrimage and indulgence.

It is noted that St. Wulfstan assisted the Domesday commissioners with their Worcestershire survey and generally ensured an Anglo Saxon voice within the bureaucracy of the conquering Normans. Although the Bishop and Lanfranc had their differences, each separate influence – at the highest level – contributed, albeit unknowingly, towards the establishment of the Bawburgh legend. There could have been any number of reasons why the story of St. Walstan might have passed Norman scrutiny, but it was the Bishop's determination to protect the existing culture which helped to ensure its survival. Of course, this is not to say that the Bishop's intent was entirely dissimilar to Lanfranc's, which was to regularise any financial gain that might derive from such a source.

THE *NOVA LEGENDA ANGLIE*

For the first mention of Walstan in any accessible Collection of saints' lives we have to leap forward 450 years, to 1516. In that year, the legend appeared in the *Nova Legenda Anglie* (NLA), published by Wynkyne de Worde. A Collection of saints' lives, in Latin, it was based almost exclusively on the *Sanctilogium Angliae, Walliae, Scotiae, et Hiberniae* (Saints of England, Wales and Scotland) by the fourteenth-century monk, John of Tynemouth, and which is now referred to simply as the *Sanctilogium*. In the same year, Richarde Pynson published his *Kalendre of the Newe Legende of Englande*, an abridged version, in English, of the same work but published independently from that by Worde. As Pynson wrote in his Prologue, the book was '... taken out of the newe Legende of the saynts of Englande, Irelande, Scotlande, and Wales for theym that vnderstande nat the Laten tonge'. It duplicated the items of the Latin edition, including an account of St. Walstan contained in fourteen paragraphs.

The importance of inclusion in these two works cannot be overstated. Without it, the integrity of the by then 500-year-old cult of East Anglia's Patron of Agriculture might have become intellectually unsustainable. A place in these definitive works ensured that, even when the huge Medieval pilgrimage traffic tailed off, Walstan maintained his stature as Saint and

Patron. The NLA enshrined him in the new scholarship which followed the setting up of England's first printing press under William Caxton in 1476, endorsed and developed by Caxton's pupils Worde and Pynson.

Not only was printing to open the door of literacy for non-clerics, but for the first time in history, more than one copy of a work could be available, to enhance the role of research and consolidate literature and history. It was also the means of establishing a standard language and, as demonstrated by Martin Luther's use of the pamphlet, a new and substantial way of reaching the masses. Any fundamental alterations and embellishments to which the legend of St. Walstan, and others, were subjected between the Norman Conquest and the dawning of the printing age were likely to have been the last. For those lives where the original documents were lost, that which appeared in the NLA became the primary source for successive historians. Each 'Life' of St. Walstan since the 1516 NLA has contained its basic elements, except one. In 1658 a copy was made of an 'ancient' triptych, which document will be examined in Chapter 7, but which for the time being has no bearing on the search for a primary life.

CAXTON AND COMPANY

The names of Caxton, Worde and Pynson run through early printing history like those of Greek gods. Prior to the middle of the fifteenth century, England was in a world of handwritten works, relying on monks and clerics whose work, in comparison to the new medium of print, was laborious, often incompetent and exclusive to the literate. William Caxton (1422-1491) was the master of the new craft, and at his feet sat the apprentices Wynkyne de Worde and Richarde Pynson. Other than family connections with the village of Cawston, in Norfolk, not much is known about Caxton's early life, but of his influence in establishing printing in England there is no doubt. In 1476, he paid his first year's rent to Abbot John Eastney, for a shop in the precincts of Westminster Abbey, which he continued to rent until his death. Such a location was fortuitous in that it was the beginning of his close association with the Benedictines, which was to reap its rewards in the easy access he acquired to their library and archives.

When, in 1484, Caxton printed his version of Jacobus de Voragine's *Legenda Aurea*, it heralded a new era of hagiology and was the means whereby legend upon legend was perpetuated and immortalised. Caxton named more than one translation, or version, of the work and omitted some of Jacobus' saints, adding some sixty of his own. This original *Legenda* was compiled in 1260 by the Italian Dominican, Jacobus, Archbishop of Genoa, but it had been revised and amended many times before Caxton's edition. After 1470 it became the first printed Collection of saints' lives and set the example for the NLA and Pynson's *Kalendre*.

After Caxton's death in 1491, his work was continued by Wynkyne de Worde, to whom Caxton had already handed over the daily management of the press rooms. Worde, a native of Alsace, was equally as competent as Caxton, having, it is believed, worked with him in the Cologne press as a teenage apprentice. As Caxton's foreman at Westminster, he is thought to have supervised the production of *Recuyell* and *Game of Chess*, two of Caxton's most famous books. Both he and Caxton might better be described as publishers rather than printers, since it is unlikely that they, or Pynson, were involved in the manual process of printing. That was better left to compositors or pressmen. After 1491, Worde remained at the Westminster shop for another nine years, when he removed to Fleet Street, to set up his establishment. There, in 1516, he published the *Sanctilogium* of John of Tynemouth as the *Nova Legenda Anglie*. It has long been assumed that the Latin Life of St. Walstan came from this *Sanctilogium*: so what of it, and its author, John of Tynemouth?

THE VICAR OF TYNEMOUTH

John of Tynemouth, who was born about 1290, was a native of Tynemouth and took his name when vicar of that town. After a university education, he became a Benedictine monk of St. Albans, of which Tynemouth Priory was a cell. Around 1340, John is thought to have moved to the Abbey at St. Albans, to begin compiling material for a Calendar of English saints. The library there was huge, with sometimes up to twenty scribes at work, copying and recording the annals of history. It was not only the busiest and largest library, but also one of the oldest, having been established by the first Norman Abbot, Paul de Caen, nephew (or possibly son) of Archbishop Lanfranc.

The task of compilation was formidable. During the twelfth and thirteenth centuries hagiology had grown in popularity and the accumulated writing of each Life, as listed in the Church Calendar, had begun to swell. Personal details about particular saints had been added to those previously required to, say, establish confessorship, or martyrdom, or to add credence for perceived miracles in the writing of a *legenda*. But there was no common consensus and no definitive Calendar. Certainly there were no common forms of spelling or accurate dating. Although there had been some attempts to add to the lists of saints' names in the old Church Calendars, notably Bede's *Martyrology*, and the Calendar of St. Willibrorg, such collections were the acknowledged saints of the whole Roman Catholic Church. But, even the St. Albans library did not contain the information John needed so he travelled to abbeys and monasteries in Ely, Canterbury, London, Glastonbury, and perhaps even to Wymondham, in Norfolk.

The Priory of Wymondham, founded in 1107, was a daughter house of St. Albans until, in 1448, it became an Abbey in its own right. Although relations between Wymondham and the Benedictine Mother House were often strained, there was necessary traffic between the two houses, as there was also at Binham, another Norfolk cell of St. Albans. During his journey round the British Isles, John of Tynemouth lived and worked at the nearest Benedictine house, where he might rightly expect a brotherly welcome. At Wymondham, however, whether as brother or scholar, his arrival might have occasioned a somewhat cooler reception than he was used to, since all too frequent visits by the Abbot of St. Albans put considerable strain on the resources of the Priory.

However, the monks would have been obliged to allow John to work there, and it is difficult to think that he could have been at Wymondham and not visit, or at least hear about, the shrine at Bawburgh. Although the Abbey itself was not a centre of pilgrimage, it was close enough to Norwich and Bawburgh to be involved in the pilgrimage traffic which traversed East Anglia.

How disappointing, therefore, to find that Walstan is not among the 157 lives in the *Sanctilogium*. Although extant in the British Library as forming part of MS Cotton Tiberius E, the manuscript was badly, and tragically, damaged in a fire during 1731. A check of a catalogue of the Cottonian Collection (which includes MS Tiberius E, of which the *Sanctilogium* is a part), compiled by Thomas Smith in 1696, reveals that there is, indeed, a *Wlf[s]tano* in the 157 lives; but it is *De S. Wlftano, Epifcopo & Confeffore* (Saint Wulfstan, Bishop and Confessor) who appears there, and is likely to be one of the first examples of Bishop Wulfstan being mistaken for Walstan. The Smith catalogue uses the form 'f' for 's' and might, therefore, have been the cause of the mistake at some point in translation or compilation.

In addition, there is no trace of the Bawburgh legend in the Bodleian Manuscript 240, a volume of 898 pages, made for the Monks at Bury St. Edmunds in 1377, its sources attributed to John of Tynemouth and others. No hint is left, either, of the extent to which John used his access to a mid-fourteenth-century chronicle entitled Manuscript Brompton, which was based on a previous compilation made by an unknown scribe from Norwich and therefore a likely source.

A footnote to the entry of the 1901 NLA confirms that the Life of *Sancto Walstano Confessore* was omitted in the Tiberius manuscript. (It is interesting to see that while the inestimable and learned Horstman has no trouble identifying Walstan with two a's, he variously uses Wulfstan, Wulstan and Wolston for the Bishop.)

It has to be assumed that John of Tynemouth recorded the story of St. Walstan elsewhere; or that the manuscript was lost on one of his many journeys; or that it was left behind in the library of one of the Benedictine houses. John had a love of vision, apparitions and legends, and was never sceptical of even the most fantastic story. He would, no doubt, have delighted in the legend of St. Walstan, but it is inevitable that much of his work failed to survive even the fourteenth century and it would seem that nothing he wrote about St. Walstan survives to this day. In 1349, John, and forty of the sixty monks at St. Albans, died of the Black Death.

FRIAR JOHN CAPGRAVE

Although Wynkyne de Worde did not credit John of Tynemouth directly, it is generally agreed that, in spite of having been tampered with in the early fifteenth century by the Norfolk monk, John Capgrave, and again in Manuscript Tanner 15 written for the Church of Canterbury in 1499, it was the *Sanctilogium* which formed the greater part of the 1516 NLA. It must now be further agreed that, although that work has traditionally been assumed to be the source of, and earliest reference to, the Walstan legend, this too is incorrect. But what of the other oft-credited source, Capgrave's *Legends*; is this also misleading?

An Augustinian friar, theologian and historian, John Capgrave (1393-1464) was born at Lynn, in Norfolk, and lived there for most of his life. Having studied at university (it is not certain which one, but probably Oxford), he was ordained priest in 1417 and became an inmate of the Austin Friary at Lynn. Soon after taking his doctor's degree, Capgrave was promoted to be Provincial of his Order in England. With such influence and position, he could not, surely, have failed to know about the pilgrimage centre at Bawburgh, and of its importance to the revenue of the Church in Norfolk.

Among Capgrave's work is to be found the adaptations of John of Tynemouth's manuscripts but he really only re-arranged the manuscript from a Calendar form to one of alphabetical order, albeit with prodigious effort. Such are the quirks of history that the Collection of saints' lives known as the *Nova Legenda Anglie* came to be credited to Capgrave himself, rather than to either John of Tynemouth or Worde. Therefore, Capgrave, to whom has traditionally been assigned the primary Life of St. Walstan, may now be discounted. In 1901, a new edition of the NLA was published, and its editor, Carl Horstman began to set the record straight.

In 1516, when Worde and Pynson published simultaneously, Walstan was included not in the main text, but as one of fifteen 'new' lives. These lives were discovered late in the publishing process and were not part of the chief source, namely the *Sanctilogium*, nor were they part of Capgrave's editing. Walstan and the other fourteen appear at the end of the NLA and are not in alphabetical order. It is clear that the legend was being published for the first time in 1516, since they had not been added in Manuscript Tanner, at the very end of the fifteenth century.

Horstman voiced his scepticism about Capgrave's true contribution to the 1516 Collection, chiefly because he was not the original author. Whether or not Capgrave did record the legend of St. Walstan has not been proved, though it would be extraordinary if he did not at least know of it. Capgrave spent most of his life at Lynn, but he was a prodigious writer and could have had access to the cartularies of the time, even though many of the documents would already have been either copied or plagiarised from other, often anonymous, writers. Capgrave's own abridgement of John of Tynemouth's work was just one such example and, according to Bishop Bale, the *Sanctilogium* itself had been modelled on work done by Guido de Castris, Abbot of St. Denis, who died in 1350. Most of the hagiographical treasures of the day were kept in the Benedictine libraries but whether or not Capgrave would have gained access there is irrelevant, since we are no longer looking to him for the source of the legend.

ADDITIONAL LIVES

In the 1901 edition of the NLA credit for the text was given to three processes: in substance it was the acknowledged *Sanctilogium*, attributed to John of Tynemouth; secondly, the same collection modified and re-arranged by Capgrave; and thirdly, the 1516 version by Worde with the additional lives. Having failed to identify the legend of St. Walstan in the first two, only the third source need now concern us.

For his NLA, Worde had used the most easily available material, as did Pynson, but at some stage late in the publishing process, the batch of fifteen lives was discovered. Where had Worde, or Pynson, found these additional lives, and when? The list of fifteen does not fall into any discernible grouping, since it includes a Welsh saint, Decuman, who died in 719, and St. Helena, a third-century Empress who was mother to Constantine the Great. Grateful though history might be to Wynkyne de Worde for providing this invaluable primary source, it would have been helpful if he had been as diligent in naming the derivation of his material as John of Tynemouth had always been. Were Pynson and Worde working from an original document, or, perhaps, from unused manuscripts by Capgrave not found until after his death? Were there maybe other relevant documents which might have been available?

From among the various collections and studies made during the fourteenth century, one from the crux of the thirteenth and fourteenth centuries still survives. It is a collection, containing forty-seven saints' lives, which once belonged to the nuns of Romsey, and known as MS Lansdowne 436. This manuscript was gathered independently of anything done by John of Tynemouth, and was not known to him. Among these forty-seven names we find *Wlstanus*. The lives are abridged, and the hand unknown; but, alas, folio 55 of that manuscript describes St. Wulfstan of Worcester. David

Rollason points to another fourteenth-century Collection of English saints'
lives in Gotha, Forschungsbibliothek, but no mention of St. Walstan is
contained in it. Having now scanned the obvious archive sources, the question
still remains: where did Worde and Pynson find the Life of St. Walstan?

THOMAS DE LA MARE

The answer must surely lie in Caxton's close association with the Benedictine
community, and in particular with the story of one Thomas de la Mare, who
was appointed Abbot of St. Albans in 1349, that terrible year in the history of
St. Albans when the plague carried off forty out of the sixty monks there,
including John of Tynemouth. It was Abbot Thomas, one-time Prior of
Tynemouth (1341-49) who sent John's manuscripts, together with other books
and study material, to the monks at Redburn, a cell of St. Albans only five
miles away, which served as a place of convalescence for sick monks.

Though the inscription was lost in the fire of 1731, it is generally
thought that John had dedicated part of the Tiberius manuscript to the
Abbot. Thomas had followed John at Tynemouth (as Prior), and over the
years the two men had formed a great friendship and a shared interest in
scholarly pursuits. To say that John of Tynemouth might have been at
Wymondham, and thus have had access to the legend surrounding the
Shrine of St. Walstan at Bawburgh, is speculation; but that Thomas de la
Mare did his apprenticeship at Wymondham there is no doubt.

Thomas de la Mare was born about 1308 into a Hertfordshire family
well versed in the religious life. His uncle was Abbot of Missenden, an
older brother was an Augustine monk at Thetford, and another brother and
their only sister became members of the Benedictine community of St.
Albans. He is described as '... cheerful, meek and humble in spirit, benign,
generous, hospitable, a lover of peace, a patron of learning, an encourager
of merit; a general favourite; of dignified presence, and fluent speech'. He
had served his probation in the cell at Wymondham before returning to St.
Albans as steward in 1335.

Having been in Norfolk, and no doubt in contact with his brother at
Thetford, Thomas was well placed to pass on to John of Tynemouth any
legends which could help in the compilation of the new Calendar. The fact
that the legend of St. Walstan did not appear in the *Sanctilogium* is not proof
that neither man recorded it. There was little time in 1349 for the two friends
to compare notes; John might already have contracted the plague when
Thomas arrived at St. Albans to take up his position as Abbot. He was, no
doubt, busy establishing himself at the Abbey and dealing with the problems
and distress caused by the Black Death. The account of Walstan might simply
have been left in the library, or sent with John's other manuscripts to Redburn
sometime after 1349, when Thomas took charge of his friend's work.

The link, then, between John of Tynemouth and the 1516 NLA is probably Thomas de la Mare, who was Abbot of St. Albans, who had been at Wymondham, and was a man of letters. It is a short hop from there to think that at some point manuscripts, or copies of them, belonging to St. Albans, or Redburn, found their way into the Benedictine library at Westminster Abbey and that one of them referred to St. Walstan. Considering Caxton's free and handy access to this library, and Worde's inheritance from his master, it is entirely plausible that it was there that the fifteen 'new' lives were found and included in the 1516 NLA.

Thomas de la Mare had been a friend of learning, and was not without connections at the other religious houses. He would have been happy for his monks at St. Albans to copy work from that library for other houses, especially if they were the legacy of his great friend, John of Tynemouth. Although Westminster Abbey is not renowned for its contribution to early English literature, it was nevertheless conveniently situated in London, which gave it a certain prominance, and was favoured by the monarchy. During his revision of *The Golden Legend*, Caxton might have discovered these additional lives at any one of the Benedictine libraries, but as likely as not under his very nose at Westminster. In spite of the fires in 1298 and 1447, which had destroyed so much, it was still a more than valid source of material. At the time Caxton might have put aside these new lives, intending to use them in the *Legend*, or for a future book, and then lost or forgotten them. Worde or Pynson later found them and, at last, remedied the ommission of St. Walstan from the list of English saints.

After 1516, the NLA continued as the single most accessible source for later authorities on legends of the saints, chief among them Bishop Bale, in *English Votaries*, and Bishop Challoner's *Memorial of Ancient British Piety* (1761). In the early years of the seventeenth century, Nicholas Roscarrock included Walstan in his huge compendium of the English saints, but the latter pages in the alphabetical sequence were subsequently torn out, the surviving manuscript now concluding with St. Simon Sudbury. However, Roscarrock for the most part drew his information from commonplace sources, and the lost entry no doubt reflected that of the NLA.

Similarly, Stanton's *Menology of England and Wales* owes much to the NLA, as do such later writers as Tanner, Blomefield, Butler, Husenbeth, the Ramsgate Monks, M.R. James, and various editors, all of whom wrote or epitomised the legend of St. Walstan in their own style.

~ • ~

Chapter Five
THE LEGEND SPREADS

'... there is no direct proportion between the legitimacy and popularity of a saint's cultus and the historical value of the written documents that testify to it ... we are therefore quite justified in being wary of a legend, while maintaining full trust in the saint.'
Fr. Hippolyte Delehaye, Bollandist

W E shall never know the true extent of Walstan's influence on the religious life of pre-Reformation England, but in spite of the upheavals preoccuping the Elmham Bishops early in the eleventh century, Bishop Aethelmar must have succeeded in publicising the Bawburgh *cultus* (from Lat. *colere*, 'to honour', and meaning 'to worship' or 'to cultivate') sufficiently to establish him as saint at least in the immediate neighbourhood of Bawburgh. As the cult grew and became established, his image, already characterised by a scythe and two calves, would undoubtedly have appeared on many more rood screens, and other church furniture, than survive today. The discovery of a fifteenth-century wall painting, depicting St. Walstan, at Cavenham in West Suffolk, together with the representation at Foxearth in Essex, enhance the view that further discoveries might yet be made. Those icons which have outlasted the ravages of time, the Reformation, and the 'cleansing' of the churches by the Puritans, are few and in consequence are precious in the search for St. Walstan.

No less important are those dedications which date from the years closer to our own time, since they stand as testimony to the continuing influence of the cult. There are few pre-Reformation English saints who inspire the establishment of monuments in the twentieth century, although the specific emblems of a scythe and two calves are often replaced now by less traditional ones, relying for identification on captions.

This chapter may be read in conjunction with Appendix I which lists all known or suggested representations and iconography attributed to SS. Walstan and Blida, and brings together for the first time dedications in Anglican and Catholic churches, pre and post-Reformation iconography, plus modern secular imagery.

THE WRITTEN WORD

Although a writer who took a certain interest in St. Walstan, the twentieth-century academician M.R. James wrote scathingly of Walstan's importance. He names him 'obscure', 'a mythical personage', and 'little known', commenting that any monuments '... will not be numerous, for the cult of St. Walstan was confined to a very small area, and had no powerful corporation to propagate it'.

Even Eamon Duffy, writing in 1992, credits the cult of St. Walstan as being contained within a seventeen-mile radius of Bawburgh, thereby highlighting the 'local' emphasis.

The fact of Walstan's inclusion in many of the standard Collections of saints' lives, compiled far beyond the boundaries of Norfolk and Suffolk, and over a number of centuries, rather goes against such opinions. It is obvious, for example, that the Prior of Norwich Cathedral would have promoted those shrines within his jurisdiction whenever possible while the practice of lay patronage can be seen to have effectively spread the cult into East and West Suffolk and Essex.

Both Wynkyne de Worde and Richarde Pynson thought the legend worthy of a place in their sixteenth-century Collections, as did Bale whose *English Votaries* was written while he lived in Germany. In the nineteenth century, Walstan's fame was to spread to the United States of America and Canada, when Butler's *Lives* was published in New York and Montreal during 1853 (complete with North American spelling), as well as being translated into French, Spanish and German. In 1925, Dom J. Baud gave Walstan a place in his *Dictionnaire d'Hagiographie*, followed by *The Book of Saints* from the Ramsgate Monks in 1947. If the cult had been so remarkably insignificant, how much more surprising it is that the legend has lasted for so long, with no help from a powerful corporation. Other saints, notably St. William of Norwich, enjoyed quite widespread notoriety until the political climate which had created them in due course failed the test of popular devotion.

Naturally enough, the Bawburgh legend did not appeal to everybody. Donald Attwater, in his Introduction to *A Dictionary of Saints* (1938), writes dismissively:

> '[Walstan] was born at Bawburgh in Norfolk and spent his days as a farm labourer at Taverham and Costessey. d. 1016. His cultus seems never to have spread beyond that neighbourhood.'

Attwater did not list Walstan in *The Penguin Dictionary of Saints*, although, in association with the Jesuit scholar, Herbert Thurston, he left an edited version in the 1956 edition of Butler's *Lives*. Michael Walsh, however, later removed the legend from both the *Lives* and the *Lives of Patron Saints*.

On the other hand, R.L.P. Milton, Fellow and Chaplain of Worcester College, Oxford, described Walstan in 1949 as having 'considerable fame, particularly in East Anglia' though he omitted to say where such fame might have been found. Milton also indexed St. Blida, though she appears there much as she is listed elsewhere, as the mother of St. Walstan.

The exclusion of Walstan from the *Acta Sanctorum* of the Bollandist Monks is thought by M.R. James to be significant, and, since Attwater was a devotee of the best-known of the Bollandists, Hippolyte Delehaye, he was presumably of the same opinion. However, when M.R. James says that the Bollandists are 'silent' about St. Walstan, he goes on to acknowledge that the Latin Life is included in their *Bibliotheca Hagiogr. Latina*. The early Bollandists did not, anyway, have access to English sources. Although they did seem to delight in disproving this or that saint's life, Delehaye himself denied waging war on legends, numbering such works as amongst '... the great unconscious natural forces'.

NORFOLK IMAGERY

In Norfolk, the Medieval legacy of dedication to St. Walstan can still be seen in churches at Barnham Broom, Denton, Litcham, Beeston-next-Mileham, Ludham, North Burlingham, Norwich and Sparham. Each of these can be thought of as representative of what was a wide acknowledgement of Walstan in East Anglia.

The inclusion of Walstan on the rood screen at North Burlingham is significant in that it is dated 1536, and is believed to have been the last screen erected in Norfolk before the pillage of the churches took place under Henry VIII. This would serve to illustrate that the Bawburgh legend was as strong as ever, right up to the eve of the Reformation.

The image at Litcham, on the south half of the Church screen, is just as significant, given the number of pilgrims who visited the Chapel there on their way to the Shrine of Our Lady of Walsingham. There is also, in All Saints Church, Litcham, a curious and ancient cryptogram which has never been properly explained and which some historians have suggested could have a connection with Walstan of Bawburgh.

The cryptogram is said to be a prayer, scratched into the wall by a pilgrim of the Middle Ages, and the signature has been deciphered as 'Wyke Bamburgh'. The similarity between 'Bamburgh' and 'Bawburgh', and a certain lack of actual clarity, has led the odd commentator to suggest a link of some sort between the Litcham Chapel and the Shrine Chapel at Bawburgh. This theory cannot be entirely discounted since it was not unknown for pilgrims to leave a permanent reminder of their visit to one or other shrine on the pilgrimage routes across Britain. At Beachamwell, for example, Mortlock and Roberts cite other, undeciphered graffiti, thought to date from the fourteenth century. However, with reference to 'Bamburgh', this could as easily be used to distinguish the place of origin of the writer, i.e. 'Wyke of Bawburgh'.

The obvious alternative to 'Bawburgh' reaches back into Anglo Saxon history for its origins, to the Northumbrian town of Bamburgh (Bamborough), once the centre of power for the eighth-century Kings of Northumbria. Only a short boat ride from Bamburgh was Lindisfarne, the one-time seat of St. Cuthbert (634-687). The cult of St. Cuthbert survived the destruction of St. Aidan's Lindisfarne Priory in 793, and his image appears in numerous Medieval illustrations and is to be found in most contemporary Calendars. A pilgrim with such distinguished connections might well have been tempted to leave his mark at Litcham, as would any devotee of another Norfolk saint, Godrick (1069-1170). St. Godrick, born in Walpole, is thought to have visited the Farne Islands in his seafaring days, and took his inspiration from St. Cuthbert.

Coincidentally, in a biography of M.R. James by Richard Pfaff (1980), St. Walstan is mistakenly indexed as 'Walstan of Bamburgh'.

Only a few miles from Litcham is Beeston-next-Mileham, where, in the Church of the Nativity of the Blessed Virgin, a figure on the dado of the mutilated south screen is considered to represent Walstan. Although the scythe outline is not particularly easy to trace it is nevertheless discernible. Knowing the proximity of Beeston to the pilgrimage centre at Litcham it is almost certain that the figure is that of Walstan. Eamon Duffy in *The Stripping of the Altars* says '... one of the figures on the dado of the south screen there appears to have been carrying a scythe, and is almost certainly St. Walstan'. Duffy is the first to credit Walstan at Beeston.

Evidence of the cult of St. Blida is, as we have discovered, very slight, although as recently as 1955, Helen Roeder credited Blida as Patron of Mothers, though on what grounds is not clear. However, in the Church of St. Mary Magdalene in Norwich, there is a sixteenth-century screen panel bearing an image attributed to Blida, next to one of her son, Walstan. Behind these two panels lies a remarkable trail of discovery and preservation, which is more fully explored in Appendix I. Suffice it to say here that the panels, thought to date from about 1515, can now be seen in the Church of St. Mary Magdalene, removed there from the original site at St. James (with Pockthorpe).

Given the history of these panels, some doubt could be raised as to whether that dedicated to St. Blida is in fact the original title, although there is little doubt that St. Walstan is correctly named. All that can safely be said is that there is no definite evidence that the figure on the panel is not St. Blida. What is less certain is that the female figure on the accompanying font is correctly named as Blida, and only appears as such by authority of Husenbeth.

One other illustration attributed to St. Blida (in Keyser, 1883, as pointed out by Miriam Gill) is a figure which featured on the screen of the now ruined church at Babingley, Norfolk. Although fire destroyed the screen in 1854, a watercolour of all the panels was done by Dawson Turner. But, although the story of the Babingley panels is told in *Sandringham, Past & Present*, Blida is not named in that account. Identification is believed to have been made by Husenbeth in the 1860s. The Church of St. Felix at Babingley was of special interest, as it is supposed to be built on the site of the first East Anglian Church, and the village has been looked on favourably by the Royal Family, since it is so close to their Sandringham home. In 1894-5, the Prince of Wales (Edward VII) built a modern Church – of blue corrugated iron with a thatched roof – but it, too, is now disused and falling into ruin.

The single undisputed relic of St. Blida remains the tiny fragment of glass which survives in a repaired window at the Church of St. Agnes, Cawston. It is pronounced to be Medieval and goes some way to proving that a cult once derived from her life. M.R. James referred to a fragment as being 'preserved in Cawston parsonage' and it is presumed to be that which was incorporated in the south aisle window at St. Agnes' Church in 1932.

Due to the plundering of the Shrine Chapel in 1538, there is almost no Medieval legacy of the Bawburgh site itself, but who knows what treasures might once have been there during the pilgrimage years? Little survives from that time, except a Poor Box thought to date from the reign of Henry II; the remains of a fourteenth-century wall painting – probably depicting St. Christopher; and, in the north-east wall, the filled-in archway which once led to the Shrine Chapel.

Bryant alone credits the survival of other ancient representation at Bawburgh; in his *Norfolk Churches* (1905) he records: 'There were formerly some good poppy-heads on the old benches, representing Angels, Saints, and S. Walstan'. However, we are not told when 'formerly' applied or what became of the bench-ends.

Although at the last count there were almost a hundred archaeological sites in the Parish of Bawburgh, many of them were only discovered in the 1980s during surveying work for the Norwich Southern Bypass and there has been little time for evaluation. However, among the finds are a number of Medieval brooches; so far, though, no pilgrim badges have been identified. Perhaps when other excavation takes place it is possible that such reminders of those halycon days of the pilgrimage traffic will be found. There might even have been pilgrim badges on sale at Bawburgh, as there were at other shrines, and maybe one or two from further away were lost in the lanes of Bawburgh, or in Earlham's Green Lane along which travellers to and from Norwich passed.

And what of the Shrine Chapel itself? It was surely no less grand than others for which there are splendid descriptions. During the late fifteenth century, there were several bequests to the Chapel and Guild of St. Walstan, and in 1505 (as pointed out by Robert Halliday) Thomas Shemyng bequeathed his soul to Walstan with twelve shillings to paint the Saint's image in Bawburgh Church and twelve shillings to the Saint's Guild. Today, only the outline of the Chapel entrance, and its ruined foundations, can be traced on the north wall of the existing Church which still has its rare dedication to St. Walstan.

ST. WALSTAN IN SUFFOLK

Evidence that the cult flourished in Suffolk is much less, but the fact that a fifteenth-century chapel was dedicated to him in St. Mary's Church, Bury St. Edmunds, establishes the cult as being far more widespread than has previously been credited. Similarly, the wall painting discovered in 1967 at Cavenham is another small step towards this author's theory that Cambridgeshire is the most obvious 'escape route' for the cult to have spread more widely through Eastern England. It would not be surprising to find representation of St. Walstan in Cambridgeshire along the westward paths leading to the important Medieval centre of worship at Ely.

The Chapel of St. Wolston is at the west end of the north or St. Peter's aisle of St. Mary's, in a recess formed by the projection of the tower into the Church of St. Mary's. It was here that the Archdeacon of Sudbury held his Visitations and Consistory Courts until 1874. As well as the ecclesiastical courts and visitations, it was customary to distribute the gifts of bread to the poor from the Chapel, which was historically separated from the nave by a screen corresponding in character to that which is still visible in the choir. In the Chapel, also, executors of wills were required to deliver accounts of their trust.

Unfortunately, although a Victorian brass plaque proclaiming the Chapel for 'Wolston, Patron Saint of East Anglian Farmers' was present well within living memory, it is now thought to be lost.

The Chapel was completed in the 1430s, and as yet no evidence has emerged which might prove that it replaced an earlier St. Wolston's Chapel in a previous Church on the same site. The older Church was, though, built by the Benedictines, which Order was by way of being Walstan's champions.

Evidence of the Chapel derives, as it often does, from contemporary wills and bequests. Thus, in 1503, the Chapel is acknowledged by one Sir William Gardener, priest of the rood altar in the monastery of St. Edmunds, and cited by the nineteenth-century editor and antiquarian Samuel Tymms in the numerous editions of *The History of St. Mary's*. In his will, Sir William bequeathed '... to the altar of saynt Walston in the church of saynt

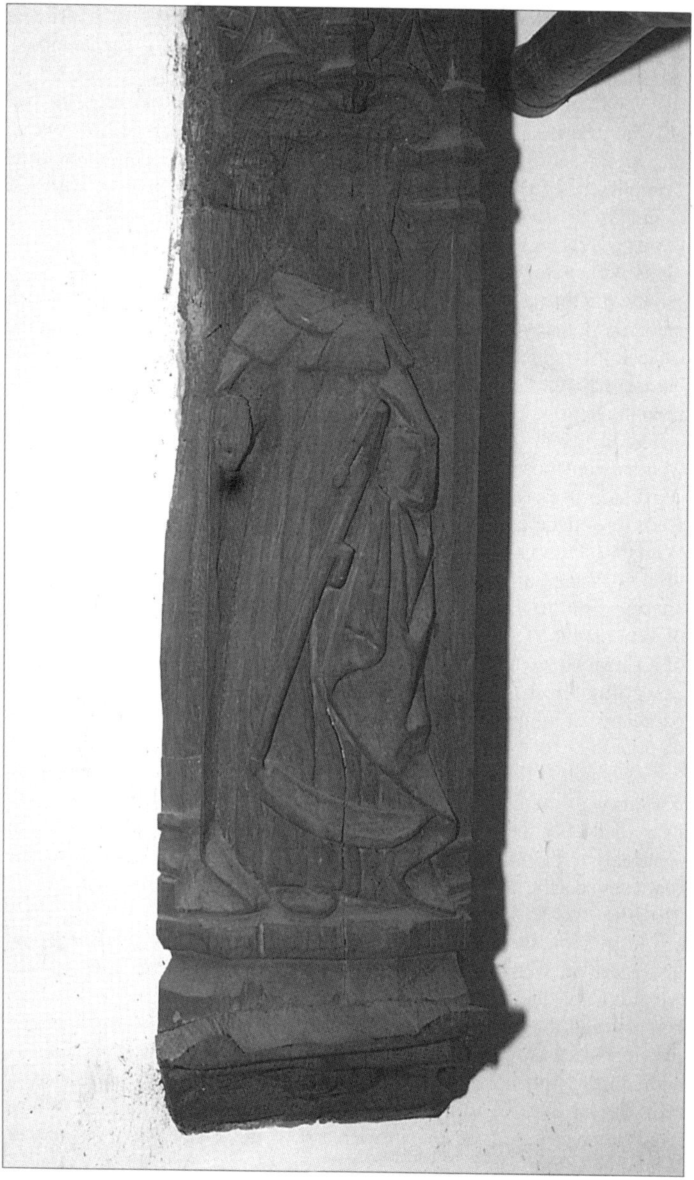

Mary' a large number of books, plus '... j peyre chalices of sylv, a vestment of blewe sarsenett, a corporas case w(it)h a corp'as in hitt, ij aught clothys' and sundry other possessions.

The Chapel dedication to St. Wolston (variously spelt Wulstan) would also have been familiar to the antiquary Thomas Tanner, who had been in the Archdeaconry of Norfolk immediately prior to his appointment as Commissary of the Archdeaconry of Sudbury and the town of Bury St. Edmunds, in 1706. He spent much of his professional life in the Norwich diocese, and two volumes of his work were used by Blomefield in 1805 for his *History of Norfolk*, which was dedicated to Tanner.

On the theme of St. Walstan's traditional association with agriculture, the glass in the west window of St. Mary's, and in close proximity to the Chapel, was coincidentally paid for by local farmers as thanksgiving for the bumper harvest of 1845. In 1920, a memorial was built in the Chapel to those from the Suffolk Yeomanry who were slain in the First World War.

In St. Mary's, too, Samuel Tymms attributes one of the famous wooden roof post carvings to Walston. However, this is likely to be a confusion between Walstan and Wul(f)stan since the carving is of a Bishop and bears little similarity to other Walstan iconography. Wulfstan, Bishop of Worcester, is the most obvious alternative, but in 962, a Wulfstan gave lands at Palgrave, Suffolk, to a Church in 'Bedrickesurthe' (Bury St. Edmunds), which date conveniently fits that of Wulfstan the Cantor, who flourished around 996. Given the existence of a Chapel dedicated to St. Wolston, a mistake could have been made in assigning the roof carving. The question must also be asked if, perchance, it might be the other way round; that is, the Chapel dedication could also be to Wulfstan.

Although in the various editions of *A Handbook of Bury St. Edmunds*, Tymms is given to uncertain interchange of the two names, there is plenty of evidence to show that he identified St. Wolston and St. Wul(f)stan separately in the matter of the Chapel (if not the carving). Indeed, Tymms footnotes specific details of the Norfolk saint 'St. Wolston the Confessor' in *The History of St. Mary's*.

In addition, the author of the current guide to St. Mary's, historian and lay reader of St. Mary's, Clive Paine, points out that the existing Church was built by the town's people, at the commencement of the fifteenth century, and they would be more likely to have chosen Walstan as their inspiration than a Bishop of Worcester or, indeed, Wulfstan the Cantor. In addition, the Abbot of the day, William Curteys (d. 1446), was appointed by the General Chapter to be visitor of all the Benedictine houses in East Anglia, two of which were at Norwich and Wymondham where the story of Walstan was familiar.

One other piece of information relating to the Chapel is to be found in the north aisle of St. Mary's where a painting can be found which is dated between 1707 and 1712. It shows that there were still then screens around 'St. Wulstan's Chapel', but as the text accompanying the painting dates from the 1930s the spelling of Wulstan cannot be considered for identity purposes. Much restoration has been done in the Church since the early 1800s and at some point the screens were removed, possibly after 1874. In 1836 an ancient wall painting was discovered on one of the Chapel walls, which had been hidden by a coating of whitewash, though its subject is unknown and there is no sign of St. Walstan on it.

However, a fifteenth-century wall painting which does depict St. Walstan is to be found at Cavenham, about seven miles north-west of Bury St. Edmunds, and is considered one of the most significant and important finds of this search. It is unique in being the only definite wall painting of St. Walstan, although the fact that it exists at Cavenham should be no real surprise. The village is on an ancient route – the Icknield Way – and has been named as being one of the places which linked Newmarket and Thetford.

The painting was discovered as recently as 1967, and the outline figure of Walstan is as definitive as it could be, with both the specific and generic emblems, a scythe and crown, clearly drawn (see page 140). It may be the only piece of a once-larger mural to have survived. Research into the origins and implications of the painting is currently being carried out by Miss Miriam Gill (see Bibliography) but, surprisingly, the identification of the figure as Walstan (by Dr. David Park of the Courtauld Institute of Art) came some twenty years after its discovery.

The painting, which measures approximately two feet by two feet eight inches, shows Walstan with – unusually – a hand raised in blessing with two small figures by his right foot looking up at him. Identification of these figures, one male and one female, has caused some discussion: are they characters in the legend – perhaps Nalga and his sceptical wife – or merely passers-by, or pilgrims? Although they are much smaller than St. Walstan, this could merely have been done purposely to emphasise just who was the more important of the three. However, although the figures appear at first glance to be diminutive adults, their features appear childlike.

One answer could lie in a legend belonging to the nearby village of Woolpit, where there was once a sizeable shrine to Our Lady of Pity and a Lady's Well near the Church. The story is summarised by William Dutt in his *Suffolk Guide*, and told originally by William of Newburgh.

One day some farm labourers were at work in a harvest field at Woolpit when they saw a boy and girl who appeared to come out of the pits known as 'Wolfpittes', which existed for the destruction of the wolves which roamed thereabouts. The two children said that they had come from a

Christian country called St. Martin's, which had churches, but where there was no sun, 'only a faint twilight ... but beyond a broad river there lay a land of light'.

That morning, while they were tending their father's sheep, they had heard a noise like the ringing of the bells at Bury Abbey, whereupon they found themselves among the reapers in the harvest field of Woolpit. The two did not return to St. Martin's and, while the boy soon died, the girl lived and married a man of Lynn.

If the two figures cannot be otherwise identified, it is entirely possible that a derivative of the Woolpit folklore was used at Cavenham where the theme of harvest was represented by St. Walstan. It must be acknowedged, however, that Clive Paine dismisses the Woolpit siblings in favour of figures representing an aspect of the legend, possibly Nalga and his wife, or the donors of the painting.

The third known Suffolk pre-Reformation imagery of St. Walstan is a fifteenth-century wood carving which is part of the impressive hammerbeam roof at St Mary the Virgin Church, Earl Stonham, although it is, in common with the other figures, minus its head. The inclusion of St. Walstan here is very much in keeping with the theme of country life depicted in the other roof carvings, which include a sturdy farmyard duck, a fox with a goose in its mouth, an owl, and a terrier.

Unfortunately, the beautifully crafted roof carvings suffered from the attention of the notorious William Dowsing in the 1640s. Arthur Mee describes Dowsing, a commissioner under the Earl of Manchester, as 'a fanatical zealot of destruction', and so he was: in just fifty days he smashed and vandalised 150 churches in Suffolk. Although Dowsing is traditionally credited with the destruction of the roof figures, Clive Paine points out that the actual work was likely to have been carried out by Edmund Blomfield, of 'Aspell-Stonham', since in his *Diary* Dowsing names Blomfield as his substitute.

It may yet emerge that Dowsing, or his subordinate, was responsible for destroying other images of St. Walstan in Suffolk, particularly if they had been included among the hundreds of stained glass windows smashed by the Puritans. Earl Stonham is in the path of those pilgrims criss-crossing East Anglia and there could well have been other such representation of St. Walstan along the same route.

So far, no representations of St. Walstan have been discovered in Ipswich itself and no claim made that the cult of St. Blida was ever celebrated in Suffolk. However, there is one more possible example of St. Walstan which, if investigated, might prove to be one of the most exciting finds to date.

In the tiny, but historic, Church of St. Mary at Ashby in East Suffolk, a series of wall paintings were listed in Keyser's 1883 *List of Buildings Having Mural Decorations*. They were said to contain The Last Judgement,

St. Catherine, St. William of Norwich, and The History of St. Wulstan – but were at time of writing '… all covered with a fresh coat of whitewash' and part, no doubt, of the renovation work which took place in the 1880s. The author of the Village History, Rev. Dr. Edward C. Brooks, writes:

> *'Early in 1973 Mrs. Eve Baker, one of the country's foremost conservators of wall paintings … visited Ashby Church … Her report was favourable towards the possibility of finding these murals … There seems to have been little disturbance of the fabric of the church over the past five centuries, so we hope their survival is something waiting to be discovered.'*

Originally, Mr. Brooks assigned the depiction to St. Wul(f)stan, but later decided to give the matter wider consideration. The Worcester Bishop is rarely depicted in East Anglia and, reasoned Mr. Brooks, 'although he stood for the Saxon episcopal excellence against the invading Normans this would not be a valid presentation at the time the murals were painted'.

There would seem to be a more than average chance that the 'History' does indeed relate to St. Walstan, rather than to St. Wul(f)stan (as at Norwich Cathedral – see Appendix IV). The list of Ashby Rectors includes one Simon de Bauburgh (1361-1390), whose Patron was Joan, wife of John de Inglose. The Inglose family came from Loddon in Norfolk, in which Church the supposed martyrdom of St. William is celebrated. The undisputed presence of William of Norwich at Ashby was acknowledged by M.R. James, although in *The Life of William of Norwich* he stated that he could find no description of the painting. If it is assumed that William of Norwich was the Patron's choice, Simon de Bauburgh – Rector at Ashby for over thirty years – would have been likely to choose St. Walstan.

It is also to be noted that later Patrons of Ashby Church were the Jernegan family, the first being William Jernegan in 1487. Another branch of this family was to receive the Manor of Costessey from Mary I, part of which lay in Bawburgh, where they were to play a large part in the continuance and survival of the legend of St. Walstan in English Catholicism.

Due to Blythburgh being named as Walstan's birthplace in the English Life (see also Chapter 7), it has been suggested, though never explored or proved, that imagery of St. Walstan existed at the Medieval port of Dunwich, once the centre of the See of St. Felix and historically and geographically linked to Blythburgh. Ancient Dunwich has long since been lost to the sea, but in early Medieval times it was an important trading port, exporting wool and grain to Europe and beyond, while importing wine, cloth, furs and timber. With eight parish churches and several religious houses and chapels, there were plenty of places for the early pilgrims to congregate on their way to and from the religious shrines of the British Isles.

Who is also to deny that pilgrims leaving Dunwich might not have taken the inspiration of St. Walstan with them far beyond the shores of East Anglia? The cult of St. Edmund was celebrated at the Basilica of St. Sernin at Toulouse, where it is thought Edmund's relics were taken by Louis VIII, King of France, in the twelfth century. And it is evident, from the extraordinary *Book of Margery Kempe*, of 1436, that the proximity of Norfolk and Suffolk ports to Europe facilitated a sizeable pilgrimage industry and that many of those who visited Bawburgh came from overseas. Kempe herself included journeys to Our Lady of Ipswich, her native Lynn, to Walsingham, as well as to Rome and Jerusalem.

AN ESSEX DEDICATION

So far, identification of St. Walstan in Essex is limited to a panel in the rood screen of the Church of SS. Peter and Paul at Foxearth (pictured opposite). Although the panel itself bears extensive Victorian renovation, its sixteenth-century origins make it as significant as the Cavenham wall painting in establishing the cult of St. Walstan beyond that formerly considered.

The screen has five female saints on the north side, and five male saints on the south side of the gate; Walstan stands between SS. Alban and Felix. The Church interior bears an extraordinary Victorian ornateness which is the direct legacy of Foxearth's rector between 1845 and 1892, John Foster, and caused the Church to be known locally for many years as the 'cathedral'. Foster was a Tractarian who used his own money to upgrade and beautify the Church by commissioning wall decorations and ceiling stencils, thus following the philosophy of the Oxford Movement for the revitalisation of the Protestant Church.

In his *Shell Guide to Essex*, Norman Scarfe attributes the panel as 'early Tudor' and describes the renovations as harsh, but the figure of St. Walstan, bearded and holding a scythe, does not seem to have been fundamentally altered. There is no reason either to suggest that the original identity of the screen saints would have been changed by the Rev. Foster nor, indeed, any reason for Walstan to be introduced or substituted in a part of Eastern England where no discernible links with the legend of St. Walstan exist. However, one fifteenth-century journey by a Bawburgh couple to Essex shows that villagers were themselves not averse to travel into Essex.

In 1445 a farmer, Richard Wright, went on a pilgrimage to Dunmow Priory in Essex, where he and his wife hoped to claim the famous Dunmow Flitch. There was, at the time, a tradition at the Priory whereby a married couple with proven fidelity were awarded a flitch of bacon. Mention of the Dunmow Flitch is made in literature as early as Chaucer's *Tales*, but that awarded to Mr. and Mrs. Wright of Bawburgh is the first on record. In the Cartulary of the Priory is a memorandum to say that Richard Wright, '... of Bawburgh next Norwich, in the County of Norfolk, yeoman, came here and pleaded for the bacon of Dunmow on the 17th day of April in the 23rd year of the reign of King Henry VI, after the Conquest, and was sworn according to the form of the gift aforesaid, etc. before John Canon, then Prior of this place'.

In Blomefield's *History of Norfolk* at the Norwich Record Office (which gives the Dunmow story) someone has written in pencil 'Chaucer mentions Bawburgh'. As yet no such reference has been found, the writer possibly confusing the Chaucerian reference to the Dunmow Flitch, or perhaps a mistake for Bawdeswell, which village Chaucer does mention. (The naming of the Reeve of Bardeswell has always been taken as an indication that Chaucer knew Norfolk well.)

FURTHER AFIELD

Just as it is not yet possible to know the full extent of the legend in the Eastern Counties of the Middle Ages, it is even more difficult to ascertain Walstan's influence further afield. While this search has now established the cult outside Norfolk, it may by no stretch of the imagination be considered to have been of any great national importance. However, a stone figure, crowned and holding a scythe, standing atop All Saints' Church at Gresford in Clwyd (formerly Denbighshire) has been named as Walstan. Although M.R. James could not believe that the fame of St. Walstan penetrated so far west, there is no reason why that should not have been the case. The Benedictine Order was a large one and wielded huge influence in Britain right up to the Reformation. Why should the cult of St. Walstan not have been promoted by the Order outside East Anglia? There were, after all, no set rules by which a cult was extended; indeed, representations invariably came about as the result of an individual's patronage or memorial. Many influential patrons held or acquired a stake in Bawburgh fortunes over the centuries, including the Norman Alan Rufus, whose estate was heavily endowed by William the Conqueror (see also Chapter 6).

Until very recently it had been accepted that the '*Wulstane*' mentioned in a 1239 Reading Calendar referred to Walstan. The inscription was for a monk called John of Fornsete, who was keeper of the Cartulary of the Abbey and whose name derived from Forncett in Norfolk. Religious life at the time was often monotonous, and as a means of light relief, minstrels were allowed into the religious houses. At Reading, an unknown discantor wrote down a piece of harmonised secular music which is now famously known as *Sumer is Icumen In*. It is popularly called *The Cuckoo Song* and being traditionally sung at May Day celebrations it served as another pointer in the direction of Walstan. Almost certainly, John of Fornsete neither wrote nor transcribed the work, but he was obviously held in some regard at the Abbey, since his name survives on the original manuscript of this first English song.

On the Reading Calendar, part of the manuscript on which the music is written, is the dedication prayer entered on St. Wulstan's Day, 1239: '*Ora, Wulstane, pro nostro fratre, Johanne de Fornsete* (Wulstan, pray for our brother, John of Forncett.)

Where a writer was unsure of his ground – for example, Arthur Mee – he simply left it at 'St. Wulstan's Day'. However, on examination of the original manuscript, which is the only copy to bear the inscription, the date is the 19th January, the feastdate of St. Wul(f)stan.

One intriguing tale about a possible lost icon of Walstan surfaced as recently as forty years ago, in the unlikely location of Rongai in Kenya, where the Anglican Church is named for St. Walstan of Bawburgh. While the story of this far-away dedication more rightly belongs in a later chapter, it is said that the dediction for the Settlers' Church was decided on after someone saw an advertisement in *World Farming* for hay-making equipment, which had on it a reference to Walstan. One young Remittance man then remembered seeing a statue to the Patron of Farmers and Farm Workers above the entrance to an English cathedral and thought the advertisement an omen. The Settlers wanted the new Church to reflect their lives as farmers, as well as linking their new lives to the old, and St. Walstan was accepted as Patron Saint of the Rongai Church.

The young man said that the figure he had seen was robed, and held in one hand a wheatsheaf. Although wheat is not a recognised emblem of St. Walstan, the description is facsimile to that which is carved on the font in St. Julian's Church in Norwich. Does a stone carving of St. Walstan still stand, unrecognised and unacknowledged, above the entrance to an English cathedral?

~ • ~

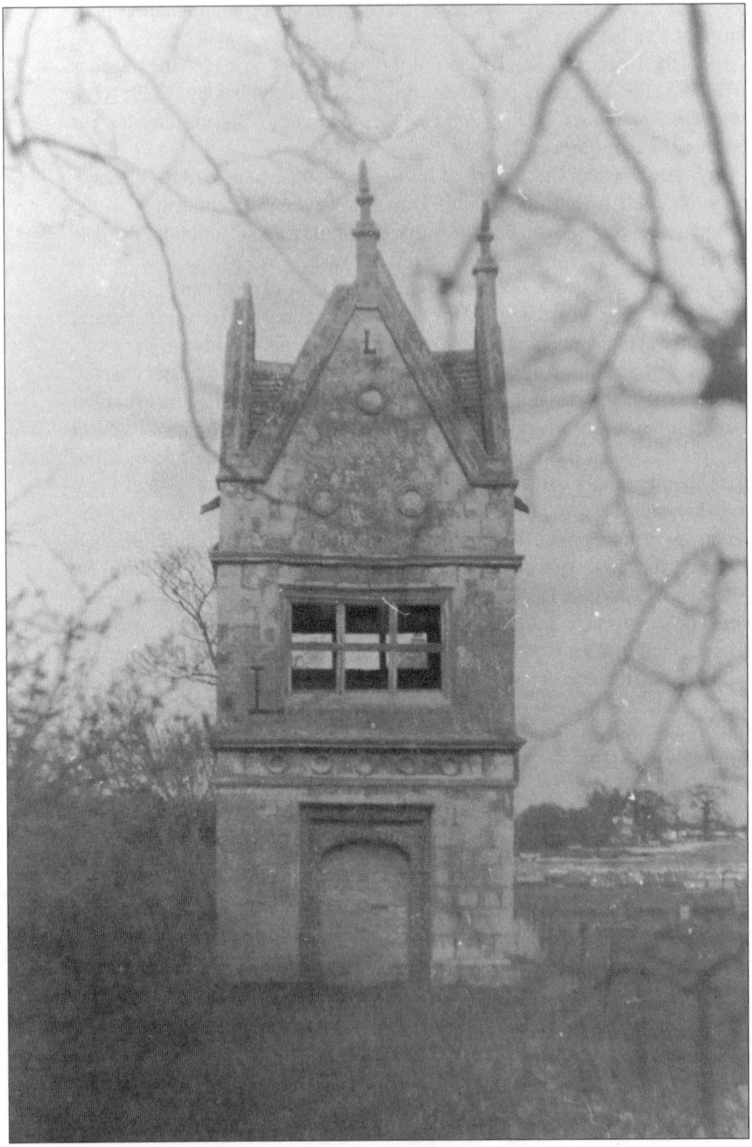

Chapter Six
TO BE A PILGRIM

'In ancient time, besides the vicar, there were six chantry priests
serving in the church at St. Walstan's altar, which Saint was
inshrined in the north chapel of this church, which was
demolished on that account at the Reformation.'
Blomefield's History of Norfolk (1805)

*I*MAGINING what it must have been like to visit Bawburgh as a
Medieval pilgrim need not tax the mind, if, with closed eyes, the modern
pilgrim stands on the site of the ancient shrine at Bawburgh and thinks film.
A twentieth-century man or woman can use a camera's eye to track a band
of Medieval pilgrims as they approach the Shrine Chapel of St. Walstan,
picking their way carefully along the dusty and uneven path which runs
along the bank of the River Yare. Most are wearing the traditional, long,
russet-coloured gown, with large sleeves, and a leather belt to which is tied
a bowl, or bag, containing the day's needs. On their heads are the large,
round hat of the pilgrims, each with a rosary hung round their neck.

For many, the last stop had been at the tiny hamlet of Algarsthorpe, a
short way back along the path, where they had prayed in the Chapel of St.
Mary Magdalene. A few had spent the previous night at the imposing
Wymondham Abbey, where early morning Mass had been said by one of
the black-robed Benedictine monks. There, a group of merchant pilgrims,
with a retinue of attendants, had met other wayfarers travelling together for
safety. That morning their procession is followed by men and women from
nearby farms and villages, anxious to celebrate the feast date of God's
servant, Walstan.

The last man in the slowly winding line of pilgrims leans on his staff
and looks back towards Algarsthorpe for a glimpse of the crumbling
stonework of the nunnery rising above the vineyards, just then pale green
with spring growth, before turning back to the final lap of his journey.
Already, he can see the crooked roof of the sturdy, wooden mill, and the
round tower of the Saxon church. As he turns, he lifts his face to the sky.
The day looks set to stay fine and bright, the few white, wisping clouds
scudding carelessly across the May sky.

As the footpath guides the pilgrims away from the river, the leader
reaches the foot of the hill. He slows his step, almost to a halt, and the

6

crowd's chaotic, excited chatter dies. Each pilgrim, whether rich, poor, foreign or native, begins to prepare him or herself for the Mass. Some nervously finger the coins which are to be offered to the Chantry Priests, kept there by the Prior of Norwich. Such tokens of intercession will be laid on the altar and prayers said for the repose of souls and for the good of the living.

A party of merchants will hope to seek overnight accommodation with the Priests in the messuage, built below the Church, while the locals – and those anxious to reach the next site – will stay only long enough to beg the Patron Saint's intercession with God for His blessing on their humble endeavours and to hear the Priest read the *legenda* of St. Walstan from the triptych in the Shrine Chapel. After Mass, those farmers and farm labourers among the company will process to the Well, there to dip their hands into the Holy Water, invoking God's healing powers in the name of St. Walstan. Each year they come to kneel before the Shrine, as their fathers and grandfathers have done, with a faith undiminished by the realities of peasantry, their hopes undimmed by the harshness of life.

As the camera of imagination stops whirring, a young man stoops to cup the glimmering, crystal-clear well water in his roughened hand, then pours it gently onto the head of a calf, lying weakly and with no signs of life, in his bare arms.

Then the vision is gone and the modern pilgrim touches again the reality of a quiet Norfolk churchyard in the fading years of the twentieth century.

THE PILGRIM WAY

To search for St. Walstan without knowing why pilgrims sought earthly answers to heavenly questions at Bawburgh is to deny meaning to the legend. Religion in Medieval times had wholly different meanings and was very much a shared occupation; indeed, if *The Canterbury Tales* are anything to go by, there was rather more fun to be had than the false piousness so often envisaged.

At Bawburgh, pilgrims were not seeking to retrace the steps of a mentor, or the founder of a religious order; they were not seeking, either, to walk the same route as Christ himself. Jerusalem, and the Holy Lands of the East, were there for those who could afford such travel. Saints were never intended to take the place of God and those who revered the Shrine of St. Walstan were not mistaking the servant for the Master. Any such idolatry would have been difficult to sustain, so long as it was accepted that God was the very reason for the Shrine's existence. Instead, those who sought St. Walstan came to be healed, to invoke God's mercy, and to beg forgiveness from sin as part of the prevailing Medieval concept and practice of Christianity.

As well, the story of a royal prince forsaking riches and power to become a farmworker had a suitably devout romanticism about it. Centres of pilgrimage were controlled by the Church hierarchy and the story of Walstan satisfied the needs for a heavenly intermediary while being inoffensive to successive political regimes.

While the fashion was still for a lifelong search for salvation by means of a pilgrimage, Bawburgh took its rightful place on the pilgrim's map. During the late thirteenth and fourteenth centuries the practice of pilgrimage was in high vogue and a visit to the Bawburgh Shrine was one part of a wide spiritual embrace of all things holy. But the holiness, or value, was not in the stone and mortar of the Chapel, rather it was carried in the aspirations brought by the pilgrims themselves. Walstan is a saint celebrated by virtue of popular acclaim, rather than by any formal canonization, and reflects a recognisable search for a comfortable immortality.

By the fourteenth and fifteenth centuries those in search of devotional or penitential pilgrimage still found in Walstan an acceptable, and by then firmly established, cult. These pilgrims reasoned philosophically that hell was just as immortal as heaven, but less desirable. Even towards the Reformation, when religious scepticism was encouraged by the Crown, the story of St. Walstan still had the power to reassure the pilgrim that Almighty God, raised in splendour above their understanding, had taken into His heaven a humble farm worker. This riches-to-rags tale was ideal for those who wished, for any number of reasons, to establish heavenly insurance but had no appetite for emulating the sentiments of Luke, Chapter 14, Verse 33, as Walstan had done.

Perception of God has always been exclusively individual by nature, but the physical route to be taken was both public and universal. A large number of Medieval pilgrims who visited St. Walstan's Shrine had undertaken difficult and long voyages in order to achieve one more step in their search for spiritual fulfilment. Shrines, or holy places, were important for some as a means of being seen by other pilgrims, and to curry favour in their home environment. As outward proof of his or her search, those fortunate enough to have them sported a collection of shrine badges. Yet those men and women of East Anglia, who perhaps had no badges from far-away places, were just as much pilgrims. There is nothing to say that a pilgrimage has to entail a long journey and there is no measure for sincerity of intent.

A CHANTRY IS ESTABLISHED

Since there were six Chantry Priests at Bawburgh, it is clear that a large number of pilgrims willingly paid for intercession, or 'indulgences', but it is unclear when the Chapel was first designated a Chantry rather than a site of parochial worship. Bishop Bale, and others, always put emphasis on attendance at the shrine by local people, but their offerings would hardly warrant six priests and the building of a considerable messuage below the Church. Blomefield wrote that the shrine was visited daily, '... not only by pilgrims from all parts of England, but numbers came from beyond the seas for that purpose', obviously bringing their temporal offerings in abundance.

In his book *Medieval Chantries and Chantry Chapels*, G.H. Cook points out that the earliest recorded Chantry was that at Lincoln Cathedral, in 1235, but it seems likely that plans for the establishment of a Chantry in Bawburgh were afoot by then, since in 1240 Bishop William de Ralegh of the Norwich Cathedral Priory thought it worthwhile to appropriate Bawburgh Rectory. In 1235 the Abbot of Bon Repos had returned the patronage of Bawburgh to the monks of the Holy Trinity of Norwich.

About 1255 (so says Blomefield) 'Beatrice, widow of John le Barber of Norwich, released to the church of St. Walstan at Bauburc ... a messuage' which was to house priests and visiting pilgrims, and was built on the north side of the church. In 1278 land was acquired by the Bishop of Norwich upon which a vicarage was built in addition to the messuage, and by 1309, revenue was such that the re-building of the chancel in SS. Mary and Walstan was put in hand and the role of the Chantry Priests enhanced; in 1488 an extension was made to the Rectory. If the Chantry Chapel at Bawburgh was established as early as the middle of the thirteenth century it would rate as one of the earliest in the country and would have owed its existence, finally if not originally, to the Norwich Priory. However, the establishment of many Parish Chantries was owed to a benefactor, perhaps royal or at least a wealthy landowner, a theme we have met before in this search for St. Walstan.

Are Benedict and Blida's 'royal' connections too easily dismissed, and was Mr. Piper right when he described the search of local landowners, in Norwich market, for 'one of their own'? Were the couple, in fact, the original benefactors of the Church?

Chantry Priests were there to say Mass, nominally for the soul of a recently departed relative or friend, and to soak up the offerings of indulgence, which began in earnest at the beginning of the twelfth century and rapidly increased after the Black Death which left behind it a stark reminder of man's mortality. A plea for intercession with God on behalf of a soul often went on beyond death, with a bequest to a Church or Shrine contained in a formal will, a practice much encouraged by the Church. The Shrine of St. Walstan is mentioned in numerous wills, and no doubt in many more now lost and forgotten, and usefully illustrate the links which Bawburgh had with other towns and villages in England and abroad.

PAROCHIAL TIES

Until the twentieth century, the fate of Bawburgh was, since at least the Norman Invasion, tied to the Manor of Costessey – William the Conqueror awarding it to Alan Rufus, Viscount of Roan and Earl of Richmond. Alan, in his turn, gave away much of the revenue, and together with Fen Drayton in Cambridgeshire, Bawburgh was passed to the Abbot of Bon Repos in Brittany. As well, Blomefield records that 'Katherine, Countess of Brittain' used revenue from Bawburgh Mill to give the monks of Norwich a rent for the souls of the ancestors of her family.

Over the centuries, entitlement in Bawburgh often reverted to the Crown, and influential men and women were awarded the patronage of Bawburgh, invariably taking an interest in its fate and prosperity. In the Middle Ages, it belonged to the powerful Earls of Suffolk, the de la Pole family, whose Coat of Arms can still be seen in Bawburgh Church. Later, in the seventeenth century, revenue from the Rectory of Bawburgh went to form part of a 'pension' for the King, during one of the several periods when it was retained by the reigning monarch.

There have always been links, too, with other Norfolk parishes, who have either shared a vicar, or had particular exchanges of revenue and tithe. Often, these parochial ties brought dividends to Bawburgh and helped to increase the assets of the Parish Church from its original settlement. In 1460, for instance, Thomas Esthawe, Vicar of Thornham and a former Vicar at Bawburgh, bequeathed £10 towards the re-building of the Chapel of St. Walstan, and Blomefield tells of a bequest in 1528, by Sir Thomas Wethyr. Master of the charnel in Norwich, Sir Thomas was buried in the Cathedral, but gave his 'close' in Bawburgh to the vicar there, and his successors, on the condition that they pray for his soul, and his friends' souls, every Sunday in the year, in the pulpit, and every Friday remember him in the Mass. If any vicar should neglect this, '... the alderman of the gild of Our Lady and St. Walstone at Baber, and the brethren shall take the close to sustain the gild, giving 4d. to the curate, and offering 1d. on his yerday for dirige and mass for evermore'.

The reason for these bequests could not be clearer: all unredeemed sinners were destined for hell, so it made sense to earn earthly remission from sin by whatever means. Pre-Reformation, there was only one religion to which all society belonged and, when it came to sin, everyone was in the same boat. The established Christianity united everyone, and in turn linked them inexorably with most of Europe. Life, religion and politics were synonymous to Medieval men and women, although much of the practical Church rule came from Rome. Pilgrimage was a universal occupation for those who could anyhow afford either the money or the time. It met the need for an indulgence of hope that temporal atonement, for any sins outstanding, might lessen a spell in Purgatory, that place between heaven and earth, where souls might finally be purged of all sin before entering heaven. God, after all, did not expect perfection from his children, but He did expect sinners to acknowledge their wrongs and repent accordingly.

ONE OF A NUMBER

Following what might now be called market forces, the Medieval pilgrim was admirably catered for by the Church in East Anglia. Norfolk, Suffolk, Essex and Cambridgeshire can all boast numerous small shrines which were available not only to those who had money to travel but also to the local penitent, plus a quantity of significant pilgrimage sites. In Norfolk, besides that at Bawburgh, there was a choice of sites of varying size and importance, many of them in honour of St. Edmund. In Fishergate, Norwich, there was St. Edmund's Church, where a piece of his shirt was preserved in a box of crystal, and visited with great reverence by pilgrims. St. Edmund, King and Martyr, was also honoured at Hoxne, where there was not one but two Chapels dedicated to him and a cult dating from 869 AD.

There were shrines, too, at Elsing, Horstead, Reepham and Cringleford. The latter was to St. Albert of Cringleford, and itemised in the will of Agnes Parker who died in 1505 and was buried at Cringleford. Albert (otherwise Ethelbert) was another King of the East Angles, although the manner of his death in the eighth century would seem hardly sufficient to have inspired pilgrimage. Local folklore recalls the story of how, in order to prevent Albert from marrying her daughter, the wife of Offa II, King of Mercia, caused a pit to be dug under the chair drapery in the guest room. When Albert came to stay, he not unnaturally tried to rest on this treacherous basis, only to fall headlong, and fatally, into the hole. More usually, Offa's wife is said to have arranged Ethelbert's murder in order to prevent the annexation of Mercia by the East Anglians.

Litcham, too, was well-known as a pilgrim's resting place and one where a depiction of Walstan survives on the church screen. The Image of the Virgin was revered at Thetford, and a relic of Our Lady resided at Red Mount Chapel, Lynn, while the Image of St. Henry could be visited at St. Leonard's Priory.

Then, too, there was the Rood of Bromholm or Bacton, which early in the thirteenth century had become a centre of pilgrimage for those seeking what was said to be a cross fashioned from the wood of the True Cross. In the fifteenth century, pilgrims to Bromholm could purchase pictures of the cross and the small monastery which housed this relic grew in fame and fortune.

In Ipswich, miracles were attributed to a Golden Image of the Blessed Virgin which attracted large numbers of pilgrims, including Henry VIII, Catherine of Aragon, and Cardinal Wolsey, while the story of Bury St.

Edmunds is too well known to need explanation. In neighbouring Essex the town of Chich was re-named in honour of the Saxon St. Osyth. She was said to have been the daughter of Frithewald and Walburga, the first Christian King and Queen of East Anglia. Another East Anglian King's daughter, St. Withburga, had lived at Holkham and East Dereham, in Norfolk, but her relics were taken to Ely Cathedral to join those of St. Etheldreda and the other Ely saints Sexburga, Werburga, Ermengild and Erkengota.

But by far the best-known of the shrines and religious houses in East Anglia was that at Walsingham, which had an international reputation and was second only to the Shrine of Thomas à Becket at Canterbury.

WALSINGHAM AND THE BAWBURGH FOLLIES

Forty-five years after Bishop Aelfgar officiated at Walstan's funeral, the Shrine of Our Lady of Walsingham was founded by Richelde of Fervaques. It began as a simple Saxon house, built of wood and wattle, to remind people of the simplicities of the Bethlehem stable and inspired by the dreams of Richelde in which the Virgin Mary had shown her the Holy House in Nazareth. A monastery was established there and, under the patronage of Henry III, the Shrine of Our Lady of Walsingham flourished to international proportions. No doubt many of the pilgrims who visited Bawburgh did so on their way to Walsingham. Those deprived of a trip to the Holy Land were at least able to visit England's Nazareth, and Walsingham's notability was invaluable in attracting pilgrims to Norfolk and Suffolk.

Part of the folklore surrounding Walsingham is the so-called Slipper Chapel at Houghton, where pilgrims are said to have heard Mass, and confessed their sins, before walking the last mile to the Shrine. At this Chapel they would leave their shoes, to walk barefooted in proper humility, recalling God's injunction to Moses that he remove his shoes before treading the holy ground near to the burning bush. At least, that is the tradition, but doubts have lately been cast on the role of a Slipper Chapel, and the Walsingham historians believe the idea is not found in print until the late nineteenth century.

Naturally enough, the idea of a Slipper Chapel seemed a perfectly reasonable one to the Bawburgh chroniclers. Not only are there appropriate references to Walstan's feet in the various accounts of his life, but if Walsingham could claim a Slipper Chapel, why should Bawburgh not do the same?

Although considerably smaller than the Walsingham Chapel, a post-Reformation folly, standing conveniently near to the bridge in the village of Bawburgh, was at some stage nominated as the Slipper Chapel.

Unfortunately, there is nothing to suggest a Slipper Chapel existed in Medieval Bawburgh, either to relieve pilgrims of their footwear or for any other reason. Indeed, many of the local pilgrims would not have worn shoes.

At an indeterminate date it was also decided that the curious-looking dovecot standing beside the Slipper Chapel must be a Hermitage. Strangely enough (or perhaps not!) there is mention of a Hermitage next to the Walsingham Slipper Chapel, just as there is at Bawburgh. However, neither of these hermits – nor the one said to have lived next to the Pilgrims' Chapel at Litcham – are likely to have lived in such a structure. The term 'hermit' is misleading and talk of a hermitage derives from Blomefield, no doubt on the basis that if there was a hermit at Bawburgh he had to live somewhere. It would have been less confusing if Blomefield had used the more apt description 'Cenobite' to describe a monk living within a community, rather than 'hermit' (or 'anchorite') whose avowed intention it was to shun the company of his (or her) fellow humans. Armstrong's *History of Norfolk* says that the hermit performed Divine Service in his own Chapel beside the Hermitage at Bawburgh Bridge. Blomefield, who does not mention a Slipper Chapel, says of the hermit:

> '*There was a hermit also placed in this parish, by the Bishop's appointment, who performed divine service in his own chapel (which was by his hermitage at Bawburgh bridge) to the pilgrims and then attended them to the town, sprinkling them with hyssop and holy water.*'

Blomefield used more than one source for his material, and does not say from where he got the reference, or to which Bishop he refers, but the use of hyssop water would be commensurate with the type of miracles said to occur at the shrine. Hyssop, used in an old Jewish rite of purification, is a herbal remedy for respiratory and nervous diseases. Culpeper's *Complete Herbal* recommends a variety of decoctions, all to be taken internally, but oil of hyssop is an ancient remedy for head lice, so perhaps the hermit, or pilgrim's guide, was performing a public service.

These two follies, which once graced the lawns of the seventeenth-century Bawburgh Hall, survived the twentieth-century demolition of the Hall and remain intact to the present day, though still erroneously described as the Slipper Chapel and the Hermitage. Until very recently, they were included as such on the Ordnance Survey maps although the 'hermitage' was placed on the road near to the bridge and not in the grounds of Bawburgh Hall, pandering to the second theory about the hermit's abode. Both, however, were built by a one-time resident of Bawburgh Hall, who acquired some dressed stone from a ruined church or religious house.

At about the time building began at the Hall, sometime in 1634, rebuilding is thought to have been taking place on the farmhouse which stands on the site of the old messuage where the Chantry Priests had lived. Soon afterwards building started on what was to be Lodge Farm, close to the Bowthorpe parish boundary. Recycled material for these projects could have come from any available ruin, and it is certainly possible that parts of the damaged shrine of St. Walstan were incorporated into one or other of the structures during the seventeenth or eighteenth centuries. At Walsingham such building materials as lead, stone and wood are known to have been sold off after the destruction of the Holy House and its Chapel in the 1540s.

THE REFORMATION

The beginning of the end for the pilgrimage era was heralded in the 1530s, when Thomas Crumwell (sometimes known as Cromwell) began his climb to power. In 1533, England declared itself competent to deal with its own ecclesiastical affairs, without reference to Rome. Not long afterwards, Henry VIII put Crumwell, one-time Chancellor of the Exchequer, Dean of Wells and Vicar General, in charge of closing down all the shrines in the country. Crumwell had been employed by Cardinal Wolsey to suppress many of the small religious houses acquired by the Cardinal to finance his Colleges at Ipswich and Oxford, and he was to use the experience, and inside knowledge, to lethal effect. He began by sending 'visitors' to all parts of the country to report on the volume of devotion at each shrine.

There is no place in this book for the cause and progress of the Reformation, or for the detail of the suppression of the monasteries; suffice it to say that towards the end of the fifteenth century there had been a decline in the appetite for pilgrimage, and by the middle of the sixteenth century the fashion was fading fast. Many of the Chantry Priests had become too greedy in the matter of indulgences, openly abusing the pilgrims' intention by charging large amounts of money to say Mass for the repose of souls.

During 1538, the Shrine of St. Walstan was desecrated and plundered. The relics of the Saint, buried with such honour in 1016 and sanctified by the Bishop of Elmham in 1047, were burned.

It was impossible that Bawburgh could have been overlooked. Not only were the 'visitors' thorough in their mission, but in 1528 the Abbey of York had released to the Dean of Cardinal Wolsey's College in Ipswich all their revenues belonging to the Priory of Rumburgh in Suffolk, which Priory had claim to a portion of Bawburgh's tithe. The Priory at Rumburgh had been founded in 1064, by the monks of St. Benet's Abbey in Norfolk, and was given as a cell to the Abbey of York by Alan de Noir (or Niger), Earl of Richmond and Bretagne, brother of the first Norman Lord of Costessey

Manor, Alan Rufus. Alan de Noir had been the first to assume responsibility for the restoration of St. Mary's in York, in which county he settled after the Conquest. At what point Rumburgh, and therefore St. Mary's in York, acquired its portion of Bawburgh tithe is uncertain, but in 1528 Rumburgh was one of twenty-two monasteries, including six in Essex, which Wolsey dissolved for the endowment of his Ipswich College.

The Cathedral Priory at Norwich was among those abolished and the Rectory of Bawburgh transferred to the new Dean and Chapter of Norwich. All over East Anglia, the purge went on: eleven men at Walsingham were executed when they tried to save their monastery and Lady Chapel, while at Ipswich agents of the King entered the Chapel of Our Lady to remove the entire contents. The statues of Our Lady from Walsingham and Ipswich were taken to Smithfield for burning and cartloads of treasure were taken from Norfolk and Suffolk to the King's London Treasury. The lead on the roof of St. Osyth's Priory was recorded to be worth £1,000 and among its 'treasures' was the silver casket in which was kept the skull of St. Osyth.

In spite of being immortalised by the Norfolk-born Reeve in Chaucer's *The Canterbury Tales*, the cult of the Rood of Bromholm was not to survive, nor was the once-popular Chapel to Our Lady of Woolpit. By 1540, the Ministers' Accounts were recording the fate of some of those ousted from religious houses: the Prioress of Marham, the Priors of Bromholm, the Holy Trinity at Ipswich and of Westacre, and the Abbot of Wendling were all dead. Many inmates had been old and sickly and were not able to cope with the changes or the hardships imposed upon them.

The turmoil of those years is too easily dismissed by a single word, Reformation. It must not be forgotten that the destruction of the monasteries and the establishment of the English Church was not simply a one-man crusade, that is, Henry VIII versus the Popish rule. The dissolute behaviour of the religious houses, and by the Chantry Priests of such shrines as that of St. Walstan, had not gone unnoticed by the population at large. Many of Crumwell's 'visitors' were disenchanted Englishmen who saw the opportunity to join in the hostility towards the rich and prosperous Church of Rome.

Generally, the ideals of reform had been met with approval in East Anglia, but it can be imagined that in Bawburgh local antagonism was mitigated by the revenue generated by the Shrine, though some might have felt that more of the profit could have gone their way, rather than to the Church. For over five hundred years pilgrims had sought the Shrine of St. Walstan and brought prosperity to the village of Bawburgh, increasing the Church's holding to almost one hundred acres of land. Centuries of prestige which had accompanied such fame and wealth were to be followed by desolation.

After Crumwell's 'visitors' had done their work there was nothing left to attract the men and women of Europe to Bawburgh. Only the villagers, and a few sightseers, were there to look on the blackened remains of the once-splendid Chapel, its treasures gone and the Church desolate. The new Dean and Chapter sent assessors to the Rectory of Bawburgh to make sure of the arrangements of new rental and tithe agreements. No doubt the parishioners missed the pilgrims, who brought with them the excitement of foreign lands, news from other communities, and the different languages and culture which for so long had enriched the lives of the men and women of East Anglia. But the effects of the Reformation on the village economy were even grimmer, and Blomefield describes it thus:

'... when pilgrimages ceased, and all such rites were abolished, the inhabitants came immediately to great poverty, and so continued till the church became so ruinous, that it was scarce fit for divine service, neither could they afterwards assemble in it, without hazard of their lives; and so it remained forsaken for some time.'

~ • ~

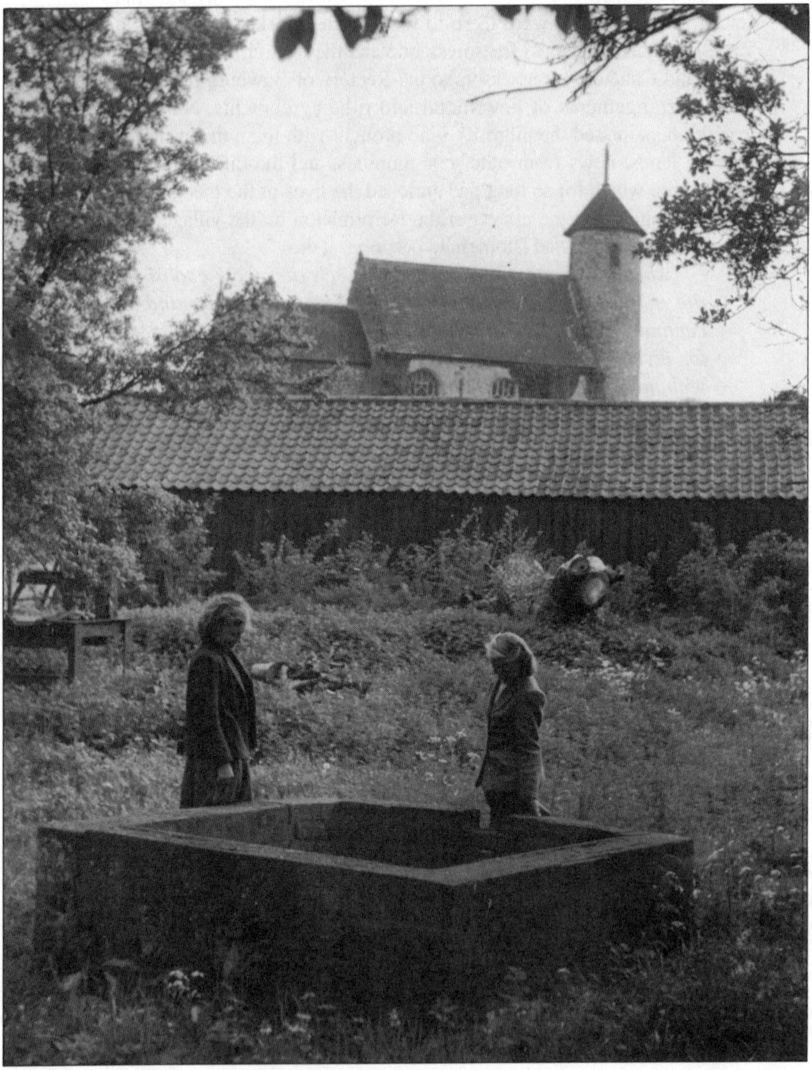

Chapter Seven
WHATEVER HAPPENED TO THE TRIPTYCH?

'The legend is in English verse. I take it from a volume of the Gibson papers in the Lambeth Library. It is a transcript made in 1658 from the original, then in the possession of a recusant named Clark, of 'Beauthorp' (now spelt Bowthorp) in Norfolk. This original was of a curious kind. It was in the form of a triptych of wood, covered with sheets of vellum, on which the legend was inscribed.'
M.R. James (1917)

O N the 29th September, 1658, a copy was made of a Medieval triptych. Entitled *The History of St. Walston*, it was in English verse and said to belong to Bawburgh Church. The work was both commissioned and executed by a person or persons unknown although the triptych was, at the time, in the possession of a Mr. Clarke, a Papist (or recusant), from the neighbouring village of Bowthorpe. A note to this effect, written on the front and back pages of the copy, together with a description of the original, was the first and last documented sighting of the triptych. Some fifty years later, the copy was included in a collection of papers given by Archbishop Thomas Tenison to Edmund Gibson, when the latter was Lambeth librarian. It was catalogued and filed as Item 8 of Lambeth Manuscript Number 935. Today, it is still in the safekeeping of the Lambeth Palace Library in London and is the second of only two known lives of St. Walstan. The original triptych has – quite simply – disappeared.

Before turning to the 1658 copy (referred to now as Item 8), let us first consider the original triptych. Nothing is reliably known about it other than the short description given on the front and final pages of the copy (which can be seen on pages 74 and 76), but it was undoubtedly the popular *legenda* of St. Walstan. It was an account of his life, and confessorship, which would have been kept in the Shrine Chapel for the edification of the pilgrims, to be read aloud on the annual feast day.

The physical form of three panels, the two side ones hinged to fold back onto the centre one, was a common form of church furniture in such a Chapel as that at Bawburgh. A written description of the triptych was given

The History of S.t Walston,

taken out of an antient parchm.t M.s,
enclosed in 3 peices of wood about a
yard long each of y.m ~~~~~~~~~~~~~~~~~
~~~~~~~~~~~~~~~~~~~~~~~~~~~~~~~~~~~~
~~~~~~~~~~~~~~~~~~~~~~~~~~~~~~~~~~~~
~~~~~~~~~~~~~~~~~~~~~~~~~~~~~~~~~~~~
~~~~~~~~~~~~~~~~~~~~~~~~~~ y.e following Form.

the owner m.r. Clark of
Beau Thorp in Norffolk.
à Papiste.

74

by the author of the copy, but much of it was crossed out and summarised by Archbishop Tenison. A rough diagram has been drawn immediately below the writing, but although the Archbishop's handwriting has been positively identified by Lambeth Palace, no one can say whether he did the drawing or if he ever actually laid eyes on the triptych. It is reasonable to assume that the Archbishop had inherited the copy from his seventeenth-century ancestor, Philip Tenison, Archdeacon of Norfolk, but if there was any accompanying information from the Archdeacon to the Archbishop it is not now filed with Item 8 and there is no note of it elsewhere in the manuscript.

Whether or not the Archbishop also obliterated the author's name is equally uncertain, but it is obvious that the words following 'by ...', which would have shown the identity of the scribe, were scratched out purposely and deliberately by someone. The 'Mr.' can still be deciphered, and although technology will some day enable this author to be identified, for the time being he remains anonymous. There seems little point in either the Archbishop or Gibson obliterating the name as late as the beginning of the eighteenth century, unless it was incriminating even then. More likely, the name was obscured by the Archdeacon or Mr. Clarke to protect the copier.

It is not entirely certain that the triptych was written in English, since Item 8 could, in theory, be a translation from Latin or French. There is, however, no reason to think that this was the case and the copy itself gives no such impression. Rather the opposite, in fact, since it is this poetic form which provides a clue as to the history of the triptych. Probably the first English version of the legend was a translation of the Latin, that being the language of the Church at the time the triptych was composed. How, then, did it come to be written in English at a time when that language was not in general use?

LANGUAGE DIFFICULTIES

For two hundred years after the Conquest, French was the language among the ruling classes in England. During the thirteenth and fourteenth centuries, Latin or Norman-French displaced English as the language of both secular and Church literature. Those who wished to marry – or even associate – with this new 'upper' class had to be at least bilingual. Gradually, English became the language of the masses and, since Latin remained the language of the Church (and therefore of the educated), native English was alive but uncultivated. Only towards the end of the fourteenth century did English begin to re-establish itself into a more widespread useage.

Had the triptych been composed after English was restored as an official language, it is less likely that it would have been written in verse, although, of course, Church poetry continued to flourish in its own right. The fact of the stanza-type construction probably means, therefore, that it

15

which ys will of God to create all thing.
but stoode & abideth in himselfe musing,
who doth these miracles but God above
yt is to be worshipped of every creature,
then unkind man, looke yt thou him love
for it is his duty & thou ensure,
wth heart both & words demure;
who so saith Nay I say Yea
Quia ipse est deus qui facit mirabilia.

O marvelous God, sitting in thy throne
in high heaven passing all man's reason
whether man be whole, sicke or groane,
by thee it releived in duly season
neither yeilding love nor thankes it is great treason,
for thou hast provided in ordinations hea
yt to thee all only honour sit & Glorie
AMEN.

Goo litle treatyse require folke of grace
yt shall have of thee inspection,
bee not too bolde to appeare in any place
of malapertnesse other psumption,
thine Author simple thorow of affection
he meanoth well, pray ym yt shall hee reade
wth Ghostly support to doe correction
Thee To reforme as they see neede.
Finis

Copied out of ye Originall
Sept. 2th Anodni 1658.

~~_____~~

The originall is in ye hands of a Recusant one Mr Clarke
&, as he saith, belongeth to ye Church of Bawburgh.
Norff.

was one of the exemptions to the rule of Latin which was granted by the authorities when it could be proved that only the use of the 'vernacular' (English) would save a person's mortal soul. This was a recognised way round the imposed, and often resented, Latinization and would tie the triptych to the late thirteenth or early fourteenth centuries.

Although Latinization tended to exclude the untutored, it was at least a common bond for those pilgrims from the wider, unified Western Christendom, whatever their national origin. There would have been a Latin scroll in the Chapel for centuries, beginning with the original by the Elmham Bishops who circulated the cult of St. Walstan to the neighbouring parishes. How many versions there have been, or when the first translation into English took place, it is impossible to know, but the original *legenda* formed the basis for both the triptych version and that in the NLA. There is no way of telling which of the two versions is the earlier but the 1516 NLA is likely to be closer to the original story as set out by the Norfolk Bishops, since it is more basic and contains only the elements of the legend while the triptych was clearly written with pilgrims in mind. Item 8 shows it to have been aimed at a popular and untutored audience although there is nothing to indicate whether the triptych included illustration of any kind which would have acted as enforcement for the illiterate.

An author could, then, compose or translate the life of a saint in soul-saving, English verse, a practice well-illustrated by the stanza-type construction of *The History of St. Walston.* Many of the Shrine Chapel pilgrims were local people who, although illiterate, could learn of the legend when it was read aloud, in their native language, by one of the priests, thereby contributing immeasurably towards saved souls, but it served, too, those literate, English-speaking pilgrims whose knowledge of Latin was thin. Towards the end of Item 8, all pilgrims – literate or not – are directed to lift their minds and hearts to heaven above, where Walstan dwelled before God. Prayers should be offered, '... though yu be unlearnd nor can nor read nor spell'. Either a word is missing between 'can' and 'nor', or the copier mistakenly repeated 'nor'; but, in any event, the line appears to confirm the function of the English Life.

THE LEGENDA POETS

At other East Anglian sites, verse similar to Item 8 was composed: in about 1450, a ballad was written at Walsingham to tell the story of Richelde of Fervaques. Although published by Richarde Pynson in 1496, this was thought to have been written in about 1460 by the celebrated chronicler, William of Worcester. However, the most famous of the *legenda* poets was a Benedictine monk named John Lydgate (c. 1370-1451) who was born near Bury St. Edmunds in Suffolk.

Lydgate's metrical *Life of St. Edmund* is among the nation's great treasures and M.R. James suggested that the Bawburgh triptych was, in fact, modelled on the verse-legends written by Lydgate; the idea that it was supervised or composed by Lydgate himself cannot be entirely discounted, although must be open to some question. There is no proof that the Suffolk monk ever visited Bawburgh, but he was persuaded to take on similar work, including an invocation to St. Robert, a boy saint whose cult began in Bury St. Edmunds during 1181 to rival that of the fabled St. William of Norwich. Since building work on St. Walstan's Chapel in Bury was completed in 1433, and a wall painting executed in nearby Cavenham in around the 1460s, it is evident that the legend was not unknown in Suffolk during Lydgate's lifetime. The year 1433 was, incidentally, one of some importance since it was then, while Henry VI was visiting the Abbot at Bury, that Lydgate presented his *Life of St. Edmund* to the young King.

Although M.R. James thought that the triptych dated from 'quite late in the fifteenth century', it is difficult to arrive at any firm conclusions purely on the description provided by Item 8, and impossible to assess its age by the form of language evidenced by the copy. The scribe would instinctively have modernised the English, since it was no doubt as ancient, and obscure, as the triptych itself. It was not unknown for similar church furniture to be updated from time to time when, perhaps, a more pilgrim-friendly version was desired or when an addition to the *legenda* was required, such as a new miracle. It was also an opportunity to amend the text, if that should have been politically expedient. Unfortunately, such 'new' versions inevitably incorporated not just changes but errors. The style of the copy was taken by M.R. James to suggest a date for the triptych but no amount of study of Item 8 will bring us any nearer to knowing the true age of the original. It is as hopeless to guess at the form of the original as to decide whether it was, in its turn, a modernising or translated version of an earlier scroll.

Since the triptych obviously pre-dates the Reformation, it is nothing short of miraculous that it survived. For that to have happened, it would first have needed someone with considerable foresight and authority to remove it from the Shrine Chapel in the years leading up to 1538. It may confidently be assumed that it was taken from Bawburgh in order that Crumwell's Visitors could not catalogue it, and it was swiftly moved to a safe house in Bowthorpe, with the intention of returning it when things calmed down. If it had fallen into the clutches of the reformers it would certainly have been destroyed. Having rescued it, these unknowns then had to keep it safe for 120 years, in order that the recusant, Mr. Clarke, should still have possession of it in 1658. Since it could not easily be returned to Bawburgh, three generations of triptych guardians had then to keep it safe, never knowing whose politics or religion would triumph. These guardians adhered to the Church of Rome, not the new English Church, and would have required considerable strength of courage to harbour the triptych during some of the most dangerous and testing years of English history.

For the remainder of Henry VIII's reign, and for the short and uncertain reign of Edward VI, it had to lay hidden in one of the nearby safe Catholic hideouts. Even when it seemed that Queen Mary was to restore Catholicism, and the old faith enjoyed a brief revival, the triptych still needed protection from those who might want to destroy it. There was no shortage of enemies who, for one reason or another, might want its destruction, not least the officers of the Puritan movement in the first Civil War. There might also have been those in Bawburgh who would have had no compunction about betraying saint worship.

Although the Church of SS. Mary and Walstan was unfit for services for many years following the Reformation, the new Dean and Chapter at Norwich had retained its dedication. There could still have been a certain sympathy for the cult, if not for Rome, among the local congregation but pilgrimage was not part of the new Protestantism. It is hard to believe that those sympathisers of reform in Bawburgh would not have missed the triptych and perhaps instigated a search although, in the prevailing confusion, it was a simple matter to say that the Visitors had already removed it. As well, those who had charge of it would have had friends in Bawburgh who were prepared to remain silent about what they knew.

Links had always existed between Bowthorpe and Bawburgh as might be expected between neighbouring villages. No doubt St. Michael's Church at Bowthorpe had been one of those parishes to whom the news of Walstan's death and canonization had been sent in 1047 by the Bishop of Elmham and perhaps representation of him formed part of the church furniture. There were other connections between the two churches, including one William Rechers – Vicar of both parishes in 1508 – who was buried in Bawburgh, where a brass memorial to him still exists.

Since Item 8 is currently the only evidence of its existence, the origins and history of the triptych will forever remain a secret and anything it could tell us about the legend of St. Walstan is lost for all time until, and if, it ever comes to light. All that can be said with any degree of certainty about the lost triptych is that which is inscribed on the front and back pages of Item 8, namely the description of its form and presentation (the original being crossed out and summarised by Archbishop Tenison); that it was 'ancient'; that its owner was a Papist named Mr. Clarke of Beauthorp (the Archbishop again amending the copy by changing Papist to Recusant); and that it belonged to the Church of Bawburgh.

We shall probably never know what Mr. Clarke did with it after the copier returned it to him on the 29th September, 1658. Was it already so ancient that it merely disintegrated; or was it passed to a new safe house; or did Mr. Clarke destroy it after handing on the copy? Since Archbishop Tenison seems to have taken some trouble to amend the title page there is an outside chance that he had more information about the triptych than exists in Item 8. In any event, he and Gibson valued it sufficiently to lodge it in Lambeth Palace.

THE LAMBETH LIFE AND 'BLYBOROW TOWN'

Item 8 consists of fifteen pages, each page approximately five inches wide and eight inches high, with straight but irregular edges, and an inch-wide margin. The paper is of góod quality, and the whole very obviously a copy, intended only as a record of the triptych, and not for exhibition or show. The writing is in black ink, with small letters which, though legible, are not particularly neat and appear to have been written in haste and done in the course of a single day. Other than the diagram there is no decoration or illustration. The pages are bound in a large, leather-covered tome kept in Lambeth Palace Library, with other documents given by Archbishop Tenison to his Domestic Chaplain, Edmund Gibson, in the eighteenth century.

Although there are certain differences between the story content of Item 8 and that of the *Nova Legenda Anglie*, it is probable that the two versions owed their origins to the same root, as has already been discussed. Indeed, if we assume that the original life was that in the Shrine Chapel, put there during the early part of the eleventh century, then all others derive from it.

Such differences as there are consist chiefly of the eleven specific miracles performed in Walstan's name, which are described in Item 8 but do not appear in the NLA, indicating that the triptych was written at the height of the pilgrimage years. Item 8 is considerably longer than the NLA and has a pilgrim-friendly feel about it, while the final verse of the NLA calls upon 'dearest Brothers', indicating a more intimate, monastic audience. Neither document gives any more information about Walstan's childhood than the name of his parents and the fact that in his adolescence he had already developed a saintly outlook on life. (Where did Mr. Piper get his information about the Confirmation service? David Rollason says that this search has been very kind in not saying outright that he made it all up!) Both credit Walstan with 'royal' birth.

The single most controversial variant between the two lives is that Item 8 declares Walstan to have been born '… in Blyborow town' rather than at Bawburgh. In the NLA, Walstan's birthplace appears as Bawburgh, and it is, of course, impossible to know whether the word 'Blyborow' was on the triptych, or if it ever appeared on any earlier versions, English or Latin. An avalanche of questions is raised by Item 8, but the somewhat astounding assertion that Walstan came from Blythburgh in Suffolk is the most intriguing, and must, therefore, be investigated.

To date, no evidence has emerged which suggests that Walstan, or Blida, had any association with Blythburgh (Blideburgh or Blythborough), and it must be said that such claims are made by agencies other than the Suffolk parish itself. The notion was encouraged by M.R. James, who published Item 8 in 1917 and commented that the Lambeth Life was '... certainly better here in saying that [Walstan] was born at Blythburgh in Suffolk'. However, the idea is unsupported by any surviving monument, or known recollection, other than this single reference in Item 8 and there is nothing to show that M.R. James did anything more ambitious than read and copy Item 8, since he cites no additional or corroborating evidence.

Blythburgh actually has no need of St. Walstan, either for publicity or patronal reasons, as it had its own saint in Jurmin (654 AD), who was buried at Blythburgh before being translated to Bury St. Edmunds. Furthermore, St. Jurmin came from an established family of saintly and royal persons, being the brother of SS. Etheldreda and Withburga, and son (or nephew) of Anna, King of the East Angles, which gave Blythburgh plenty of scope for patronage. There is nothing in history which links Anna with Walstan or Blida and there are no perceptible similarities to other legends or folklore associated with the area.

The likeness in spelling between the name of Walstan's mother, Blythe (as given in Item 8), and the placename Blythburgh, is the most obvious place to look for common error on the part of the copier. (The NLA names her as Blida.) While Blyth is familiar to the East Anglian vocabulary, the English word 'borough', and corruptions thereof, is itself common enough in placenames. It will not have gone unnoticed that the river flowing into Suffolk, originally from the Medieval port of Dunwich, is named Blyth, upon which lies Blythburgh, and it would follow that if Walstan's mother came from Blythburgh it was likely to be his birthplace. Blythburgh has a history as rich as any village in East Anglia, having once been a prosperous town, with a priory, a busy fishing industry and a flourishing weaving trade, while Dunwich was, by the late twelfth century, one of England's largest ports. However, during the thirteenth century ferocious storms began to alter the coastline and the mouth of the River Blyth became shallow and eventually blocked with stone and sand. By the early sixteenth century, Dunwich was not even in the top fifty towns. In 1658 the commercial histories of Blythburgh and Dunwich, glorious as they had once been, were already very much in the past and most of Dunwich by then under the sea.

Similarities between the spelling of the two villages Blythburgh and Bawburgh cannot be overlooked, either; besides the usual meaning of borough, an incorporated town or village, the word did once refer to an ancient custom by which real estate passed to the youngest, instead of the eldest, son. In the event of there being no sons, a daughter could inherit. If it was in any way important to associate either Benedict or Blida's identity with Blythburgh, for social or other reasons, the copier might just have been doing the job he was entrusted with, namely to heighten Walstan's profile, further enhanced by the three direct references to him as a king's son.

While offering no explanation of his own, M.R. James is critical of Husenbeth's apparent ignorance of Blythburgh as Walstan's birthplace in his nineteenth-century book on the story of St. Walstan, but there is proof that Husenbeth had studied both Item 8 and the NLA carefully. He made his own copy of Item 8 in December, 1858, which he took from one made by Canon J.C. Morris earlier in the same month. Both men dwelled on the possibilities of Blythburgh versus Bawburgh and Husenbeth, having looked in vain for any other reference to Blythburgh, came to his conclusion and wrote 'Babur' (a nineteenth-century form of Bawburgh) in the margin beside 'Blyborow'. Neither he, nor Canon Morris, saw any good reason why the traditions of Walstan's birthplace should be challenged, especially in view of the other small, but obvious, errors made by the copier, plus the general roughness of the work. For example, the Bishop of Norwich is mentioned as having attended Walstan's funeral, but the first Norwich Bishop was appointed only in 1091. Also, Walstan is mistakenly given a 'sithe' (scythe) with which to harvest wheat, instead of the more correct sickle. This can be compared with the Walsingham ballad, where William of Worcester wrote that the Holy House was built in 1061, but records show that the Walsingham Priory was established in about 1153 and the Holy House built in the early years of that century. Such harmless inaccuracies were almost bound to occur; for instance, in Lydgate's *Life of St. Edmund*, one illustration of the King's death includes several rabbits, which in 1433 were bred in warrens round Bury. However, in 869 – the date of Edmund's martyrdom – there were no rabbits in England.

The possibility of error is advanced if we consider that in 1858, exactly two hundred years after the copy was made, it was again re-shaped; first by Canon Morris and then just a few weeks later by Husenbeth, who both made simple, but potentially relevant, alterations. For example, in the fourth miracle of Item 8, a woman from 'Crowthorpe, a town here beside' is pronounced by Husenbeth to be 'Bowthorpe'. He obviously decided from the start that it was Bowthorpe, as it appears thus on his own copy, possibly in honour of the origins of Mr. Clarke. However, the village of

Crownthorpe, a few miles west of Wymondham, is the more likely candidate. This exchange of Bowthorpe for Crowthorpe has heightened importance in that it increases the possibility that Blyborow was substituted for Bawburgh in Item 8 as a result of logical conclusion. Such a change could – in time – crazily lead to some future suggestion that Walstan was born at Crownthorpe!

Husenbeth also recorded on his 'translation' of Item 8 that he had modernised the old spelling and no doubt Canon Morris had done the same, while M.R. James made other alterations. The 1658 copy is no less likely to have attracted changes of one sort or another and we do not know what condition the triptych was in when the copy was taken; it could have been stored in a damp room for a hundred years, or have been flaking with dryness for half a century.

Our copier may be imagined as an earnest and diligent sixteenth-century scribe, possessing a certain degree of education but not, perhaps, a true scholar. The squeak and rasp of the quill echoes down the nearly three hundred and fifty years which have passed since he sat down to the task of copying the ancient and precious triptych before him. He guided his nib nervously across the white sheets of paper, stopping only to dip into the ink with annoyed frequency. He was engrossed in his task, aware that time was not on his side. It was already the 29th September, and the dusk came earlier each afternoon.

His usual work was to update manuscripts written in his native English, although this one was older than most he saw, and many of the words obscure. He worked on, mechanically transferring each word onto the paper, his eye moving quickly back and forth, scanning the triptych for his place. It was his skill as a speed writer, rather than any degree of education, which had brought him to this task, and he had a reputation for integrity above the average.

The autumn light distorted the writing on the triptych; the words were often difficult to read and in some places the vellum was thin with age and mould. He shuddered as a blast of cold wind found its way through a loose pane in the window beside him. What if he was caught? Fear spurred him on ... he worked hurriedly ... there was still much to be done ... the word 'Blyborow', and then 'Blythe', fell easily onto the page. In seconds he was onto the next line, and the next, occasionally missing out or adding a word, modernising where it could easily be done and filling in a likely meaning where the parchment had cracked.

When the dusk had turned nearly to the night darkness he knew his task was complete. But there was almost half a page left empty: was there time for some words of his own? He pushed the triptych to one side and began to write:

'*Goe, litle treatyse, require folke of grace*
yt shall have of thee inspection,
bee not too bold to appear in any place
of malapertnesse, othir presumption
Thine Author simple thorow of affection
he meaneth well, pray ym yt shall thee read
wth Ghostly support to doe correction
Thee to reforme as they see need. Finis.'

We can view this tired but satisfied scribe with some amused affection, since he seems to have had some notion of reaching out to those who might read his teasing words 'thine Author ... meaneth well'. The verse was no part of the triptych and betrays a mischievous sense of humour, perhaps even a code as yet unbroken. Having surveyed his handiwork, he triumphantly – and without thinking – signed his name and laid down the pen. He had now to deliver the parchment to the man Clarke before getting well clear of the village and away from danger.

Item 8 is the only known occasion, before or since 1658, on which Blythburgh is authoritatively named as Walstan's birthplace and the assertion is not borne out by a single item of evidence from any other source. It should also be recalled that there are the strongest possible reasons for supposing that the legend of St. Walstan had been taken from an older, more ancient devotion associated with Bawburgh. Nor is there any trace of a St. Blida in Blythburgh history, whether as Walstan's mother or as saint, and no surviving monument or icon to either saint in the Church or village. The wafer-thin possibility of a link between St. Blida and St. Brida of Westhall, a village just a few miles north-east of Blythburgh, is the unlikely starting point for such an investigation.

Each Blythburgh reference now found in literature is either taken directly from the Lambeth Life or copied from the transcript published in 1917 by M.R. James, who might be thought to have given the matter better consideration than he did. (M.R. James also claimed Item 8 as 'new' in 1917 but of course Husenbeth, Canon Morris, and others, were familiar with it.)

Butler makes mention of 'an old manuscript life' although, assuming that he had read it for himself, gave no details which depend on it and he did not use Blythburgh. Blomefield appears not to acknowledge the Lambeth manuscript at all, nor to have known of the triptych. Since he took his version from Tanner, presumably he, too, knew nothing of this alternative birthplace.

On balance, and having searched in vain for any reference to the contrary, it must be assumed that, whether or not Bawburgh is correctly named as Walstan's place of origin, Blythburgh most definitely is not. Only if such alternative evidence comes to light and is authentically pre-1658 can the assertion be taken seriously and further research instigated.

THE REBELLION

There were any number of reasons why the unknown scribe would not want his day's work talked about and his signing of the copy must have been an aberration. On the day that Item 8 was made the news of Oliver Cromwell's death was news indeed. Although Cromwell had died on the 3rd September, some twenty-five days previously, England was still ruled by a Commonwealth Government. Neither our copier nor his sponsor were to know that the country was just two years away from the Restoration of the English Monarchy. All the fragmented loyalties of Church and State were soon to be shaken once more in a kaleidoscope, no one knowing what new pattern might emerge.

In 1649 Charles I had been beheaded and England proclaimed a Commonwealth, but by then destruction of church treasure had been as great as it had been at the Reformation. During 1643-4 the zealot William Dowsing rampaged through Suffolk, smashing painted windows and destroying beautiful and ancient church furniture in the name of Puritanism. The damage caused by the Cromwellian troops to the material, as well as the spiritual, Church has often been overlooked in the shadow of the Reformation. In the first wave of civil war, church buildings were ransacked, and communities split, though some made valiant attempts to outwit the new reformers who came to strip the parish churches of their 'false images'. Parishioners of the Church of St. Edmund at Fritton in Norfolk endured the destruction of their ancient church glass but had the wit to whitewash one wall painting and so hide it, a good ploy since the Puritans were rather keen on whitewashing. (The painting was to remain secret until restoration work was carried out in the early part of this century.) The wall painting of St. Walstan at Cavenham in West Suffolk was only discovered in 1967 although many others which survived the Rebellion were covered in the Victorian era of church renovation.

What began in the 1640s as a purifying of the Church ended with the powerful Westminster Assembly abolishing the use of the Prayer Book and Charles I choosing death rather than give up episcopacy. Cromwell had appointed Commissioners to approve and examine the preachers, in time resorting to persecution and ultimate removal of some priests from their parishes. Undoubtedly there were genuine abuses of power and misuse of church buildings: merchants stored their wares in churches; churchwardens held banquets there; and in some churches the floor was constantly being disturbed for burials. Puritan ministers were put in charge and the practices of church life went underground. As early as 1596 the Vicar of Bawburgh, Daniel Howes, had been identified by the Puritan leaders as being more interested in hunting than in his parochial responsibilities but was only one of a number of Norfolk and Suffolk clergy who were exampled in an effort to prove that laxity existed.

The state of many churches was disgusting and, to their credit, the Puritans did a much-needed job of cleaning them. Most village churches were damp, often with saplings undermining the foundations and roofs leaking. In 1633 the roof of Bawburgh Church was re-tiled, in the hope of making it at least weather-proof, and in 1640 the Dean and Chapter of Norwich, as patrons of the vicarage and improprietors of the rectory, nominated curates and held the living in sequestration until the Chapter itself was dissolved six years later by the Parliamentarians.

The ideas behind the Puritan movement had found sympathy in the Eastern Counties generally, and Oliver Cromwell's East Anglian connections are fully explored in a number of books, most notably Ketton-Cremer's *Norfolk in the Civil War*. Among those clergy who were removed from their living was Philip Tenison, Archdeacon of Norfolk and Vicar of Hethersett and Foulsham. Tenison had the misfortune to be vicar in the home village of one of Cromwell's foremost supporters, General Philip Skippon, who lived at the Old Hall, Foulsham and was a much-loved soldier of the Cromwellian army. There was to be no help from Hethersett, either, since Blomefield tells us: '... 1647 Philip Tennison, ejected at the Rebellion to make way for one Jeremiah Coleman, who was buried at Hethersett, 1658'.

This Jeremiah Coleman, a predecessor of the Jeremiah Colman who was to begin his illustrious milling career at Bawburgh Mill in 1802, was not the only prominent Norfolk man to support Cromwell. Sir Henry Jerningham, of Costessey Hall, sought – and got – protection from Cromwell himself. It was on behalf of Sir Henry that in January, 1648, Cromwell sent a personal directive from Whitehall to the effect that nothing of Sir Henry's was to be molested or plundered. At the time, most of Costessey, Bowthorpe and Bawburgh belonged to the Jerninghams, having been part of the Manor of Costessey since before Domesday. To unravel the secrets of Mr. Clarke, and thus restore a missing link in the chain of events which led to the 1658 copy, this search must now turn its attention to the history of recusancy at Costessey and Bowthorpe.

THE JERNINGHAM CONNECTION AND THE BOWTHORPE RECUSANTS

The notoriously Catholic Jerningham family had come to prominence during the previous century when Queen Mary rewarded those loyal to her cause with lands. The first Jerningham to arrive at Costessey Manor – the family name was then Jernegan – was Sir Henry Jernegan (1509-1572). The family is thought to have come from Horham, in Suffolk, which in the twelfth century was called Horham Jernegan. Sir Henry was loyal to Mary Tudor and one of the first in Norwich to proclaim her as sovereign. In support of her claim to the throne, he led a group of his own retainers first to the Duke of Norfolk's estate at Kenninghall, where the future Queen stayed in the week following the death of King Edward, and then to Framlingham Castle where she gathered her forces before entering London. Sir Henry later held the posts of Vice-Chamberlain, Master of the Horse (and Household) and was appointed a Privy Councillor. In 1553 the Queen granted him Costessey Manor and thus began a family connection with Norfolk which was to last until 1918, and which had an important role to play in the continuation of the legend of St. Walstan.

However, at Mary's death in 1558, those Catholic supporters who had played so important a role in placing her on the throne returned to their country seats, many of them in East Anglia. As well as the Catholic Dukes of Norfolk, the Bedingfields, Petres, Cornwallises and Waldegraves were displaced at Court, their loyalty to Church and Monarch once more the cause of their being social outcasts. The Jerninghams retreated to Costessey, where their staunchly Catholic loyalties remained as strong as ever, and where they carried the support of some of their tenants in the villages of Costessey and Bowthorpe. There had been, no doubt, a tradition of pre-Reformation pilgrimage to Bawburgh among the farmers of Costessey and Bowthorpe; indeed, perhaps Mr. Clarke was one of those whose ancestors had worshipped at the Shrine Chapel and been entrusted with the safe-keeping of the triptych. The name of Clarke (Clark or Clerk/e) is common enough in the area; even a cursory look through the records shows that the Rector of Intwood and Keswick, with Gowthorpe Chapel, was a Richard Clerk, who died in 1680, and at Bowthorpe there had been a vicar named Andrew Clarke from 1605 until 1612.

When Sir Henry came to Costessey was he told about the triptych which by then had already lain hidden for several years? He had not owned the Manor in 1538 but his intense Catholic sympathies might have persuaded those guardians to seek a safe place for it at the rebuilt Hall, with its priest holes and secret Chapel. But trust is not easily given in Norfolk and questions about loyalty might well have been asked in 1578 when the Protestant Queen Elizabeth visited Sir Henry's widow at Costessey Hall. In spite of denouncing other prominent recusants in her sweep through East Anglia in 1578, she left the Widow Jerningham at Costessey rather than in Norwich gaol, which was the destination for other less fortunate persons of the same Catholic persuasion.

Life for these recusant families changed dramatically when Elizabeth I came to the throne and immediately reversed the fortunes of the Catholic men and women in her realm. Although the Church at Bawburgh survived, that at Bowthorpe became a ruin. In 1560, two years after Elizabeth became Queen, the Church of St. Michael was desecrated, though it was not done with any retaliatory vengeance. At a time when it was compulsory for all society to attend the Church of England, the solution for displaced recusants was obvious: if the Parish Church was in ruins, no one could be expected to attend it. Together with the Churches of Costessey and Bowthorpe, those at Easton, Earlham, and Runhall were similarly reduced to a ruinous state. The Manor of Costessey had not only the Jerningham influence but Bowthorpe Hall had, since the 1570s, been the property of the Yaxleys, of Yaxley and Mellis in Suffolk, a wealthy and staunchly Catholic family and stubbornly recusant. The Catholic Waldegraves also lived at Bowthorpe and in 1600, Charles Waldegrave married Frances Yaxley and moved into the Hall. There is every possibility that the Yaxley and Waldegrave families were instrumental in hiding the triptych. The arrival of the Jerninghams in Costessey did not just reinforce the existing adherence to Catholicism but also made it possible for the Old Faith to survive effectively.

During and beyond Elizabeth's reign the Catholic faith was kept by priests – usually French Jesuits – brought to England by the Catholic gentry. At Costessey Hall, the south stairs were known as Chaplain's Stairs, as they led to the priest hole used by many who ministered to the faithful in secret. Information about these priests is understandably scarce but in 1582 it was reported that a 'Mr.' Pratt was living at Costessey Hall. This Mr. Pratt was a Catholic priest, and sometime after 1588 another priest named John Gerard is thought to have been at Costessey, Kimberley and possibly Bowthorpe Hall.

John Gerard, born in 1564 to Sir Thomas Gerard of Bryn, in Lancashire, was a member of a family obstinantly and uncompromisingly recusant. Although he had the opportunity to acquire great education, he preferred instead to become proficient in field sports and falconry. After being ordained a Jesuit priest in 1588, he began his mission to England, landing on the Norfolk coast somewhere between Happisburgh and Bacton. (It was common for priests to take an alias when travelling and Fr. Gerard turns up in Norfolk during 1595 as Robert Thompson, attendant to Edward Yelverton, 'Gent of Woolverton'.)

A little later, another young priest, Henry Floyd, was to follow in Fr. Gerard's footsteps. Fr. Floyd went by a number of 'Mr.' aliases – including Fludd, Smith, Rivers, and Seymour – and is thought to have been the tutor named Bullen, living with the Waldegraves of Bowthorpe in 1614. In that year the Yaxleys, their servants and the tutor Bullen, were presented to the Bishop as Popish recusants. Jessopp, writing in 1879, believed Bullen to be Fr. Floyd. When the Yaxleys left Bowthorpe to succeed to the Suffolk property, 'Bullen' went with them.

All during those troublesome and dangerous years, the triptych containing *The History of St. Walston* lay hidden. When persecution of recusants became the occupation not only of Protestants but of the new and fervent exponents of Puritanism, the risks were immense. After Elizabeth came James I and with his reign the rumblings of civil unrest. By the time Charles I was crowned, recusants were beyond the pale of a wider society already split between King and People. In Norfolk the Catholics were persecuted mercilessly by Matthew Wren, who was appointed Bishop of Norwich in 1635, their only consolation being that he was equally disinclined towards Puritanism. It was Bishop Wren who restored many Norfolk churches to a useable condition, including that at Bawburgh, though he was unsuccessful in restoring St. Michael's at Bowthorpe. In spite of repeated threats, and in 1637 declaring that the Church must be fit for a monthly service, St. Michael's quickly reverted to a ruin once the Bishop was removed from Norwich after only a little over two years.

SEPTEMBER, 1658

In September, 1658, then, the communities of Costessey, Bowthorpe and Bawburgh held their breath. The Catholic Sir Henry Jerningham was a supporter of Cromwell, but, with the Protector dead, the safety which that allegiance had afforded was now in question; the Norfolk Archdeacon of the Established Church, Philip Tenison, who included Bawburgh among his favourite and beloved churches, was deposed and eager to see an end to Puritan rule; and, somewhere in Costessey or Bowthorpe, Catholic recusants were hiding an ancient, pre-Reformation triptych which still belonged to the Protestant Church at Bawburgh. The precise whereabouts of the triptych was known only to a few in Bowthorpe who had followed the Catholic persuasion of the prominent families but who, of late, had been confused by Sir Henry Jerningham's sympathies.

There seems little doubt that sometime during, or before, the beginning of September, 1658, Archdeacon Tenison and the Bowthorpe recusants made contact. The Archdeacon had been stripped of his position and living by the Puritan rulers and had a grievance shared with the Catholics. But they were united against a powerful enemy, and in a moment of panic as the news of Cromwell's death reached Norfolk, Mr. Clarke no doubt confided his worries about the safety of the triptych to Philip Tenison. As Archdeacon, Tenison would normally have had control of the Church fabric and some power over the administration connected with the parish registers.

Tenison acted immediately: with Cromwell dead there was no telling what would happen in Whitehall and with all speed he requested Mr. Clarke to contact a trusted scribe and, in all practicable haste, make a copy of the triptych. If the triptych itself could not be saved, for reasons of its age, condition, or the fear of its discovery, then at least a copy should be made.

The mission was to be kept secret from Henry Jerningham since it would be just the thing with which to curry favour with the new Lord Protector. The Yaxleys, on the other hand, were known to the guardians and unquestionably trustworthy, as were the Waldegraves.

Mr. Clarke did as the Archdeacon asked and immediately sent a message to Suffolk followed by another to Bowthorpe Hall. Early on the morning of the 29th September, a copier arrived in Bowthorpe and was set to work without delay. He was a man worthy of trust and his sympathies did not lie with the Puritan ideals.

1660 AND RESTORATION

On the 29th May, 1660, King Charles II rode through London to the accompaniment of church bells and bonfires on street corners. The arms of the newly-restored Monarch were raised in churches across England, including that of Bawburgh. But, although Archdeacon Tenison had been awarded his own grant of arms, and was restored to his living at Foulsham, he was not to witness the re-birth of the Established Church. He died on the 15th January, 1660, and a plaque to his memory can still be seen in Bawburgh Church. His papers, among them the 1658 copy of *The History of St. Walston*, were eventually passed to his grandson, Thomas Tenison, who amended and corrected Item 8. Afterwards it was passed to Gibson and thus into Lambeth Library.

So many unanswered questions still arise over the matter of the triptych and its copy, and naturally much of the above is no more than guesswork masquerading as answers and should be read as such. But what of the copier? Who could this anonymous scribe have been and why was Mr. Clarke so blatantly described as 'recusant' in Item 8? There is no attempt to disguise his identity, as there is that of the copier. If Mr. Clarke, or the copier, was a priest it would hardly have been relevant in the Archbishop's time and the possibility of tracing such priests is limited, since Jessopp points out that the last list of presentments of Popish recusants in the Bishop's Registry is dated 1616. 'Mr. Clarke' might anyway be another pseudonym. The 'Clerke' named in Item 8 was the self-same priest who ministered the Last Sacrament to Walstan at Taverham. Thus, may we say that Mr. Clarke of Bowthorpe was also a priest?

It is a safe guess that if the scribe had been a priest, he was a successor to those Jesuits who had lived under the protection of the Waldegraves, Yaxleys and Jerninghams. In his fascinating book, *One Generation of a Norfolk House*, Jessopp explores the relationships and movements of the Norfolk Catholics at this time and notes particularly the tutor Bullen, alias Fr. Floyd. By 1658 Fr. Floyd would have been over ninety years of age, and thus unlikely to have been the copier, but by association with the Yaxleys his successor would have been beyond reproach and might have consented to save *The History of St. Walston* for posterity.

A possibility as yet undiscussed is that the mysterious copier was none other than Archdeacon Tenison himself, who adopted the Jesuit practice of an alias. If Thomas Tenison had that information before him, or even a suspicion of it, that would be reason enough for him to prevent identification of the scribe, he being an outspoken critic of the Papacy. If the Archdeacon was, in fact, the 'owner' of the triptych, he might have taken the name of Clarke from Wethersfield in Essex, in which parish he was instituted in 1642. The Clarkes, or Clerkes, of Wethersfield were a well-known family with several monuments in the Parish Church.

Just as Philip Tenison's other associations with Bawburgh have not been fully explored, there remains the question of who raised the shroud brass to the Archdeacon in the Church at Bawburgh. He died some months before the Restoration, and had not officiated as Archdeacon for some years in the Protestant community at Bawburgh. Why, then, was he so important to that community and who made sure that his memory was not forgotten?

~ • ~

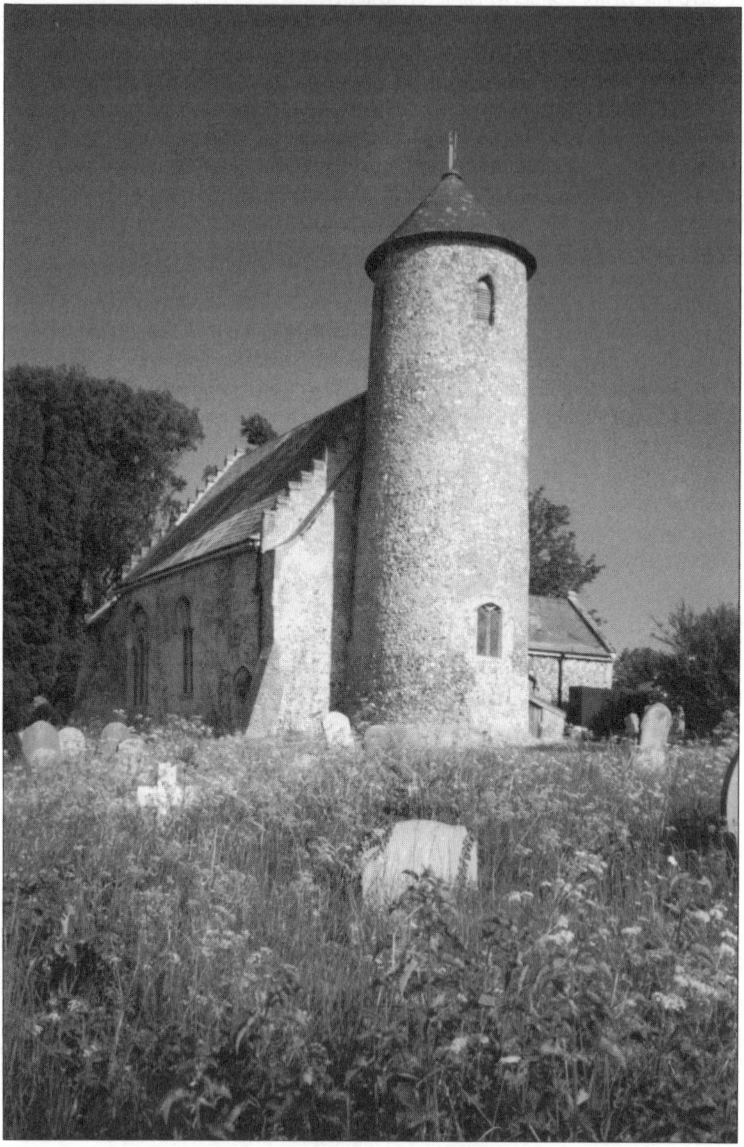

Chapter Eight
THE MIRACULOUS WELL

'St. Walston's soul out of the world did passe ... his body doth
rest in Bawburgh kerke, where many fold miracles all Mighty
God doth worke. Blind men made to see & looke on ye sunne,
Crooked both & lame right up for to goe. ye deafe man perfectly
his hearing hath wonne, damned spirit cast out of man also,
Leprosy, Fevir, Palsy, wt many sicknesses mo be cur'd & heal'd
in this holy place.'
        Item 8, MS Lambeth 935 (1658)

*I*N the aftermath of the Reformation, the Shrine of St. Walstan lay in
ruins. The prosperity which it had brought to Bawburgh for five hundred
years was gone, as were the Chantry Priests. In burning the relics of St.
Walstan, and reducing the Chapel irrevocably to rubble, the reformers
sought to give local proof of the greater destruction, that of the broken unity
of Western Christendom. The days of a religion common to all Europe were
ended. After 1538 it became difficult for recusants (as adherents to Roman
Catholicism came to be called) to travel, due in large part to the harsh Penal
Laws, and pilgrimage was hardly destined to become a feature of the new
Protestantism; veneration of the saints and of the Blessed Virgin Mary fell
under the edict of prohibition, and it was to be some 300 years before a
revival of English Catholicism could begin.

After Henry VIII died in 1547 the guardians of the new king, Edward VI,
continued the war against pilgrimages, the glorification of holy relics, or other
examples that the Roman Church still practised saint-worship, including any
wells declared sacred or dedicated to a saint. Although there is some
indication that a trickle of pilgrims continued to visit the ruins of Walsingham,
Canterbury, and possibly Bawburgh, the new church rulers were adamant in
their opposition to pilgrimage. Henry VIII had ordered that all mention of
Thomas of Canterbury be erased from the liturgical books, and where even
small sites of worship were tentatively repaired they were again dismantled.

When Queen Mary came to the throne in 1553 it was by no means
certain that the Church of Rome had, after all, lost its hold on Britain, but
there was barely time for affiliation to the doctrines of the Papacy to
manifest itself. Even supposing it had been possible, the people of
Bawburgh would not have rebuilt the Shrine Chapel: it was just too

dangerous to contemplate, especially since the reward of doing so was of dubious merit. Once the Rectory of SS. Mary and Walstan was transferred to the new Dean and Chapter in Norwich, it was only a matter of time before the spirit and legend of the Patron Saint of Farm Workers and Agriculture would, for better or worse, translate to Protestantism and possible extinction.

Yet tradition died hard; just as it had been difficult for the new Christian Church to remove the old Pagan customs and festivals, Henry VIII did not entirely succeed in his intent. The fact that many shrines were eventually rebuilt, and the King had continually to repeat his orders relating to their destruction, meant that devotion to the old ways persisted. Whatever human needs the shrines and pilgrimages had satisfied lived on; so, if they were to be forbidden to the people, something was bound to take their place.

WATER CULTURE REVIVAL

By the end of the sixteenth century, that something had matured in a new form of hydrotherapy. Spas and mineral springs became fashionable and were re-discovered all over the country, while thousands of wells formerly associated with the saints found a new role. The Holy Well of St. Walstan was one of them, though mercifully it retained the dignity of holiness rather than degenerating into a 'wishing' well, the miserable fate of so many other sacred wells. At such places, where people might previously have offered a prayer, or oblation to the Church, they instead made a wish, usually of a more temporal than spiritual nature. The best which can be said for these formerly holy places is that the new 'pilgrims' were nevertheless carrying on an association between water and human ritual, which can be traced back to the Bronze Age, and beyond. Even now, the custom of tossing coins into wells and fountains is an ancient ritual still carried out daily all over the world.

In western countries today the significance of water as a tool of life is usually forgotten until, for some reason or other, a shortage occurs, but in the years following the Reformation a reverence still existed. Gradually, during those troubled and turbulent years of the bedding down of the new religion, tiny shoots of optimism, inspired by water culture, began to appear in Bawburgh. A new phase of the legend was beginning, one which reached back to Roman and Pagan cults where water had been acknowledged a necessary part of spiritual and secular life. Such aspirations were about to regain their pre-Christian relevance, set to emulate waves breaking on the beach, when the water is as old as time but each wave is new. The people of Bawburgh harked back to the instincts of their forbears by honouring the old union between man and water, manifest by the Well below the Church.

When it existed, the Shrine Chapel had naturally been the focus of attention. While Mass was said in the adjoining Church, it was always the Shrine which had attracted the indulgence-paying pilgrims; it was there that the triptych had hung and its walls contained the hopes and prayers of generations of men and women. But after those walls had gone, a new, outward sign was needed if the cult of St. Walstan was to be seen to exist. Conveniently, Taverham, Costessey and Bawburgh all lay close to river beds, and the legend of St. Walstan was steeped in a tradition of springs, wells and rivers. Had it not been the miraculous water of St. Walstan's Well which pilgrims had sought in times of sickness; and had it not been to the Well that local farmers had brought their animals? In the absence of the saint's mortal remains, and without the machinery of organised religion, the Well became the replacement focus for the legend of St. Walstan in post-Reformation Bawburgh.

Henry's reformation might have tackled religious ills, but disease of the body still existed in all its ghastly forms. Medical science was a long way behind faith healing and post-Reformation men and women were only beginning to separate earthly comforts from spiritual needs. Medieval pilgrims had looked for miracles relating more to the after-life than the contemporary journey, but late sixteenth- and seventeenth-century pilgrims combined their search for God with one of human hopefulness, through whatever medium was available. Those visiting Bawburgh found the medium there to be the water from a Holy Well and the legend of a humble farm worker, which once more served the needs of humanity, this time a generation emerging from spiritual numbness. After all, not only was the theme of curing illness with water thoroughly in vogue, but St. Walstan's Well already possessed a long tradition of miraculous healing of both mind and body.

PRE-REFORMATION MIRACLES

The ancient miracles which acted as the credentials necessary for the Well's new character reach back to the eleventh century, although in such matters we are naturally in the hands of uncertain witnesses. It is now impossible to verify such proceedings and would be impractical, to say the least, to investigate whether two oxen pulled a waggon bearing the body of Walstan from Taverham to Bawburgh; that, with the rest of the legend itself, can only be discussed in the wider context of the origins of folklore and Anglo Saxon hagiology. Instead, it is the use to which these miracles were put, in the second half of the sixteenth century, that mirrors the essence of the legend, this requiring little change to redirect its emphasis. There were miracles said to take place in Walstan's lifetime and at his death (the increased seed corn, the perfumed and trampled briars, the taming of the 'opprobrious' wife, the visions, and the passing of the cart through the wall of the Church), but it was the water-related miracles which achieved increased importance for the men and women who visited the Well in post-Reformation Bawburgh.

According to Item 8, it was on the 30th May, 1016, that the first spring – at Taverham – appeared miraculously, to be used by the Parish Priest during the celebration of Walstan's last Mass in the hayfield. The second spring (but the first in the NLA, since no mention is made there of water needed for the Priest) came shortly after the crossing of the River Wensum by the funeral cortege. It is said that an impression of the cart tracks was for years afterwards apparent on the surface of the water, marking the place at which the waggon crossed its surface. (In the NLA this incident took place on a pool in the wood.) Using the evidence of the English Life, the triptych hanging in Bawburgh Church told the pilgrims:

'The soul of Walston Angells bare to heaven;
Oxen wth ye body to Costesey took ye way:
Over a great river went in yt stevyn;
a great miracle folkes present say:
ye Cart wth ye corse & people passed on hey
upon ye overpart of ye water wthout drowning
God made ym to passe, without stowning.'

Back on dry land, they only went a short way before one of the oxen 'staled', and immediately another spring occurred (the NLA says this took place on a hill top):

'Another thing marvelous remaineth in yt place
ye print of ye wheel yet at ys day,
as men say, appeareth before their face:
ye oxen upon ye hill tooke ye right way
towards ye lodge as fast as they may:
the one ox staled, a marvelous case:
there sprang a well by Gods grace.'

A well was built over the second spring in Costessey wood to mark the place and to guide pilgrims in their search for St. Walstan.

Eamon Duffy (1992) highlighted the word 'staled', which he took to mean 'urinated' rather than the more usual interpretation of 'stalled'. (The word 'staled' is now more usually associated with horses than oxen or cattle.) However, David Rollason, who translated the NLA entry for this search, points out that the Latin words used for the oxen standing where the wells appeared are *persisterent* (to persist, stand still) and *fecerunt stationem* (they made a stop), and although there are words in the translation which could carry a slightly different meaning from that used, such is not the case with the oxen.

The third spring, mentioned in both Lives, burst forth at Bawburgh, just below the Church, where the oxen again stopped to rest. Once the Shrine Chapel was built and pilgrimages commenced, the Bawburgh spring was enclosed in a well, which became filled with Holy Water. Although three wells (only two in the NLA) are associated with the legend, only the one at Bawburgh is credited with miraculous properties and no doubt that has much to do with its location.

Through the intervention of St. Walstan, water from this final well healed men and beasts alike. Miracles of no mean account were said to have occurred: blind men were given renewed sight; lameness righted; hearing restored; spirits were cast out; and leprosy, fever, 'Palsy', and many other sicknesses were cured and healed. Farmers carried off phials of water from St. Walstan's Well to give to sick animals, in the hope of curing their illness or infertility.

The Oxford Dictionary of Saints understandably says that such cures were explicable in terms of faith-healing, auto-suggestion, or inaccurate diagnosis – suggestions which can be used to explain any placebo effect, ancient or modern. Trials carried out this century have proved that patients invariably feel better, and in some cases were better, as the result of taking an inert 'drug'. However, real or imagined, the occurrence of miracles would have done much for the prestige, and therefore prosperity, of Bawburgh's Holy Well. Miracles were, after all, expected of a saint and such tales could only encourage visitors to the village. Sir Thomas More recorded that it was not unknown for a priest to stage a fraudulent miracle if business was slack at a particular shrine.

It was a specially good advertisement if the healed person was prominent and advantageously rich. Item 8, for example, records a certain knight, Sir Gregory Lovell, who came to Bawburgh '... wth great sicknesse & great bone ake'. Sir Gregory had spent a great deal of silver and gold in a search for easement of his pain and in pursuit of good health. Luckily he acquired some holy water from St. Walstan's Well, which he used to good effect, namely the restoration of his well-being.

As well as adding a third spring to the legend, Item 8 also records eleven specific miracles, none of which appear in the Latin Life, when all manner of sicknesses are said to have been cured. In a spirit of one-upmanship, the sixth miracle concerns a Canterbury man who had failed to persuade St. Thomas to cure his lameness. A fellow pilgrim suggested the man visit St. Walstan's Well instead, persuading the poor afflicted man that if he could get there, he would find release from his pain.

In due course, and after much travail, the man arrived in Norwich, and then in Bawburgh, where he prayed before St. Walstan. Those with him declared that he did indeed depart for home with both leg and body fully mended.

One of the eleven miracles inevitably concerns the raising of the dead:
'A man in Bawburgh wch a thaxtr was
down fell backward in a deep pond:
two days lay there, a marvelous case,
in depthnesse of ye pit upon ye sond
up take, fast knit in deaths bond,
& to Church borne buried to be,
his neighbours following yt for to see.

'before Walstan's tomb ye beer was set
soon after men prayd he made moving:
up they him take anon wthout letting,
to God & St. Walston they made loovyng.
this holy Walston's name doth spring
in diverse & many mo countries yn this
for these & many mo miracles, I wys.'

BISHOP BALE

Of all the cures and blessings associated with saints, holy wells and miraculous healing, there are several references to one unique facet of cure at Bawburgh which is not to be found in other or contemporary legends. It was Bishop Bale who assigned to the water of St. Walstan's Well the dubious honour of being able to restore what the Suffolk-born Bishop called men's 'prevy parts'. Since there is a passing mention in the NLA of *'genitalibus membris'* (fruitful or generative limb/genitals) it is possible that the idea was not entirely Bale's own, but it is at the door of this colourful man of the cloth that blame must be laid for an unfortunate comparison of St. Walstan with the Greek God, Priapus. This, in the Bishop's *English Votaries* of 1546, was copied by Blomefield, who recorded the entry in his 1805 *History of Norfolk*, repeating the information that both men and beast '... who had lost their genitals' were made whole and entirely cured at Bawburgh.

That Bale should have emphasised miracles relating to such matters reflects his somewhat eccentric attitude to life, religion and sex, and a lifelong attempt to convey his own ideas to the popular mind. Born in 1495 in the village of Cove near Dunwich, Suffolk, John Bale was sent for education to a Carmelite convent in Norwich, where he was an enthusiastic and zealous Roman Catholic. After being sent to Jesus College, Cambridge, however, he took St. Paul's advice on the matter of marrying rather than burning: he renounced his monastic habit – and vows – and married a young woman named Dorothy. On consideration, he also transferred his energies from championing the cause of Catholicism to that of the new Protestantism.

By 1540 he had made so many enemies by his outspoken sermons and unorthodox behaviour (one description speaks of his rude vigour of expression, and his want of good taste and moderation) that he and Dorothy, with their children, had to seek refuge in Germany. There, amongst other works and plays (said to be distinguished by a total lack of decorum), he wrote *The Actes of Englyshe Votaryes*. After returning to England he was for a time promoted to the vicarage of Swaffham, Norfolk, but soon afterwards Edward VI sent him to Ireland, an uninspired choice since most of the clergy there remained faithful to Roman Catholicism and therefore to clerical chastity. Having occasioned considerable scandal by advising his fellow priests to marry he finally left Ireland. Bale, known as 'Bilious Bale' by his contemporary scholars, died at Canterbury in 1563, leaving behind him a presentable amount of work although much of it is said to be marred by misrepresentations, inaccuracies and what might be called his 'earthy' turn of phrase. In *English Votaries* this opponent of anything he considered to be sentiment or idolatry wrote of St. Walstan:

> *'Saynte Walstane of Bawburgh iii Miles from Norwych, was neyther Monke nor Prest, yet vowed he (they say) to lyve Chast without a Wyfe, and perfourmed that Promyse, by Fastynge of the Frydaye and good Sayntes Vygyls without any other Grace or Gyft gyven of God. He dyed in the Year of our Lord a M. and xvi. in the thyrde Calendes of June, and became after the maner of Priapus the God of they Feldes in Northfolke, and Gyde of their Harvestes, al Mowers and Sythe folowers sekynge hym ones in the Yeare. Loke his Legende in the Cataloge of Johan Capgrave, Provyncyall of the Augustyne Fryeres, and ye shal finde there, that both Men and Beastes which had lost their Prevy Parts, had newe Members again restored to them, by this Walstane. Marke thys kynde of Myracles, for your Learnynge, I thynke Ye have seldome redde the lyke.'*

It was typical that Bale should both ridicule the miracles in general and highlight those relating to 'prevy parts' in particular. The mention of Priapus was not called for, but is no doubt related to the concept of fertility which features in the Greek legend. Priapus was a mythological god of fertility, with the phallus as his symbol, who was worshipped in both Greece and Italy. When even the Greeks outgrew their fascination for Priapus (the ass, being the symbol of lechery, was sacrificed in his honour) his role was changed from that of a god to something resembling a cross between a scarecrow and the patron god of gardens. Statues of Priapus as a crude, misshapen man, with enormous genitals, were regarded as amusing by those who had formerly worshipped him as a god of fertility.

Considering the likelihood of links between the Bawburgh well and Roman and Saxon times, there is no reason why such a manifestation of the concept of fertility should not be part of the legend. Fertility meant survival, but is at odds with the Christian intent to encourage the idea that celibacy is desirable for those attaining sainthood or earthly sanctity.

The Christian stance on purity is shown by the huge number of women who chose death rather than lose their virginity, whether or not they were married, and the exclusively male clergy were expected to practice celibacy. The conundrum of squaring universal virginity with the continuance of the species was never entirely solved, except in the necessity of a virgin birth by Mary, Mother of Christ, and chastity was generally acknowledged to be more holy than otherwise. Previous cultures had less of a problem, as can be seen in various Celtic legends relating to the Goddess Epona (Macha in Wales and Rhiannon in Ireland) to whom is attributed the triple characteristics of mother, virgin and female aggressor. Folklore surrounding Bishop Wulfstan dwells on the measures he took to control his urge to propagate the species. During his lifetime, Wulfstan expounded much energy in espousing the virtues of a celibate priesthood and to improving the monastic observance. Bale seems rather scornful that, although Walstan was 'neyther Monke nor Prest' he nevertheless lived chastely without a wife.

This particular aspect of the Bawburgh legend is, then, a combination between man's need and desire for virility, and the Church's stated requirements of celibacy for its officers and representatives. Just how the tradition of miraculous restoration for male 'members' survived in the legend is miraculous in itself. It is easier to trace the link of fecundity with the agricultural nature of the legend and the synonymous desire for productive and healthy crops and livestock. The month of May has traditional celebrations which centre on the theme of fertility, and the transition of spring into summer, often symbolised by the white flowers of the hawthorn.

Uncertainty surrounds the source which Bale used, but he is known to have studied the manuscripts of John Leland and no doubt he had access to the NLA or Pynson's *Kalendre* in Germany.

There is no '*genitalibus membris*' reference in Item 8, although it is obviously impossible to know whether the 1658 copier sanitized the contents of the triptych for a less earthy audience. There is one oblique reference to 'members' in the miracle of Sir Gregory Lovell, but this is taken to mean his arms and legs.

ST. WALSTAN'S BUSH

However, for those pre-Reformation pilgrims seeking cures at the Shrine – whether or not they were hoping to improve their fertility – or have parts of their bodies 'restored' – there were many rituals to be observed. Among them is one which accounts for a reference in Bryant's *The Churches of Norfolk* (1905):

'Years ago, an old thorn bush stood close by [the Well], called St. Walstan's Bush.'

Few other chroniclers have mentioned St. Walstan's Bush, but there is no reason why it should not have existed. Pilgrims would often end their prayers or rituals by leaving an offering, sometimes a pin or a stone, or a piece of their clothing which they would hang on a nearby tree or bush. The significance of such an offering has not been fully determined, but since St. Walstan's Well was associated with healing serious illness, the sufferer there might hope that as the material rotted away so would the disease. No excavation has taken place to find out if pilgrims ever left any more substantial gifts in or beside the Well, but if so they are still buried nearby. It is unlikely that they would have been stolen, since the ill luck of the donor would then be transferred to the thief.

POST-REFORMATION

This tradition of healing was, then, the legacy which the post-Reformation pilgrim inherited and Bawburgh village sought to exploit. Petitions for the cure of just about any ailment were brought to Bawburgh, much as they were to other sites in East Anglia, notably at St Withburga's Well, East Dereham, which is in the churchard close to St. Nicholas' Church. St. Withburga's remains were stolen and taken to Ely in 974, but traces of her Chapel can still be seen and it is said that a bath-house was built late in the eighteenth century to accommodate those seeking to be healed by the holy water.

The wells at Walsingham Abbey fared less well than those at Bawburgh and East Dereham. There they became wishing wells, where the wisher knelt on a stone and dipped a hand into one of two wells while silently making a wish. However, the ancient well at the Anglican Shrine, Little Walsingham, was restored in 1931 and is now incorporated into the new shrine where it retains a holy status.

Some wells, like that of St. Mindred's, at Exning near Newmarket in Suffolk, are shrouded in mystery and are little more than place names on a map. No one now knows who Mindred was, but the rumour is that St. Etheldreda was baptised at one of her three Exning wells. There were Holy Wells, too, at Woolpit in West Suffolk, where pilgrims attended the Lady's Well, and at Wymondham in Norfolk, where the Well is dedicated to St. Thomas of Canterbury.

Throughout the seventeenth century, the new pilgrims visited Bawburgh and the Parish Church of St. Mary and St. Walstan, albeit in smaller numbers than in previous centuries and for different reasons.

No doubt some were Catholics, who had no freedom of worship but sought consolation in the deserted, but still holy, site at Bawburgh. Were the brave guardians of the ancient triptych among those who went secretly to the Church and surreptitiously took the waters of the Holy Well? If so, their secret is well kept and they achieved the anonymity they hoped for. Perhaps they stood nearby, quietly watching the repairers re-tile the Church roof in 1633, and again during 1637, when the notorious Bishop Matthew Wren ordered further restoration of the Church. Who knows how many 'recusants' from Bowthorpe and Costessey were there in 1660 when the shroud brass to Archdeacon Philip Tenison was dedicated?

The legend of St. Walstan, kept alive so well by the Archdeacon and the Catholic guardians, continued to appear in anthologies and collections of saints' lives and was included in the massive compendium of English saints compiled early in the seventeenth century by Nicholas Roscarrock. The legend continued to appear in print during the Hanoverian period: in 1756 the Rev. Alban Butler published *The Lives of the Fathers, Martyrs, and Other Principal Saints*, to give new emphasis to the old legends. Bishop Challoner followed this a few years later by giving Walstan a place in his *Memorial of Ancient British Piety*, thereby acknowledging, as did Butler, the special status given to those saints who gained popular acclaim.

THE GENTLEMAN'S MAGAZINE

In the eighteenth century, the old practices of hydrotherapy achieved a second revival and visiting healing wells again became fashionable, this time accompanied by the contemporary interest in matters of science. In 1763, the miraculous cures at St. Walstan's Well became the subject of discussion in *The Gentleman's Magazine*. This renowned journal was published monthly, and concentrated on academic – and especially antiquarian – subjects. It sold well during the eighteenth and nineteenth centuries and, during the 1760s, its editor was one Sylvanus Urban, Gent.

The discussion about St. Walstan began in July, when the magazine carried articles on springs, baths, etc. and their various medical properties. Debate on the subject continued in the August issue, when bilious cholic was examined in some depth, with instances of how the disorder had been lately cured at Bath. Also, there was consideration of a document emanating from Bristol regarding diseases of the stomach. Generally, these inquiries into the science of theraputic waters were of an interested and inquisitive, rather than sceptical, nature. The September issue carried a review of *Attempts to Revive Ancient Medical Doctrines*, by Alex Sutherland, M.D., followed by a letter to the Editor. The correspondent, signing himself 'X.Y.Z.' wrote to Mr. Urban that on the subject of spring water he could report that the virtue of the water of Bawburgh spring was still held in as great an estimation as ever. He continued:

'My business has very lately obliged me to make a tour through this country, at all the market towns, and even at every village I stopt at, I was informed of its wonderful efficacy in curing all disorders. The resort to this spring has been very great all this summer. I was assured by a person who was on the spot, that there were frequently 2000 people there at a time, particularly on Sunday mornings; and that the spring was frequently emptied, not so much by the quantity drank on the spot, as what was put into bottles, casks, and barrels, to be transported to the remotest parts of the county.'

Mr. 'X.Y.Z.' went on to declare that it was his duty to pass on this account of 'Catholic medicine', but regretted that he, for his own part, had no faith that St. Walstan could produce such extraordinary effect in the water. He appealed to a chemist to analyse the water, as a favour to the world. However, if any such chemist was found, he failed to report back to Mr. Urban, or at least his account appears not to have been published.

It must be wondered as to the accuracy of the person 'on the spot' who supplied the information that two thousand people frequently visited the Well on a Sunday morning. Two thousand people is a lot of people. Who were they all and what were they doing at Bawburgh? Perhaps Mr. X.Y.Z.'s informant was the man about whom Husenbeth wrote in 1859:

'An old man died not long ago at Babur, who was known to the writer, and in his younger days kept an inn there, which was frequented by crowds of visitors to St. Walstan's Well'.

If one report in the *Norwich Gazette* is anything to go by, large numbers of these visitors were up to no good. In 1763 the *Gazette* recorded a 'concourse' of people at the Bawburgh Well, and 'much confusion ensued … and many heads were broken in the scuffle'.

Many twentieth-century writers have recorded that bottles of the Holy Water were sold on the streets of Norwich, though no price is ever quoted and none of the expected dire consequences are recorded for any who peddled miraculous cure for profit. Doubtless it was profit which accounts for the huge quantities of water taken in 'casks and barrels' as reported to Mr. Urban. Obviously, those who could not visit the Well had the Holy Water brought to them by contemporary entrepreneurs. The nineteenth-century *Index Monasticus* (Taylor, page 20) in Norwich Library observes that '… waters of St. Walstan's Well have been retailed in the streets of Norwich, even within the memory of its present inhabitants'.

While there is no evidence that any specific miracles were chronicled during the years when hydrotherapy was at its height, there is one which took place in March, 1819, and for which detailed witness statements still exist. Included in the papers of Fr. Husenbeth in the Bishop's Library, Northampton, is a twenty-three-page document giving a full description of the proceedings written in the hand of the happy recipient, Mr. Francis Bunn – a manuscript which would no doubt have fascinated Mr. 'X.Y.Z.' and occasioned a further Letter to the Editor.

THE MIRACLE OF MR. BUNN

In 1787 Mr. Francis Bunn was born in Wymondham, Norfolk, and for most of his early life suffered from lameness and agonising pain in one leg. In his statement he wrote of a lifelong but unsuccessful search for healing of both body and soul. For his body he tried doctors in Wymondham and Norwich, and for his spiritual health he tried the Methodists, the Independents, the Baptists and the Established Church. While serving in the army he was sent to Ireland, where he naturally had a terrible time with his health, but managed to woo a young Irish girl named Mary, the future Mrs. Bunn, and bring her back to Costessey. Although his new wife was a Catholic, Francis remained a member of the Methodist Church, but Mrs. Bunn, wishing to attend the Catholic Chapel at Costessey in thanksgiving for their second child, set about persuading her husband to accompany her.

Poor Mr. Bunn was suffering as usual from the continuous wound in his leg, as of course he had done for most of his life. But, on Easter Sunday, 1817, the couple set off for Costessey. Mr. Bunn was in a state of immense trepidation and anxiety as to what might happen to him if he entered a Catholic Chapel. He had always protested vigorously against the Roman Church, and its sanction of image worship, going so far as to declare it was no more a sin to kill a papist than it was to kill a dog.

However, on entering the porch of the Chapel, Mr. Bunn was struck not by the expected bolt of lightning but by an immediate realisation of the error of his ways. He subsequently consented to have his daughter baptised by the Priest and set about reading books on the Catholic faith. To cut a long and endearing narrative sadly, but necessarily, short, in 1819 Mr. Bunn was cured of his affliction after visiting St. Walstan's Well, and remained in good health until his death thirty-seven years later.

Witness to these events came from a variety of sources, including Sir George Jerningham and his former Chaplain, Fr. Samuel Jones; Protestant doctors from Norwich and Wymondham; various members of Mr. Bunn's family; and from Mr. Bunn himself, who in 1820 signed his occupation as 'Bombazine weaver'.

Some time after 1820 the declarations were put together by the hand of Fr. Husenbeth, the new Chaplain at Costessey Hall. He seems to have gone to great lengths to collate evidence of times, dates, and reliable witness, adding his own corroboration that he personally knew Mr. Bunn from 1820 until the man's death in 1856 and that the much-discussed leg remained cured. It is known that Fr. Husenbeth had it in his mind to submit this, and other documentation, to the Vatican in order that canonization of St. Walstan might be formalised. Towards the end of *The Life of St. Walstan* he wrote:

'It is most desirable to revive the ancient tradition to the Saint, principally in his immediate locality. With this object, a petition has been presented to the Holy See by the Bishop of Northampton, in whose diocese this part of England is comprised, the purport of which is, that, as our saint is not inscribed in the Roman Martyrology, the Holy See would approve of the religious veneration of him as a Saint, which has been paid to him in England from time immorial'.

It is, however, proving difficult to find evidence of this submission to the Vatican. Unfortunately, the papers of the contemporary Bishop Wareing of Northampton no longer exist and are thought to have been destroyed, while few of Husenbeth's notes or correspondence survived the dispersal sale of his library which took place shortly after his death. A request for such information as is available is currently before the officers of the Holy See in order that the details might be known.

However, it is certain that as well as that of Mr. Bunn, two other miracles were similarly catalogued, one concerning an Ursuline Sister and the other a Benedictine nun. Both incidents took place in a Hammersmith Convent and an account of all three miracles appear in the Husenbeth book.

In the first of the Hammersmith miracles, Sister St. John Chrysostom set out from Edinburgh in October, 1839, to return to her own convent at Chavagnes, France, but was taken ill. She was removed to the Benedictine Convent at Hammersmith where she was attended by various doctors. Though practically at death's door, Sister Chrysostom resolutely declined the suggestion by the Mother Abbess that she should seek a cure through moss from St. Walstan's Well. Instead, she preferred to put her faith in a medal of the Blessed Virgin Mary. But, in the words of a writer in the *Norwich Mercury* (1898):

'... [Sister Chrysostom] applied the medal to her stomach, and instantly heard these words as if proceeding from the medal, "drink some water poured on the moss from St. Walstan's well". This she did at once, and then swallowed the moss, instantly exclaiming, 'I am cured".

Thus restored, Sister Chrysostom had for her supper eight oysters with bread, some bread and butter pudding, and wine and some water to drink.

Two years later, in 1841, an inmate of the same Hammersmith Convent fell desperately ill; Dame Mary Magdalen McDonnell had consumption. The sister prayed to Our Lady for help and made a Novena, composed of the *Memorare* Prayer with the aspiration *Sancte Walstane, ora pro nobis.* The Mother Abbess sent to Fr. Husenbeth for some water from St. Walstan's Well and, having drunk it, Dame Mary Magdalen regained her health. As testimony, the Abbess sent all details of the case to Fr. Husenbeth, with the news that the doctors had pronounced the patient to be 'most decidedly better'.

~ • ~

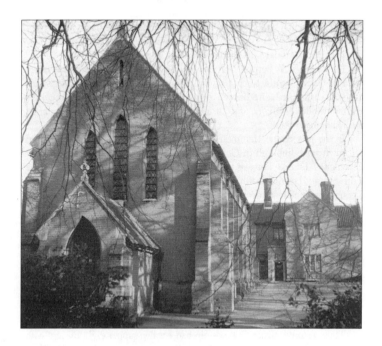

Chapter Nine

A CATHOLIC SAINT

'The hand of God is not shortened, and he is still wonderful in his Saints. Devotion to St. Walstan has been rewarded even in our days by singular favours and blessings.'
Fr. F.C. Husenbeth, D.D.

*E*AST Anglia has always been in the forefront of religious discussion and opinion, and as we know from the story of the lost triptych the villages of Bowthorpe and Costessey have most especially been associated with the survival of English Catholicism. Those links between Costessey, St. Walstan and the Old Faith were strengthened and made permanent in July, 1820, when the young Father Husenbeth arrived in Norfolk at the invitation of the Jerningham family of Costessey Hall. Fr. Husenbeth took up the post of temporary Chaplain to Sir George William Stafford Jerningham with the intention of returning to teach at his old school, Sedgley Park in Staffordshire. In January, 1821, however, he consented to remain at Costessey as full-time Chaplain to the future Lord Stafford, where he lived until his death over fifty years later. In 1841 he opened St. Walstan's Chapel in Costessey and in 1859, while Provost of Northampton, wrote *The Life of Saint Walstan, Confessor.*

FATHER HUSENBETH

Frederick James Husenbeth was born on St. Walstan's Day, 1796, the son of Frederick Charles and Elizabeth Husenbeth, in the City of Bristol. His father, who had been born at Mainz in the Grand Duchy of Hesse, arrived in England during 1787, a scholar and teacher of classics, with the aim of improving his English. But, after the events of the French Revolution prevented his return home, he stayed in Bristol and set up as a merchant in wines.

Although the young Husenbeth was named Frederick James at birth, James being his mother Elizabeth's maiden name, he later changed it to Charles, and was known throughout his adult life as Frederick Charles (the same as his father). Might this have been to do with the early death of his mother – Frederick was only nineteen at the time – and the death of an older brother? Elizabeth had been a non-Catholic at the time of her marriage but was received into her husband's Church in 1806, when Frederick James was ten years old. Her death in 1816 came at what was no doubt an emotional time for the young man about to commit himself to the priesthood, and it is possible that Elizabeth had been preoccupied with the dead son at the expense of Frederick.

In February, 1820, Frederick (now Charles) Husenbeth was ordained priest and in July of the same year he took up a temporary post as Chaplain to the Jerningham family. The following year he visited his old school, hoping for a teaching post, but returned almost immediately to take up permanent residence in Costessey where he was to spend the rest of his life.

The year 1820 had been one of change for England: George III had finally died and the Prince Regent, George IV, acceded to the throne but failed in his attempt to divorce Queen Caroline. At Costessey Hall the Jerninghams were also in mourning: Sir George's second son, William Charles, had died at Dunkirk and his body brought back to Costessey for burial. Fr. Samuel Jones had been at the Hall for seven years and his departure left the Jerninghams without a Chaplain. It was this, combined with the Dunkirk tragedy, the knowledge that the Jerninghams were to assume the Barony of Stafford, plus the lack of a definite job at Sedley Park, which conspired to persuade Fr. Husenbeth to move permanently to Costessey.

No sooner did he arrived in Norfolk than he set about removing the Chaplain's residence from Costessey Hall into the village. He quickly gained the confidence of the local Catholic community, and was so successful in his work that in the first few years of his ministry, he increased the Catholic community from 200 to 500. But, as the congregation grew, so did the anxiety of Lady Stafford and Fr. Husenbeth. Services at the Hall Chapel of St. Augustine became crowded and uncomfortable and in 1831, Lady Stafford decided to do something about it: she and Lord Stafford offered the opportunity for a new Catholic Church in the village of Costessey. In April, 1832, Fr. Husenbeth wrote to a friend:

'The great increase of Catholics in this mission has rendered a new Chapel absolutely necessary. I have undertaken to erect one with the sanction of the Rt. Rev. Dr. Walsh, and with the approbation of Lord Stafford, who have both handsomely contributed. I have already collected a considerable sum; but after great exertions to raise a sufficient fund, I have found the resources of many exhausted by repeated calls of a similar kind, and in too many other instances, the charity of many grown cold.'

Nevertheless, a fund was set up and a variety of people contributed including the Earl of Shrewsbury, Catherine Lady Throckmorton, Sir H. Bedingfield (who only gave £5 while Lady Bedingfield contributed £38 5s.), many small but valuable contributions from parishioners, and £20 from

Fr. Husenbeth's father, Frederick. By May, 1834, enough money had been raised for building of the new Chapel to begin and the foundations of St. Walstan's Chapel were laid, though sadly Lady Frances was not to see it as she had died in 1832.

It is clear that Fr. Husenbeth had few doubts as to what to call the new Chapel. He had from the first been captivated by the story of St. Walstan in a village so historically a part of the Costessey Manor and the Old Faith. 'The venerable remains of the [Bawburgh] Chapel,' he wrote, 'are still visited by devout Catholics with pious reverence, and the writer has seen a holy Bishop from the far Western diocese of Natchez, in North America, detach a small fragment from the ruined wall, to carry home with him as a sacred memorial of St. Walstan'.

The tradition of worship at nearby Bawburgh meant that St. Walstan was the first name on everyone's lips. The connections between the Jerninghams and Bawburgh are now well-known to readers of this search, and Fr. Husenbeth's own interest is fully evident. During his time at Costessey he not only accumulated statements of witness to the celebration of Walstan as a saint in Costessey, Bawburgh and Taverham, from both the Catholic and Protestant sources, but used St. Walstan consistently as a tool in his enthusiastic promotion of the Gospel. Since it was Samuel Jones who 'introduced' Husenbeth to St. Walstan, it may be presumed that he, too, was a devotee and that there was a general acceptance of St. Walstan by the Jerninghams.

It was hoped that the new Chapel would open on St. Walstan's Day (and Husenbeth's 45th birthday) 1841, but that year it coincided with Whit Sunday; the opening ceremony, therefore, took place on the 26th, the first solemn service being performed on the 30th May. Holy Water was taken from the Well at Bawburgh (then called Babur) for the Blessing.

Fr. Husenbeth continued his Costessey mission with grace and diligence, becoming a much-loved figure in and around the parish. He explored and documented local Church history and became St. Walstan's third biographer. His book *The Life of St. Walstan, Confessor* was published in 1859 and he lost no opportunity to interpret folklore or suggested fact to the clear advantage of his cause. Even when it came to Bishop Bale's outrageous comparison of Walstan with Priapus, Husenbeth distilled it down to Bale's mention of 'wonderful cures received through the Saint's intercession' and succeeded in making the Bishop sound positively respectable! Nothing is made of Bale's mockery and all mention of 'prevy parts' is removed, leaving only '… those who have lost eyes and other members' to have been cured, and there is no mention of the urinating oxen of Item 8.

Much of the book consists of extracts from Item 8, but he and Canon Morris spent some time collecting and processing the material, with help from James Bulwer. He commented ruefully on not being able to include any drawing of the representations of Walstan, due to the expense, and was right in thinking that there was more iconography than those he mentioned, which were at North Burlingham, Ludham, Barnham Broom, Sparham, Denton, and Norwich (St. James).

Commenting on *The Life of St. Walstan* in 1917, M.R. James remained critical not only of what he saw to be an ignorance of Blythburgh as Walstan's birthplace, but also accused Husenbeth of going to some lengths to explain how Benedict and Blida were unaware that their son was living only a few miles away at Taverham if they lived in Bawburgh. In fact there are only a few lines of 'justification' on the subject and, while James claimed to have compiled a better list of effigies from Husenbeth's later works, he in fact misses out that at Litcham (although he later included it in *Suffolk and Norfolk*). He is also at variance with Husenbeth in saying that the feast of St. Walstan occurs in the *Manual* of 1708, two years later than the date given in the book (see Appendix V).

Publications other than his book on St. Walstan were several, but Husenbeth's authoritative *Emblems of Saints: by which they are distinguished in Works of Art*, published in 1850 and many times thereafter, became a classic of its kind. In addition to his parochial duties he accepted the post of Grand Vicar for Norfolk and Suffolk from Bishop Walsh, and in 1842 was appointed Vicar General for the whole of the District by Bishop Wareing. He also found time to indulge his hobby of keeping snakes, toads and parrots, and is said by Norgate to have been responsible for the introduction of several new plants to this country. Pope Pius IX conferred on him the honorary title of Doctor of Divinity by a decree dated 4th July, 1850, and in June, 1852, he became the first Provost of the newly created Northampton Cathedral Chapter and was thereafter known locally as Provost Husenbeth.

When the first Westminster Provincial Synod was held at Oscott in 1852, Provost Husenbeth attended as Bishop's Theologian and Chapter Delegate, and he appears on the unfinished painting by James Doyle at Oscott.

The presence and influence of St. Walstan's Chapel gradually became an integral part of Costessey life; many local people had been involved in its construction, either as sponsors or as tradespeople, and the name Walstan continued to be given to Catholic sons. Among the subscribers to the Chapel Fund was Walstan Hastings, organist, who donated 6d. to the cost of the sanctuary lamp and later, in 1861, paid for repairs to the organ. Even today, the use of the name Walstan can be seen on headstones in the Chapel graveyard, a witness to the tradition of naming a child for one who has found favour with God.

At his death, in October, 1872, Provost Husenbeth was owner of St. Walstan's Chapel. During 1871, the Rt. Hon. Henry Valentine Lord Stafford had made over the whole of the Chapel land, cemetery, Chapel, house and buildings to Husenbeth and he, in his turn, willed it to the Bishop of Northampton. Glowing and affectionate obituaries appeared in the Catholic Press including that in the *Northampton Catholic Magazine* which contained an account of the last hour of his life:

> *'The annointing in the name of the Lord took place, the Holy Viaticum was administered, and a little after eight o'clock in the morning of the 31st of October death placed his cold chilling hand on the heart of the Very Rev. F.C. Husenbeth, D.D., Vicar-General and Provost of Northampton, and his pulse beat no more. The melancholy tidings quickly travelled from house to house, and that day big grief filled many a soul.'*

Provost Husenbeth had lived, worked and preached in Costessey for over fifty years and was a true, if sometimes uncritical, champion of the legend of St. Walstan.

RELIGIOUS DISSENT AND DISCUSSION

Father Husenbeth's arrival at Costessey Park had coincided with the emergence of Catholic revival taking place in the country at large. Husenbeth himself wrote at the time '... the ancient faith of our land is steadily regaining its hold on the minds and affections of the people'. By the 1830s, the Church in England had, in its turn, become unpopular and such grievances as existed found a voice in the oldest of the established and traditional centres for clerical learning, the University of Oxford. Generally named the Oxford Movement, dissenting members of the State Church united under John Keble, the son of a Gloucestershire vicar, one intention being to take up arms against Roman Catholic Emancipation and restore faith in the Established Church. Fearing a schism, the Rector of Hadleigh in Suffolk instigated a significant four-day conference which he, and three of his fellow clergymen, hoped would influence the direction to be taken in defence of the Church. The Rev. Hugh James Rose, who had gone to Suffolk in 1830, organised the Hadleigh Conference in 1833 and it was from this humble gathering that some of the greater ripples of the Oxford Movement originated. Among the delegates was Richard Froude, an enthusiastic English Catholic, who brought John Keble and J.H. Newman (later Cardinal) together.

The awakening of religious debate paved the way, eventually, for a wider tolerance of those who did not desire worship under the banner of the Church of England or who had been denied religious freedom since the Reformation. In Bawburgh it appears that the Parish Church had successfully translated from the Church of Rome since in the seventeenth century, while Bishop Wren had only minimal success in restoring the fabric of the churches in Bowthorpe and Costessey. His efforts appear to have been welcomed in Bawburgh when, during 1637, the Church was considerably renovated. In spite of the fact that the Catholic Jerninghams were the chief landowners in the parish, the village indicated a diplomatic measure of support for the Established Church, whereas in Costessey and Bowthorpe many more stuck to Catholicism as an alternative to Protestantism. Yet there was, typically perhaps, no religious docility in the birthplace of St. Walstan; dissenters in Bawburgh and the neighbouring village of Marlingford joined forces to look for salvation not through Catholicism but through Non-Comformity under the banner of Wesleyan Methodism.

The Bawburgh Methodists, who eventually became part of the wider Norwich Circuit, established themselves as a group during 1822 and united with others from Marlingford. As was common practice in the early days of Methodism, services were held in cottages or houses. Perhaps old habits do die hard, since it was in the month of May, 1866, that the new Chapel was opened for regular workship, built only a few hundred yards from the Parish Church. (After the 1849 split which occurred in Wesleyan Methodism, one of the places allied with the new 'rebel' Reformers was Bawburgh. The word Chapel now has a certain ambiguity, since a Shrine – or Chantry – Chapel and a Methodist or Catholic Chapel represent different concepts. Indeed, the word is extended to include those who worship in a Non-Conformist Chapel and the Chapel of St. Walstan at Costessey is now referred to as a Church.)

Although the Established Church flourished in Bawburgh, the politics and religion of the Jerninghams had nevertheless continued to play a part in the life and fate of the legend of St. Walstan right up to the nineteenth century. The influence of Sir Henry Jerningham, by his alliance with Oliver Cromwell, possibly saved Bawburgh Church from further desecration, and his ancestors had, in 1634, enhanced the village by the construction of Bawburgh Hall. In the 1800s this tradition of recusancy had brought the learned Fr. Husenbeth to Norfolk, and the cult of St. Walstan reaped the rewards of lasting influence from old fortunes.

Equally, it was to be part of a burst of exuberant and fundamentalist religious opinion in the shape of Joseph Leycester Lyne, better known as Father Ignatius, Order of St. Benedict. While the good Father Husenbeth was quietly going about his pastoral and literary business in Costessey, he no doubt heard of the activities in Norwich of this energetic and colourful man, who entirely deserved the title 'eccentric', and who was taking advantage of contemporary religious dissent and discussion. Among the action-packed adventures, and hectic events, which took place during the nearly three years that Fr. Ignatius spent in East Anglia, his pilgrimage to St. Walstan's Well in 1864 was among the most memorable.

FATHER IGNATIUS AND THE THIRD ORDER

It is likely that when Father Ignatius founded his Third Order of monks in Norwich, in 1864, he already had more than a nodding acquaintance with the legend of St. Walstan. He was a devotee of Butler's *Lives of the Saints*, and seems to have taken literally the romanticised image which Butler attributed to his sainted persons. Donald Attwater points out with some emphasis that *Lives* was prescribed reading for the Third Order brotherhood and was one of only two or three books allowed to the Monks of Llanthony, the community founded in South Wales by Ignatius in 1870. Passages from *Lives* were read aloud to the monks of an evening, no doubt in emulation of St. Ignatius of Loyola, whose name and example Joseph Lyne had adopted. St. Ignatius had been touched by God while reading saints' lives and had therefore advocated such a practice to his followers. However, as a boy Joseph Leycester had 'preached' to his cousins on the lives of saints and Christian martyrs, often to the intense annoyance of other family members.

The life and beliefs of Joseph Lyne are the subject of three detailed books, whose authors show him to have been a committed exponent of the religious life, orthodox in the truest sense. Born in 1837, he claimed to have known from an early age that his calling was to become a clergyman out of the ordinary – which ambition he more than fulfilled. After securing a free place at St. Paul's Cathedral School he hardly used it to its best advantage, having devised his own very firm idea of piety well in advance of interference from his tutors. He considered secular learning superfluous to basic church doctrine and by his late teens, Joseph and his father had fallen out over what Mr. Lyne Senior considered was his son's unhealthy preoccupation with High Church ideas to the detriment of any thoughts on the subject of earning a living. In the end, it was left to sympathetic patrons to pay for Joseph to attend Trinity College, Glenalmond, where he developed the idea of reviving monasticism in the Church of England.

In truth, the idea of monastic revivalism was not all his own. An offshoot of the Oxford Movement had been a revival of religious orders in the Established Church. In 1841 the first Protestant woman to take religious vows since the Reformation was Marian Hughes, and she was followed by other women eager for the cloistered life, including Lavinia Crosse, who founded the Community of All-Hallows at Ditchingham, Norfolk. Religious communities for men were rather slower to get established, but in 1866 came the Cowley Fathers (Society of St. John the Evangelist) and later, in 1892, the Community of the Resurrection. In the course of his life, Joseph Lyne was to commune with several men and women who heard this call from God, especially Priscilla Lydia Sellon, who had set up the Society of the Holy Trinity of Devonport in 1848, and who took rooms at Samson & Hercules House in Norwich where she founded the Sisterhood of Mount Calvary.

By the time Joseph Leycester arrived in Suffolk, during November, 1862, he was an ordained deacon, a follower of the Rule of St. Benedict, and had taken to wearing the habit of a monk. He was ostensibly acting as deacon to the Vicar of Claydon-cum-Akenham, the Rev. George Drury, who had thoughts of establishing a new monastery in Ipswich. At the invitation of the Rev. Drury, Joseph visited Ipswich and shortly afterwards established himself and three 'brothers' in the Claydon Vicarage. The immediate increase in the degree of ritual services which then took place at Claydon Church did not endear 'Brother' Lyne to the Bishop of Norwich, a Bishop much attached to the Low Church, the village of Claydon then being in his diocese.

Soon, even the Rev. Drury had begun to find his new deacon trying, to say the least, but hopes that the brotherhood would soon move to Ipswich were dimmed by the absolute lack of funds. But, still enthusiastic for the possibilities of an Ipswich monastery, George Drury suggested a hierarchy for such an establishment. Thus, without a word to the Bishop of Norwich, and in spite of the fact that he was not yet ordained priest, Deacon Lyne became Father Ignatius of the Order of St. Benedict. The 'Rule' which he inflicted on his followers, but did not impose on himself, was impossibly strict and utterly impractical.

The Rev. Drury and his long-suffering wife, who had envisaged Joseph's stay at the Vicarage to last a week at the most, were finding the whole business something of a strain. Locally, the hell-fire and damnation sermons were not at all popular and smacked of Catholicism, although Drury himself was High Church. Parishioners were not so well-disposed towards the new Order as was their Vicar and Father Ignatius was dubbed 'Father Blazer' in the solidly Protestant broadsheets of the day. Pressure was also coming from the increasing strength of the Non-Conformist movement which found East Anglian soil a most fertile environment in which to grow and whose philosophy was at odds with the High Church ideal.

In the event, George Drury was not to have his dream of an Ipswich monastery fulfilled. Following the 'divine' intervention of a High Churchman from Norwich it was eventually agreed that the new Order should be not in Ipswich but Norwich. It was there, in 1864, that Father Ignatius founded the Third Order of lay brothers and sisters in the Elm Hill 'monastery'.

Ignatius' own interpretation of what he saw as the revival of the true Order of St. Benedict in the Church of England was both fundamental and ritualistic, and reflected his acclaimed belief in the disciplines of pre-Reformation monastic life. His arrival in Norfolk gave a clear indication to the Bishop of Norwich, under whose very nose he chose to establish his eccentric interpretation of these disciplines, that he was not to be ignored. Ignatius always claimed to have restored the true Benedictine Order and made a point of adhering to the 'old' Saxon form of monastic hood – soon to be a familiar, if not particularly well-loved, sight on the streets of Norwich. The brothers were a mixture of Catholic and Protestant, but the Superior of this new Order – Father Ignatius – was as yet not ordained priest in either faith and was still, technically, a deacon in the Church of England, which institution was getting more than a little fed up with him.

Perversely, instead of putting off new recruits to the Third Order, the strict regime set by Ignatius attracted new converts and numbers flourished. Priscilla Sellon's 'Sisterhood of Mount Calvary' was extended to become the centre for the 'Sisterhood of the Third Order' and with almost every new day, controversy and division began to develop between the various religious factions within Norwich, stirred up by the antics of Father Ignatius. At one point the Catholic Church made overtures to Ignatius and, after an incident at St. Andrew's Hall – which Ignatius still considered to be the Church of the Black Friars of Norwich – the scepticism of the Protestant community escalated into horror and indignation. The families of those who were made to do public penance for having attended a secular ball at St. Andrew's Hall – Ignatius thought such a function to be blasphemous – were not slow in withdrawing their support for the idea of monastic revival in Norwich.

That Ignatius should employ the flamboyance of a pilgrimage to Bawburgh in order to advertise the Third Order was typical; a procession to the pre-Reformation shrine of St. Walstan would satisfy the need to be seen in action by the people of Norwich, in particular the Bishop. St. Walstan, with his feet firmly planted in Anglo Saxon England, had other certain attractions and was bound to appeal to a man with a message looking for a medium. Walstan's father was named Benedict, and the legend had certainly flourished under the Benedictine Order, while the historic destruction of the Shrine Chapel in 1538 lent an air of authentic martyrdom. It also took the brotherhood outside the City of Norwich and to a wider audience.

Even if Ignatius' acquaintance with the Bawburgh legend had previously been sketchy, the memory of the pilgrimage he led to St. Walstan's Well in 1864 would no doubt be restored to him when later, at Llanthony Abbey, on each 30th May, the night's reading from *Lives of the Saints* would be that of St. Walstan. The Baroness de Bertouch in *Monk of Llanthony* begins her account of the pilgrimage:

'*A public pilgrimage in full feather to St. Walston's Well – a said-to-be miraculous source of water, four miles out of Norwich referred to on the programme of old-world religious revivals. It was hundreds of years since a single pilgrim had dipped his cup into that long-forgotten spring, or breathed a prayer to its derelict Patron; so the occasion was an historical one, and worthy of the pageant with which it was commemorated by the Monks and their contingent.*'

The Monks Pilgrimage to BAWBURGH,

Or, the VISIT to the HOLY WELL!

Why what in the world are these Monks now about,
They've lately been having a rare grand turn out,
To astonish the joskins the whole country round,
Such a set of poor simpletons elsewhere can't be found.

Last week they slipp'd out of Town one by one,
And people were puzzled to know where they'd gone,
In a fly there fine dresses and gimcracks were carried,
And some said that Blazer was gone to get married.

But soon they all met upon Earlham road,
And some of the finery began to unload;
Pockthorpe famed Guild this rum lot would beat,
All it wanted was Old Snap to make it complete.

And when all were muster'd under the trees,
Down went the whole lot right on to their knees,
On the dusty road Monks and Women were seen,
With their fine Sunday dresses and smart crinoline.

Then up they all got and made a great noise,
For some began singing at the top of their voice,
Each village they came to the people turned out,
For they could not imagine what 'twas all about.

But at Bawburgh 'tis said they have found out a Well,
The Water of which all others excel,
It will cure all complaints of those that receive it,
And keep out the Devil if you can believe it.

When they got there, with fasting they turn'd very faint,
All were eager to drink at the Well of the Saint,
And some of the simpletons were heard to declare,
They could do without victuals the rest of the year.

Such a sight there was seen when they got to the Well,
For flat on there faces these Pilgrims all fell,
And began kissing the ground as if they were crazed,
While the poor country people looked on amazed.

Brother Magnetia then said, that when the Saint died,
(Though between you and me I think that he lied)
The water was seen from that place to run,
And that thousands of cures by it had been done.

Then down of the Well the country Johns got,
To gather the moss and they did get a lot,
The Monks paid them well and also did say,
They should want plenty more on some future day.

There's Old Ginger Giles he vow and protest,
That he wont work for farmers the Monks pay him best,
Seven shillings a week is not worth looking arter,
He can get twice as much by selling the water.

The People of Bawburgh they never are ill,
And dont know the want of a Doctor or Pill,
But if it is true what they tell unto me,
'Tis by using the water in making their tea.

There's Old Mother Smith that lives by the Cock,
Declares that whenever she washes her smock,
With the water although she's now getting old,
If she puts it on wet she never catch cold.

Brother Stumpy too met with a wonderful cure,
You remember the wooden leg he had to be sure.
After bathing it well for an hour or two,
A beautiful new leg appeared to his view.

Poor neighbour Goose who in St. Lawrence now dwell,
Strange is the tale I'm about for to tell,
Though the mother of eight children, of late it is said,
Through drinking Holy Water, looks more like a maid.

The blind made to see, the lame made to walk,
The deaf made to hear, and the dumb made to talk,
If you like to believe all the cures they tell,
That's done by the water and moss from this Well,

Now take my advice, don't be gull'd by such stuff,
Of Monks and of miracles we've had quite enough,
If you go to their Chapel and learn at their schools,
You'll find that they think you a great set of fools.

They'll make you believe every pulk hole they find,
Sprung up where some Saint died if they have a mind,
But I hope folks know better in this present age,
And wont join the Monks in their next Pilgrimage.

Printed for Robert Cullam, Norwich

The Baroness' assessment that it had been hundreds of years since anyone had taken any notice of the Well, plus her description of Walstan as 'derelict', was either uninformed or intentionally misleading; in any event, it was not true. Indeed, question marks hang over much of what the Baroness wrote, since it was more or less dictated by Ignatius himself, and both of them no doubt wished he had been the first pilgrim to visit the Well for hundreds of years. Ignatius was obviously not in touch with Fr. Husenbeth or he would have known of the miracles occurring in Costessey and Hammersmith Convent and of the considerable interest being exhibited in the matter of St. Walstan and the miraculous water.

The vision of holy serenity thus engendered by the Baroness contrasts with the views of the author of the broadsheet entitled *The Monks Pilgrimage to Bawburgh* (pictured opposite), printed for Robert Cullum of Norwich. The doggerel was typical of the general attitude of Protestant Norwich to the activities of the Third Order and echoed the tone of the press of the time. The pilgrimage to Bawburgh went ahead amid theatricals which Norwich had come to expect from Ignatius: hailed triumphant by the Baroness and ridiculed by the critics. It was suggested by the authorities that a special body of constables should be placed at various crossroads between Norwich and Bawburgh, to reduce the risk of accidents. But '... the Reverend Father would have none of these precautions!' says the Baroness. Instead, the 'Reverend Father' marshalled the assembled pilgrims – a party of over four hundred, according to the Baroness – and led them in complete order to Bawburgh.

The excitement of the day was matched only by a grudging admiration for the audacity of Ignatius, and the impact made by the extraordinary procession. Ignatius led, to be followed by members of the community, and thereafter a long procession of the brothers and sisters of the Third Order, each carrying a banner. Since Ignatius did not enjoy robust health it is to be wondered whether he did actually walk there and back, as stated, especially since following them were what the Baroness described to be 'wealthy members of the community' in carriages. Behind them came a host of the poorer (and more revivalist, perhaps!) pilgrims, on foot. The Baroness, with Ignatius at her elbow, tells us:

> 'The crowd of pilgrims and spectators was so great that it moved as one long flexible column through the town.'

The thoughts of the villagers is suggested by the broadsheet – 'the poor country people looked on amazed'. No doubt those Non-Conformists who looked on were strengthened in their resolve by such a parade. Their prime motivation had, after all, originated from antagonism to such Popish rituals. There is no record either of what the Rev. Hicks Thomas Deacle, the new Vicar of SS. Mary and Walstan, thought of such proceedings.

However, all went according to plan and 'no *contretemps* occurred to jar the day's devotion'. A service was held beside the Well, which was decorated with lights and flowers. Says the Baroness:

'Many and various were the vials and vessels filled with the holy-
well water, for future dissemination in home circles'.

It would seem that the water was still a source of revenue, at least for Old Ginger Giles who, says Robert Cullum, declared that he made twice as much money by selling the Well water for the monks as he did working for the farmers. Much fun was had, too, in the recounting of the miraculous qualities of the Well water and the 'miracle' of Brother Stumpy's leg:

'Brother Stumpy too met with a wonderful cure,
You remember the wooden leg he had to be sure.
After bathing it well for an hour or two,
A beautiful new leg appeared to his view'.

Unfortunately for Fr. Ignatius, his well-intentioned pilgrimage to St. Walstan's Well had dire consequences for the Third Order. Following this audacious affront to the authority of the Bishop, cries of 'No Popery' began to sound in the city. An anonymous letter was sent to Ignatius, telling him that the Priory would be set on fire, together with all who were inside, and it became clear that a mob was collecting to attack the Monastery. The Baroness takes up the story:

'... some ladies of the Third Order made their appearance –
armed. In especial, says the Reverend Father, he remembers that
Sisters Faith, Hope and Charity distinguished themselves by
characteristic and truly beautiful displays of individual courage
and strategy.'

The armoury of the Sisters was mixed; Sister Faith brought her rosary; Sister Hope carried a magnificent rolling-pin; but Sister Charity was made of sterner stuff – she brought a kettle filled with vitriol (sulphuric acid)! However, this was just one of the many battles between the Third Order and its opponents in the city and, later in 1864, Ignatius had far more serious things on his mind resulting from the scandal of a young boy who was, said the *Norfolk News*, being lured away from his mother.

Eventually, in 1866, after serious illness and an acrimonious battle with his old ally, George Drury, Ignatius left Norwich. He returned only briefly, twenty years later, and spent some time in recuperation at Sheringham shortly before his death. Fr. Ignatius was an easy target for ridicule, and more often than not made life difficult for even his most devoted supporters; but in truth he was possessed of an unshakeable faith in God, if unfortunately accompanied by a naive method of realising what he saw to be God's intent for his life's work.

~ • ~

Chapter Ten
NINE HUNDRED YEARS
LATER

*'The study of the saints is a living thing. They are still among us. Because
they have stood like spires among the small villages, they have come to
symbolize, not only the facts of their own lives, but the hopes and fears
and poetry of the little people around them. They have the authority of
history and the power of myth. They can divulge surprising secrets in any
place where they may be found and invoked and understood.'*
Helen Roeder, 1955

WHEN Queen Victoria's long reign came to an end in 1901, Edward VII
swept away the lingering sentimentalism of the nineteenth century,
and only a few years later, in the aftermath of the First World War, a new
realism was to dawn which changed society irrevocably. Surely when the
Edwardians looked for inspiration to match their thinking, the 1900s would
see an end to the legend of St. Walstan and the Victorian custom of reviving
Medieval traditions. What relevance would a humble, tenth-century farm
worker have for those who wanted, and needed, to keep pace with a rapidly
changing world? Miracles were a thing of the past and twentieth-century
men and women could be expected to look back in amusement, if not
amazement, to the story of Nalga on his Taverham farm, to the Bishops of
Elmham, and countless pilgrims who over the centuries sought eternal
redemption through the intercedence of St. Walstan.

While the Church of England has, since the Reformation, administered
the Parish Church of SS. Mary and Walstan, Husenbeth and others had
made sure that the legend was not lost to the Catholic Church which created
it. The differences between the two Churches had, since the sixteenth
century, been real enough, but towards the end of the nineteenth century,
and at the highest levels, thoughts of reconciliation were already stirring. In
Norfolk the process had already begun: during November, 1898, a writer in
the *Norwich Mercury* hinted at the new ecumenicalism:

*'That the water from the miraculous well is effectual to cure oxen,
cows, sheep, and horses, of many maladies is a belief widely
spread throughout this part of Norfolk, and Mr. Sparrow, the
present tenant of the farm where the well is found, Protestant as*

*he is, shares the general conviction of his neighbours respecting
its extraordinary virtue.'*

Mr. James Sparrow, whose daughter Charlotte lived in the village until
she died aged 85, was Churchwarden at the Parish Church and tenant at
Church Farm, which was built on the site of the old messuage, once
inhabited by the Chantry Priests. He and his contemporaries (Mr. Sparrow's
son was also Churchwarden) were united by an understanding of the cult
and history of the legend of St. Walstan, symbolised by the Church and
Well. The Rev. Gabriel Young, Vicar at Bawburgh from 1892 to 1931,
confided to members of the Norfolk and Norwich Archaeological Society,
on their visit to St. Walstan's Well in 1927, that '... the water of the well
has a curative power in it. A late farmer here, Mr. Sparrow, who was
Churchwarden many years ago, had a mare with two great sores and wanted
to have her killed. But a boy prevailed on him to let him have her. The boy
washed her morning and night for about ten days, and at the end of that time
the sores had disappeared'.

The church of Bawburgh had found a new champion in the Rev. Gabriel
Young who, on taking over the Parish, had immediately set about renovating
the Church and resuscitating village life which had, at its heart, a place of
worship dating from at least the very origins of English Christianity. The Rev.
Young and his wife, Caroline, with their three daughters and son, Annesley,
contributed to the Parish in much the same way as vicars everywhere did in
those days. The Rev. Young extended a measured acceptance of the legend,
and used St. Walstan in his ministry just as Fr. Husenbeth had, but in an
understated way as befitted Protestantism. Gabriel Young was not a scholar,
but a practical, hardworking and dutiful vicar.

A new age was beginning for the legend of St. Walstan; in 1901,
Wynkyne de Worde's 1516 *Nova Legenda Anglie* was re-published, still
containing the Latin Life of St. Walstan. Editor Carl Horstman confirmed
Walstan's place in hagiology and in his Introduction it was clear that he had
explored fully what remained of John of Tynemouth's *Sanctilogium*; it was
dismissed as the source of the legend and, at last, Friar Capgrave was put in
his rightful place. Almost one hundred years later, the myth that Capgrave's
Legends is the Primary Life of St. Walstan still persists, but, as readers of
this search will know, tradition dies hard.

A few years into the new century, in 1909, the Duke of Norfolk's
windows – one of which contained a medallion of St. Walstan – were
dedicated in Norwich at St. John's Catholic Cathedral, and in the same year
a carving of St. Walstan was included in the new pulpit at Gaywood
Church. In 1912 over five hundred men and women joined in a pilgrimage to
the Holy Well of St. Walstan. It seems that far from falling into obscurity,
the legend was gaining strength.

THE THIRD NATIONAL CATHOLIC CONGRESS

In August, 1912, a pilgrimage to St. Walstan's Well was the crowning event of the Third National Catholic Congress, held in Norwich during that year, and which event is recorded in *A Great Gothic Fane*. Although the first modern pilgrimage at Walsingham did not take place until 1922, there had been a certain amount of preparation in hand for its revival since the 1850s, when the then owner uncovered the site of the Priory Church. It was, therefore, widely expected that the climax of the Conference would be a visit to that once-great place of worship and prayer. But it was to Bawburgh, not Walsingham, that the pilgrims went.

Organisers of the pilgrimage, Fr. Philip Fletcher and Mr. Stafford Jerningham, of Costessey Park, were amazed at their own success: over five hundred pilgrims took part, many of them travelling in 'brakes' from Norwich. *A Great Gothic Fane* notes:

> *'The village of Babur was the place of assembly, and the procession to the Well was marshalled by Father Philip Fletcher, Father Filmer, and Mr. Lister Drummond. It was headed by a pre-Reformation crucifix from Costessey Hall, and comprised the party from the Hall (Mr. and Mrs. Stafford Jerningham, the Earl and Countess of Gainsborough, etc), the Sisters of Charity of St. Paul, Costessey, and the Little Sisters of the Assumption, Norwich.'*

The Rev. Gabriel Young gave his support and Mr. Sparrow again accommodated the visitors who congregated at the Well. Many drank the water ('which, by the way, always remains at the same level, however much is taken away' said *Fane*) and bottles were provided for those who wanted to take some away. Afterwards the pilgrims went on to Costessey Hall where Benediction was given in the Hall Chapel.

A Great Gothic Fane gave the usual account of the legend of St. Walstan with no deviation from what by then had become the definitive version. Much of the legend had anyway been arrived at by a process of logical conclusion; for example, as Walstan died in 1016, and was 'royal', therefore he must have been related to Edmund Ironside. It is, therefore, no surprise to read of such detail as Walstan reaching Taverham via 'a dense pathless forest'; or of Walstan 'macerating his body with frequent and vigorous fasts out of his zealous affection of holy chastity'.

English Catholicism had come a long way since the reign of Elizabeth I. Reflecting on the Congress, Mr. Frederick Hibgame wrote of the emotion generated by the sight of a Cardinal, many Bishops and priests, all gathered together in Norwich. On the night when the Lord Mayor of Norwich welcomed a Catholic Cardinal to St. Andrew's Hall (what would Fr. Ignatius have made of it all?) Mr. Hibgame met 'a grey haired old man ... who had come many miles to be present' who told him:

'I remember when we used to call the Mass 'prayers', and when, if ever, we had a High Mass – which was very seldom – a load of hay used to be drawn in front of the door of old St. John's Chapel, to prevent people's attention being drawn to it, because of more people than usual going in'.

It was as a result of the Congress pilgrimage that one of the first chronicled miracles of the twentieth century took place. A man who had come from London to attend the Congress had taken away with him some of the moss and water from St. Walstan's Well. Later in the same year his eyes began to fail and specialist after specialist was unsuccessful in restoring his sight. Thinking of his time in Norfolk, he one day remembered that he still had the moss. That evening he placed the moss on his eyes and for the next four days bathed his eyes with the water. By Thursday of the same week his eyesight was restored and his doctor told him that he was cured of blindness. As a token of gratitude, the man pledged to make a second pilgrimage to Bawburgh and the following September made good his intent.

By this time, his story had been repeated among the Catholic community of Norfolk and on the 7th September, 1913, a second pilgrimage took place in thanksgiving for what was the first of many recorded miracles to be performed in St. Walstan's name this century. Mr. Sidney Porritt, of Bawburgh Hall, allowed over three hundred Catholics from Wymondham, Norwich and Costessey to gather in his grounds and the procession to the Church was watched by many who stood beside the road. Sir Henry and Lady Jerningham were present and Father Byrne from St. Walstan's Church in Costessey preached the sermon. Mr. Sparrow at Church Farm was again on hand to make suitable arrangements for the pilgrims to take some of the water away with them, though one young man might be thought a little too enthusiastic since he produced a gallon-sized beer bottle for filling. The reporter from the *Eastern Daily Press* suggested that he carried off this barrel 'with an air of comfort and safety in store'!

It was the Irish Father Byrne of Costessey who is credited with the ownership of a print, apparently Victorian, which depicts St. Walstan kneeling in front of Taverham Church. The cart and two oxen are nearby, and his scythe on the ground, as he receives a vision from an angel (see page 16). Although a reproduction of the print appears in *A Great Gothic Fane*, and postcards were made from it, the print itself cannot now be found and seems to have gone the way of the triptych. What remains a mystery is, if that which was in the possession of Father Byrne was a print, where was the original, who had drawn it, and what happened to it?

Sometime in the 1920s or 1930s St. Walstan was again depicted in contemporary religious art, this time on a 'Holy Picture' which also included representations of the Shrines at Walsingham and Bromholm and St. William of Norwich. St. Walstan is depicted in a green robe, kneeling in prayer.

Other miracles were recorded, and many of them simple, personal tributes to faith, which did not aspire to full-scale pilgrimage. In 1949, the diary of the Rev. Benjamin John Armstrong was published by his son. Writing his entry for the 22nd November, 1868, the Rev. Armstrong described what happened after he had returned Husenbeth's *Life of St. Walstan* to one of his five Catholic parishioners, a Mrs. Skerritt:

> *'I was much interested in the book, but was surprised that the Doctor vouched for the reality of some of the miraculous cures which had been effected by some moss growing in St. Wulstan's Well. Mrs. Skerritt said that she had been herself miraculously cured by this means. On applying some moss to a very bad sore overnight she found it completely healed in the morning, leaving only a scar, as from an old wound.'*

However disbelieving or sceptical he might have been, the Rev. Armstrong, vicar at Dereham from 1850 to 1888, humoured Mrs. Skerritt by complying with her wish to be given some water from the Well of St. Withburga.

WORLD WAR AND RECONSTRUCTION

Only a short time after the happy and successful pilgrimages of 1912 and 1913 the country was plunged into the Great War. Perhaps, during those years, the continuity of devotion to St. Walstan helped the morale of a population suffering the upheaval and uncertainty of war, although the initial increase in church attendance during 1914 was not maintained. In 1917 M.R. James published the two lives of St. Walstan, a transcript of Item 8 appearing in print for the first time, and in the same year the ten screen panels were reinstated at the Church of St. James (with Pockthorpe).

After 1918, the honour formerly extended to saints was given instead to the fallen heroes of the 1914-18 war, personified by the Unknown Soldier. This was veneration of a different kind from that previously held for individual Christian heroes and heroines, and memorials to the glorious dead were raised in churches where only monuments to saints, clergy and donors had been seen. Immediately the war had ended the Church came in for a certain amount of criticism over its role in encouraging the military spirit, while simultaneously preaching Christian pacifism, forgiveness of conscientious objectors and charity towards the enemy.

In the prevailing mood of reconstruction which followed a peace fraught with guilt and anxiety, a Faculty was raised in Bury St. Edmunds to

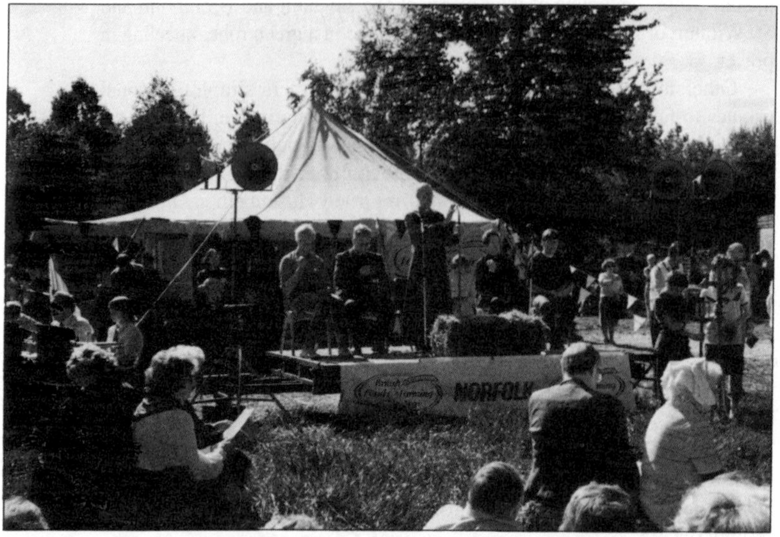
NORFOLK

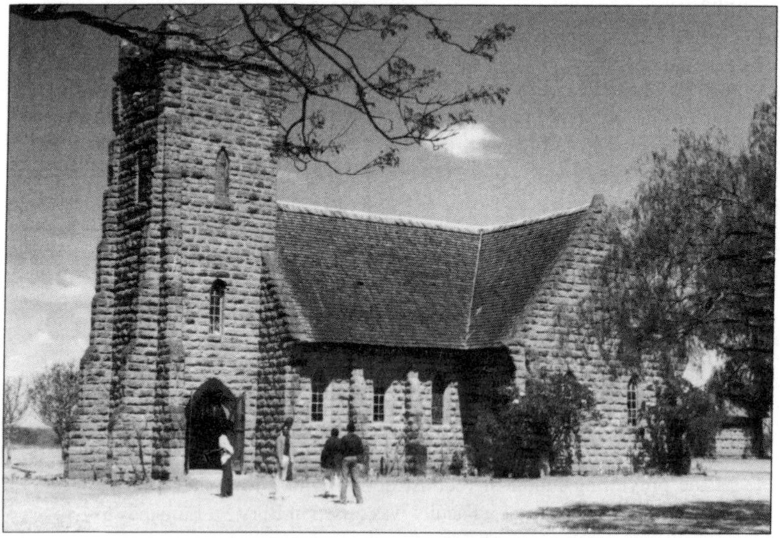

confirm the erection of a cenotaph in the Chapel of St. Wolston in St. Mary's Church during 1920, in memory of the men from the Suffolk Yeomanry killed in the Great War. And at Great Ryburgh in Norfolk an image of St. Walstan is among those on the screen erected in memory of those men who had died in, or had not returned from, the First World War.

ECUMENICAL PILGRIMAGE

During the inter-war years the spirit of religious understanding thrived, encouraged by the Lambeth Conferences of 1920 and 1930. Perhaps someone in Norfolk had been a delegate at the 1930 Conference, because in 1931 an account of an Anglo-Catholic attempt to revive devotion 'to the almost forgotten St. Walstan', was reported in the *Eastern Daily Press*. Pilgrimage had not been part of Henry VIII's reformation, but was to be part of the new ecumenity. This event of 1931 saw Protestants in pilgrimage to Bawburgh for the first time this century. There were no fanfares, and probably few realised the significance of this eventual defeat of Henry's bigotry. Leader of the pilgrimage was the Rev. W.E. Duxson, rector of St. John Maddermarket, who was joined by the vicars of St. Giles' and St. Peter Mancroft. Nuns from St. Augustine's Lodge – and the Rev. A. Hope Patten, vicar of Walsingham – walked in the procession which was met at the gate of Bawburgh Church by the Rev. Gabriel Young. Pilgrims of the 1930s viewed their religion differently from those in 1538 and there was no criticism of idolatry and no awkwardness of a union with 'papists'. Each pilgrim accepted the occasion on his or her own terms, the consequence and celebration of religious freedom.

Both the 1931 newspaper heading of 'Reviving Devotion to Little Known Norfolk Saint', and the subsequent reference to St. Walstan being 'almost forgotten' typify claims of a similar nature found in the writings of the nineteenth and twentieth centuries. Father Ignatius thought that his had been the first pilgrimage for 'hundreds of years', and, indeed, in *The Enthusiast*, Arthur Calder-Marshall says of the 1931 event that it was the first since the pilgrimage of Father Ignatius 'sixty-seven years before'. If he meant the first Protestant pilgrimage since 1864 it was not made clear, but at any rate it takes no account of the fame of the Well water in the matter of Mr. Bunn's leg, or the Hammersmith miracles, or of the considerable gatherings at St. Walstan's well in 1912 and 1913. In fact, the pilgrimage of 1931 took place exactly nineteen years to the day after that of the Catholic Congress.

The Baroness de Bertouch had also referred to Walstan as a neglected saint, the more to emphasise the graciousness of attention from Ignatius, whose intention of reviving pre-Reformation religious life included reviving St. Walstan. M.R. James referred more than once to Walstan as 'obscure' and 'little known', and even N.V. Pierce Butler calls him 'shadowy'.

It is as if these writers craved the recognition due to pioneers or discoverers, though in all cases it could only be the re-discovery of a very ancient legend. Similarly, an article in the *Norwich Union* (1903), which described a Head Office outing to the Bawburgh home of a London Manager, Mr. Charles Noverre, reported that after tea '... there was a visit to the ancient miraculous well of St. Wulstan, recently re-discovered.'

However, the 1931 pilgrimage was a complete success and a charming account of the day appeared in the local press. It seemed that pilgrimage suited twentieth-century men and women and three more notable events followed, in 1934, 1935 and 1951.

The Pilgrim's Service of 1951 saw the Rev. A. Barwood of St. Edmund's Church, Taverham, join with the Rev. H.L. Davies, Vicar of Bawburgh, and the Rev. Handel Llewellyn of St. Peter's, Cringleford, and handbell ringers from Hethersett, in a procession from the Church to the Well. Having, perhaps, read Blomefield's *History of Norfolk*, the Rev. Barwood used a branch of yew to sprinkle the pilgrims with water from the Well, though no mention is made of hyssop and there were no obvious hermits present.

Only a year later a considerable amount of discussion was to take place about the benefits, or otherwise, of the Well water, in which the Rev. Davies took part. The *Eastern Daily Press* gave an account of the pilgrimage, saying that St. Walstan's Well was 'recently revived', and reported a meeting of the Forehoe and Henstead Rural District Council held in July, 1952. Minutes of the Public Health Committee were read which gave details of the publicity 'lately given' to the Well and noted that an approach had been made to the Public Analyst regarding the quality of the water which was being sent far and wide by the Vicar of Bawburgh.

'As the water was being used for drinking purposes' said the report, 'a sample was taken for analysis and the preliminary report indicated that the water was unfit for drinking purposes.'

It was not revealed just who had approached the Public Analyst, but presumably it was not the Rev. Davies, as an article appeared in the newspaper the following day to the effect that the Vicar would 'Retain His Faith in Power of St. Walstan's Well'.

Mr. Davies had been unimpressed by what he had heard at the District Council meeting but stated that he would think over what had been said before he sent out any more water. However, it seemed that demand for the water was as great as it had ever been. Mr. Davies stated that during the previous month alone he had received letters from 'people throughout the country saying that they had derived benefit from taking water which had come from the Well', but that he would take advice and opinion from his friends before sending out any more. People had, he said, been taking water which came from the Well for literally hundreds of years and miracles were reputed to have been performed during the Middle Ages, as well as during the last century. The healing potency of the Well, continued Mr. Davies, was not affected by the Public Analyst's report 'as these healings had undoubtedly taken place in spite of the supposed unsafe condition of the water' and the report was anyway based not on the new analysis but on one carried out fifty years previously which had described the water as 'neither fit for man nor beast'.

In an attempt to widen the discussion, Mr. A.M. Blake asked if there was any authority for the presumption that holy well water came under the Public Health Acts and, although it appeared that swimming pools were covered, no answer was obtained on the subject of holy wells and vicars of Bawburgh continued for many years to distribute the Well water to those who requested it.

Whether or not the waters were curative, the Well at Bawburgh continued to attract inter-denominational interest until pilgrimage reached new heights in 1976 when parishioners from three churches in Costessey, St. Edmund's, St. Helen's and St. Walstan's, and those from St. Edmund's, Taverham, walked in pilgrimage to Bawburgh. There they were met by the Rev. Robert Loveless of Bawburgh who conducted the service for a congregation of something over one hundred pilgrims.

Yet another landmark was reached in 1982, when members of the Bawburgh Methodist Chapel joined in prayers with the Protestant community at the St. Walstan's Day service in Bawburgh Church. Sadly, the Bawburgh Chapel had its last service in May, 1994, but in 1992 the Methodist Minister, the Rev. Peter Sulson, preached at the annual Patronal Service of the Parish Church. When he left Norwich for pastures new in 1993, he wrote in the *Bawburgh News*: '... apart from the regular pattern of Sunday worship, highlights have been special moments ... and the times when we have shared in celebrations for St. Walstan at the end of May each year – real community occasions!'

Shortly after the final service the Chapel altar table was presented to the Church and remains there as a tangible reminder of 170 years of Methodism in Bawburgh.

Away from Bawburgh, the influence of St. Walstan is to be seen in other representations made since 1900 which can be found in churches at Kenninghall, Great Melton, and Fritton, where images of St. Walstan reflect the continuity of centuries. At Taverham the members of the Women's Institute gave the village a new sign, with a St. Walstan based on the Medieval representation at Barnham Broom. And in the 1970s, Harry Carter was commissioned to design a sign for what was then the Norfolk School of Agriculture (now Easton College) which incorporated the images of what must still be one of man's most vital occupations, farming, and depicts Walstan on his last journey from Taverham

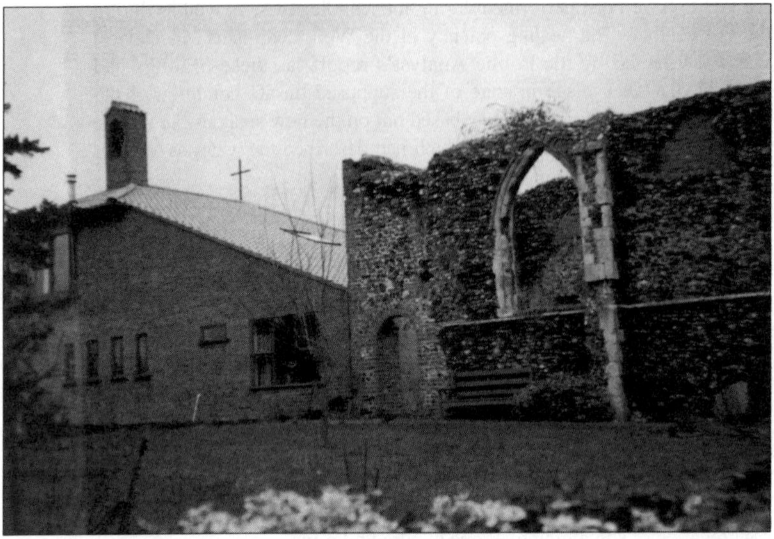

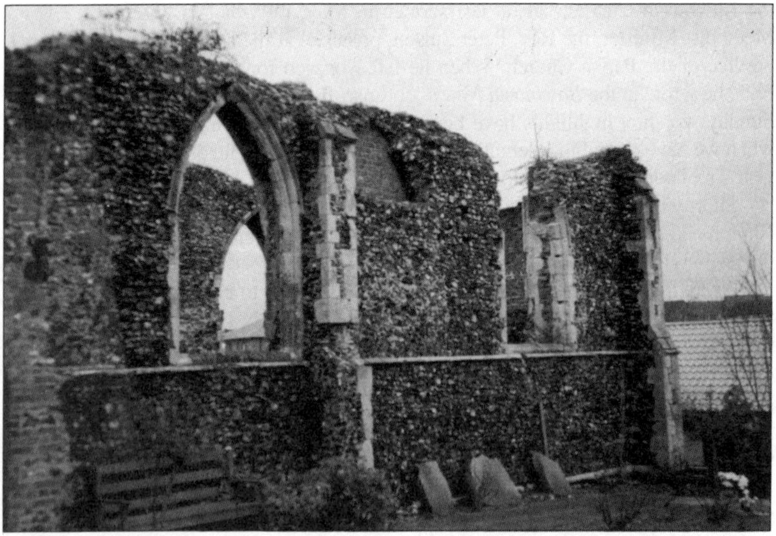

to Bawburgh. However, what no one could have predicted was that the legend of St. Walstan would, in the 1950s, touch the lives of a community thousands of miles away on the continent of Africa.

ST. WALSTAN IN AFRICA

The establishment of an Anglican Church in Kenya dedicated to St. Walstan of Bawburgh (pictured opposite) has already been mentioned, but from the original indecision over the Church dedication has grown a strong and decisive community of Kenyan parishioners whose interest in their Patron Saint is undiminished by geography and cultural differences.

As readers of this search will by now have come to expect, there are at least three versions of how the Anglican Church in Rongai came to be named for St. Walstan. Variously the European settlers were said to come from Bawburgh, or Norfolk, but the Reverend Canon Ken Sharpe, Vicar of the Mau during the 1960s, confirmed that a regular attender at the Church was an Army Captain whose father had been a Vicar in Norfolk though not, he thought, at Bawburgh. Many of the Rongai farmers had been Remittance Men, mostly from ancient families in England or Scotland who had sowed wild oats and were dispatched to 'make good' in Kenya. Most were cultured and some had been British army officers. These men worked the Rongaian farms alongside the Greek immigrants who ran the vast sisal estates on the plains falling away from Mau mountains.

Canon Sharpe also passed on the story of the Miracle of St. Walstan, which happened the day before the Church was consecrated and which is now folklore in Rongai:

> '*A party of parishioners were tidying up the grounds and there was a big pile of stone under the tower; a distance away was a pile of sand ... all tidy, of course. On the tower was an African stone-mason; suddenly, a thunderstorm developed and he slipped and fell. He should have gone on to the stones and been killed, but a great gust of wind blew him onto the sand, and he broke a leg.*'

The story of the miracle was repeated to Peter and Margot Markham, parishioners from Great Melton, who visited the Church in 1986 and heard again how Mr. Blackwood had seen the hay-making advertisement in *World Farming* which led to the final dedication of the Church (see Chapter 5). The fabric of the Church is not designed in any way to represent that at Bawburgh; it is instead a solid stone cruciform building with a tower, the stone quarried by a local farmer on his own land. One of the early Churchwardens (who Canon Sharpe remembers always described himself as 'the younger son of an impoverished Laird') copied the design of a church on his family's Scottish estate. However, a framed description of

Bawburgh, together with a piece of stone from the round tower of SS. Mary and Walstan, is kept in the Rongai Church and links between the two communities continue, unbroken and little affected by distance or time.

BRITISH FOOD & FARMING YEAR

In 1989 – over one thousand years after Walstan was born to Benedict and Blida at Bawburgh – he was again elected Patron Saint, this time for British Food & Farming Year. 1989 was also designated 'St. Walstan's Year' by the Norwich Diocessan Board of Social Responsibility and in January of that year one of the most original representations of St. Walstan was dedicated at Bowthorpe.

The year-long celebrations began in Bowthorpe, where, over three hundred years earlier, the copy of the Bawburgh triptych had been made under the eye of Mr. Clarke. The modern Bowthorpe is as different as it could be from the village of the seventeenth century; St. Michael's never entirely recovered from the neglect and ruination of Bishop Wren's time and is now only the merest heap of stones. But Bowthorpe now has a new spiritual heart, and one which includes St. Walstan. Here, close to the Worship Centre which embraces philosophy and religion from Methodism, Catholicism, the Society of Friends and the Church of England, stands the most modern – and certainly unique – representation of St. Walstan.

At the Service of Dedication, the sculptor of the concrete monument, Jeremy Dearling said: 'I was inspired by a carving I saw on St. Michael's Mount, Cornwall ... the design is executed in a primitive early Saxon style, the head being disproportionately larger than the body to denote importance. The figures on cither side of the cross are sexless to enable observers to make up their own minds as to who stands beside their cross. The figures are expressionless, but contain their own expression.'

Commissioned by the Priest, the Rev. Ray Simpson, the three-sided concrete memorial took several years to complete, each four-feet-high side weighing half a ton. It stands near the entrance to an old cart shed, which was converted into a Prayer Cell and within sight of the ruins of St. Michael's Church.

~ • ~

POSTSCRIPT

THE very exciting news about a Medieval wall painting of St. Walstan in West Suffolk was brought to my attention by Dr. John Blair almost at the end of my researches. It necessitated a re-write of at least two chapters, but that kind of thing was only to be expected and was welcomed since it justified the task and made it ever more enthralling. A few weeks later, Miriam Gill alerted me to the Essex screen dedication; later still, the possibility of other wall paintings at Ashby emerged. However, I was not prepared for a new morsel of evidence which followed a letter in the Suffolk Local History Society newsletter asking for last-minute information about the Suffolk dedications.

Mr. Robert Halliday, who had been interested in St. Walstan for many years, and whom I had met when he attended Bawburgh's Patronal Service in 1984, wrote enclosing his recent article on St. Walstan (which contains several Medieval bequests previously missed), and asking whether I knew about a window once dedicated to 'St. Wolstane' in an ancient church at Walberswick. My hopes rose and fell in the same moment. Not only was the book at indexing stage, but the histories of Walberswick and Blythburgh are inseparable, and the original site for this window appeared to be a church dating from the Norman Conquest. Was everything I had written about the Lambeth Life and its reference to 'Blyborow town' about to be turned upside down? Since Walberswick is just a short drive away, it was only hours after receiving Mr. Halliday's letter that I parked the car outside St. Andrew's, Walberswick – to make one last search for St. Walstan.

The reference to the window of St. Wolstane comes from Thomas Gardner's *An historical account of Dunwich, Blithburgh, Southwold, with remarks on some places contiguous thereto*, published in 1754, in which he writes:

> 'The windows of St. Christopher and St. Wolstane seem to have been taken from this [the old church] and set up in the latter Church, where all the Images, with the Tables of Saint George and King Harry, accompanied them.'

The old church referred to, says the Church Guide, '… stood on the border of the marshes some three or four hundred yards to the south of the site of the present Church', the last remains of which were finally destroyed in 1728. The move away from the marsh site to the new building took place in 1473, though it seems to have been some twenty years between the destruction of the old marsh church and the completion of the new one.

It was to this new church that the windows of St. Christopher and St. Wolstane were removed, along with other church furnishings.

Gardner gives no more detail other than an extract, in the same chapter, from the Church Warden's receipts for 1487. An amount of 8s.4d. was paid 'for mendying Seynt Krysteferys Wyndown' while a lesser sum of 9d. was 'for mendying Seynt Walsteneys Wyndown'. Both windows have long since been destroyed. In the present Church of St. Andrew's the remaining fragments of fourteenth- and fifteenth-century glass have been made into one light of a window in the south wall, having been discovered only in the 1930s. They are tiny, unmarked, fragments of coloured glass which give nothing away.

The author of *In and Around the Village of Walberswick*, Merle Tidey, named this Wolstane as 'St. Wulstan, the Ploughman's Saint'. Her use of the 'u' and the unfamiliar naming of Walstan as the Ploughman's Saint is interesting, as is the fact that Walstan's supposed relative, Edward the Confessor, held Walberswick as Lord of the Manor. Henry I and Henry II both had jurisdiction here, and both gave it, at various times, to the Bishop of Norwich under whose eye was the Shrine Chapel at Bawburgh.

Then, too, we find that a John Norwiche, Esq. was buried at Walberswick in 1428, and his wife Matilda in 1418, only a few years before the demise of the marsh church. Might the couple have brought the legend of St. Walstan from Norfolk, the dedication perhaps being to Matilda Norwiche? In the 1470s, an early fifteenth-century window would have been much easier to move than something contemporary with an ancient, pre-Conquest fabric. The Domesday Book evidences the existence of parish churches in Blythburgh and Walberswick long before the founding of the Blythburgh Priory in 1130, although there is as yet no proof that the church which originally housed the two windows was pre-Conquest. There is, as well, a limit on how early such a window would have been made; glass was known in the first century AD, but plain glass became known in England only around the seventh century and coloured glass was not in general use until five centuries later.

One other detail to be found at St. Andrew's is mention of a Mr. Nathaniel Flowerdew, who arrived in Walberswick in 1652 when the Church had been desecrated and the tithes of '... Bliburgh, Walberswick and Blyford' lately removed, bringing ruin to the area. Nathaniel is described as an 'intruder', who made several reports to Cromwell on the Walberswick area, including one during 1654, just four years before the Bawburgh triptych was copied. Is it another coincidence that the Flowerdew family hailed from Hethersett, whose Vicar had been the Norfolk

Archdeacon, Philip Tenison? It was one John Flowerdew who had been entrusted with the demolition of Wymondham Abbey, and some stripping of Hethersett Church, at the Reformation, and the landowning Flowerdews of Hethersett and Wymondham had played a prominent role during the Kett Rebellion.

The question inspired by this Walberswick reference is crucial. If this 'Wolstane' was in fact St. Walstan – rather than St. Wulfstan – might it have something to do with naming 'Blyborow town' in Item 8? Would the existence of the window, and the reason for its dedication, have been known to the copier of the triptych, or is it all just coincidence? After all, the tale of such a window in any other part of East Anglia would have no such significance attached to it. It is also tantalizingly easy to see that the first three letters of Walberswick are the same as those in Walstan. With Blythburgh only a stone's throw away from Walberswick, is this where the confusion arose, or was it the inspiration for deception on the part of the copier or his patron? And what has all this – if anything – to do with Walstan's supposed mother, Blythe?

If, then, 'Wolstane' or 'Walsteney' is proved to be St. Walstan, are we to explore the trail again for an explanation of why 'Blyborow' should have been named as his birthplace? Or should the matter still be treated as unconnected with either Blythburgh or the ancient See of Dunwich?

There are no obvious answers to any of these questions, but it is certainly the place to start a new search. To begin with, there are many ways of spelling Blythburgh but in history it is invariably spelt 'Bli-'. References in the Suffolk Archdeacon's book of 1663, for example, use 'Bliburgh', and Gardner uses 'Blithburgh'. In the 1528 Papal Bull for the suppression of five East Anglian monasteries, it is named 'Bliborow' (the others being 'Felixstow', 'Bromehil', 'Montjoie' and 'Romboro' – this last being the Benedictine Cell at Rumburgh which held a portion of the Bawburgh tithe). As well, 'Blyborow' is similar to Blyford (also called Blythford), a small parish just north of Blythburgh, where thirty 'superstitious pictures' were destroyed by Dowsing in 1643 and whose past is interwoven with that of Walberswick and Blythburgh. (The Church at Blyford is to 'All Saints', a dedication often indicating that the original was forgotten, perhaps after a period of ruin. All Saints was invariably used where churches were re-dedicated for whatever reason, particularly following a sacrilegious act having taken place in the church.)

This is as far as the discussion can go, for the moment, and I have made no changes to Chapters 5 or 7 following either Mr. Halliday's letter or my trip to Walberswick. On the evidence so far, the Walberswick dedication to St. Wolstane does not significantly add to the theory that St. Walstan was born in Blythburgh, though it undoubtedly increases the mystery surrounding the 1658 copy of an ancient triptych known as the Lambeth Life.

This search now draws to a close, but with the end in sight, how near have we come to finding the root of the legend of St. Walstan? There will be criticism from some about the lack of safe primary evidence, and I freely admit that ideas have been thrown in the air like tennis balls, in the hope that one or two might land in court. In some places, the story lapsed into no more than a plausible way round the lack of solid evidence. But is the figure of St. Walstan still shadowy, or little known, or obscure; and has there been any hint of why this legend should have prevailed for almost one thousand years? Readers will come to their own conclusions and no doubt this book is just another step along the way, specialist local historians adding to the story, correcting it where necessary, and probably discovering more ancient and forgotten dedications.

Shortly after I finished writing this search for St. Walstan, fire engulfed Norwich Central Library. In the matter of an hour or two, accumulations of the county's history were gone, some for ever ... the pencilled footnote in Blomefield's *History* ... a rare copy of Fr. Husenbeth's *Life of St. Walstan* ... press cuttings ... parish records, and so much more. Some of my references, therefore, might be difficult to trace until a new archive is formed, though some must be taken on trust. When such a disaster occurs there is only one way to go, and as the 1st August 1994 became yesterday, the process of recording history had begun again, and plans were afoot to re-stock the Local Studies Library.

In 1994 Bawburgh, too, felt the wind of change when villagers witnessed the closure of the Methodist Chapel, 170 years after Non-Conformity was established in the parish. The Methodist presence was the tangible evidence of the right to religious dissent, a subject more often discussed at a national level than a local one. But local dissent did exist. For example, the relationship between the Chantry Priests and those who we think of today as the country parson is as yet unexplored. As Jessopp points out in *Studies by a Recluse* (1893) '... until a man has got rid of the delusion that monks built parish churches and served them and were working clergy, he will never be able to understand English history'. Those at the Bawburgh vicarage might well have been at odds with the Prior's men serving the Shrine Chapel of St. Walstan.

On the roof of the so-called Hermit's Chapel, which once graced the lawns of the now demolished Bawburgh Hall, are the remains of a stone figure of the Blessed Virgin Mary. She is seated and looks across the river to where the Saxon Church, its conical roof bearing the Eternal Flame, can clearly be seen against the skyline. It has never been established where the figure came from, or who put her there, and when. Maybe she was once in the Shrine Chapel, and like the triptych, was saved from the iconoclasts. She is worn down now, by rain, wind and sun, almost to nothing, but perhaps whoever placed her there did so in defiance and in hope. This weathered image of St. Mary maintains her vigil even now, on the brink of a new millennium.

After the 1994 Patronal Service held in the Parish Church of SS. Mary and Walstan, Bawburgh, a villager was observed drawing some water from St. Walstan's Well. The tradition of pilgrimage to that place simply will not die.

~ • ~

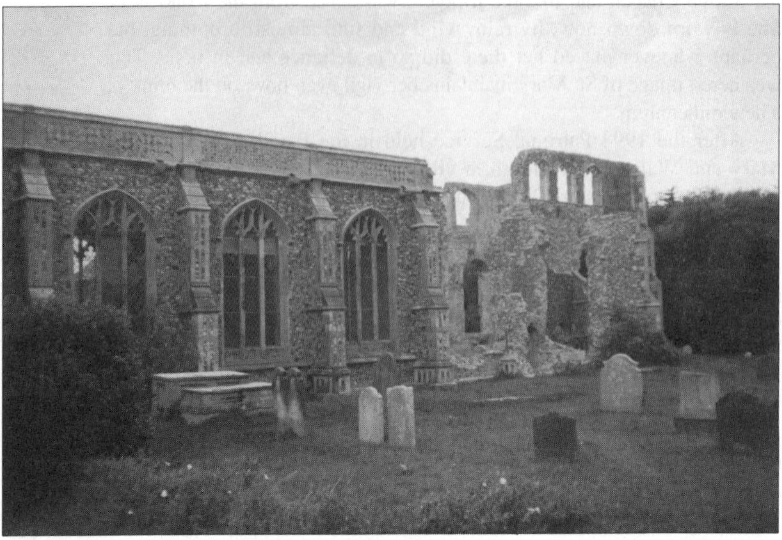

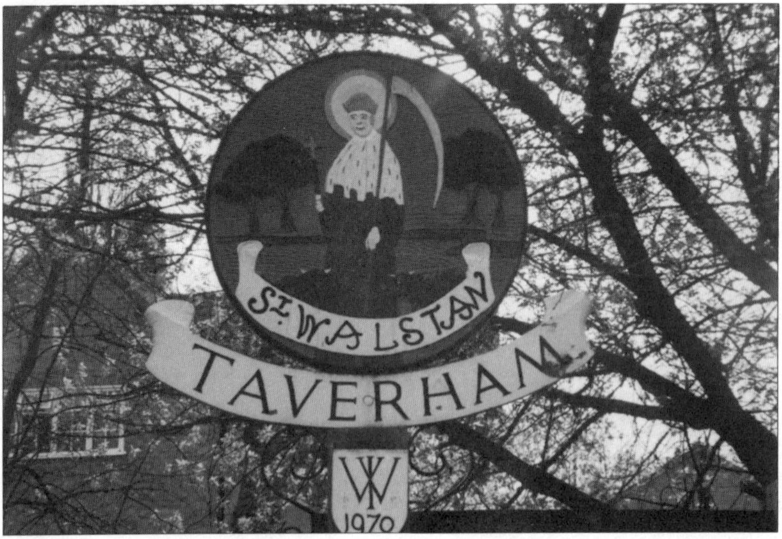
ST. WALSTAN
TAVERHAM
1970

APPENDIX I

GAZETTEER OF REPRESENTATIONS OF SS. WALSTAN AND BLIDA IN NORFOLK, SUFFOLK AND ESSEX, INCLUDING ANGLICAN AND CATHOLIC PLACES OF WORSHIP AND SOME SECULAR IMAGERY

St. Mary's, ASHBY, Suffolk. A series of wall paintings, said to contain 'The History of St. Wulstan', was recorded in the last century as having been 'all covered with a fresh coat of whitewash' (Keyser, 1883). Although no safe identification can be made until the murals are revealed, the accompanying presence of William of Norwich, and a 14th-century Rector named Simon de Bauburgh, increases the possibility that the hidden paintings portray St. Walstan.

St. Felix, BABINGLEY, Norfolk. Although the Medieval screen was destroyed by fire in 1854, it contained a number of saints, one of which is attributed to St. Blida (Keyser, 1883). The Church is thought to have been built on the site of the first church planted in East Anglia by St. Felix although it has now been derelict for over a century. However, drawings of the screen were made by Dawson Turner shortly before the fire from which identification was made (by Husenbeth). A good account of the screen is given in *Sandringham, Past & Present*, (by Mrs. Herbert Jones, Sampson Law, 1883), but no mention is made of St. Blida. The modern tin and thatch Church of Babingley (built in the 1890s by the Prince of Wales, Edward VII) is following its predecessor into decay and is no longer used for services.

SS. Peter and Paul, BARNHAM BROOM, Norfolk. On 15th C screen, St. Walstan appears with two calf-like creatures at foot; green robe with white collar and cuffs; face obliterated. Used as model for 20th-century painting, and statue, in Bawburgh Church; also Taverham Village sign (1970).

BAWBURGH, Norfolk. Birthplace of Walstan. Wooden village sign (carved by Alex Whammond) depicts Walstan with animals. Commissioned in 1977 to celebrate Queen's Silver Jubilee, the artist's monogram, A.W., is entwined with Elizabeth II on the reverse side.

SS. Mary & Walstan, BAWBURGH. Site of Shrine Chapel on north side (external). Inside are two anonymous paintings, circa. 1960s, in the style of those panels showing Walstan at (a) Sparham, with two calves at foot, crowned, carrying scythe and sceptre, clothed in ermined, gold cape; and (b) Barnham Broom, with scythe and wearing a green gown. Both paintings were found in the Church vestry by the Rev. John Watson in 1983, which incumbent had them individually framed. Painting (b) has an additional cameo of Bawburgh Village in the background. Barnham Broom also used as model for the wooden statue of Walstan, carved by Anton Wagner, which stands in the north-east window and dedicated in 1981.

St. Walstan's Well and St. Walstan's Bush, BAWBURGH. The Well is situated below the Church and is the only one credited with 'miraculous' water. It was last renovated in 1980. Bryant (1905) says: 'Years ago, an old thorn bush stood close by [the Well] called St. Walstan's Bush.'

The Nativity of the Blessed Virgin, BEESTON-NEXT-MILEHAM, Norfolk. Although the painted figures on the 15th-century screen are badly defaced, Duffy writes that one of those on the dado of the south screen appears to have been carrying a scythe, and is therefore identified as St. Walstan.

Holy Trinity, BLYTHBURGH, Suffolk. Mentioned in the 1658 copy of the English Life as being the birthplace of Walstan. No other evidence offered and no claim to, or mention of, Walstan, Benedict or Blida can be found in the Church.

St. Walstan's Prayer Cell, BOWTHORPE, Norwich, Norfolk. Concrete sculpture, dedicated on 24th January, 1989, by the Bishop of Lynn, stands at the entrance to the Prayer Cell close to the Worship Centre. One of the three panels of the obelisk tells the story of Walstan (somewhat inaccurately) and another depicts him in primitive design with scythe. The same design was used for wooden, 6-inch high, hand-carved souvenir 'Walstans'. A modern icon, by Anna Dimascio, depicting Walstan in Saxon dress, with crown to denote princely birth, was placed in the Cell during January 1989, but it was stolen in 1992. Postcards of the icon are sold continuously.

Assumption of the Blessed Virgin Mary, BURY ST. EDMUNDS, Suffolk. St. Wolston's Chapel, north side of the West Door, completed in 1433. Until 1874 the Archdeacon of Sudbury held his Visitations and Consistory Courts in the Chapel. A Victorian brass plaque which declared the Chapel for 'St. Wolston, Patron of East Anglian Farmers' was removed in recent years and is now thought to be lost. Also, one of the 15th-century roof carvings is attributed.

St. Andrew's, CAVENHAM, Suffolk. Here, on the north wall of the aisleless nave, is the only safely identified wall painting of St. Walstan (see page 140). It was discovered in 1967 and eventually identified by Dr. David Park of the Courtauld Institute of Art. It dates from the latter half of the 15th century and has an outline drawing of St. Walstan, crowned, holding a scythe in his left hand, with his right hand raised in Benediction. Two small figures are at his feet. Questions about the future hang ominously over this Church, which is in need of repair and preservation – as is the painting itself. The Vicar and village community hope that the right decisions will be made by those with the power to do so. The features and history of the painting are discussed in full by Miss Miriam Gill in her article submitted to the Suffolk Institute of Archaeology.

St. Agnes, CAWSTON, Norfolk. South aisle window, restored in 1932 by Kings of Norwich, contains a piece of medieval glass bearing the name 'Blida'. This is presumed to be the fragment referred to in 1930, by M.R. James, as being 'preserved at the [Cawston] parsonage'.

Catholic Church of Our Lady & St. Walstan, COSTESSEY, Norfolk. Opened by Fr. Husenbeth in 1841 as St. Walstan's Chapel; water from St. Walstan's Well, Bawburgh, was used in the dedication Mass. It was built under the Patronage of the Jerninghams, when their own chapel at Costessey Hall became too small for the Catholic community, with additional public subscription. East end window dedicated to *Walstanus*, depicted in red robe carrying scythe. Memorial in Churchyard to Fr. Husenbeth, author of *The Life of St. Walstan, Confessor*. In 1947, a parochial seal was made, with St. Walstan's Well in the centre surrounded by lillies, with the inscription: *'Sigillum ecclesiae S Mariae et S. Walstani apud Costessiciam'*.

A Victorian print (and/or the original) is said to have belonged to Fr. Byrne, Priest at St. Walstan's, Costessey, who died in 1924. However, neither the print or the original has been seen since the early 1900s when it was used on postcards (see page 16). It is suggested by Costessey historian Ernest Gage that the postcards were made by Frank Welch, who bought and ran a tobacconist's shop in Costessey from 1906 and whose hobby was photography. Mr. Welch was responsible for most postcards of Costessey until his death in 1942.

St. Walstan's Close, COSTESSEY. Road leading off Bawburgh Lane, and once linked Costessey and Bawburgh, but it was sealed in 1992 when the Norwich Southern Bypass was built.

St. Walstan's Well, COSTESSEY PARK. Site for the second of the three wells, reputed to have been a stopping place for travellers and pilgrims until

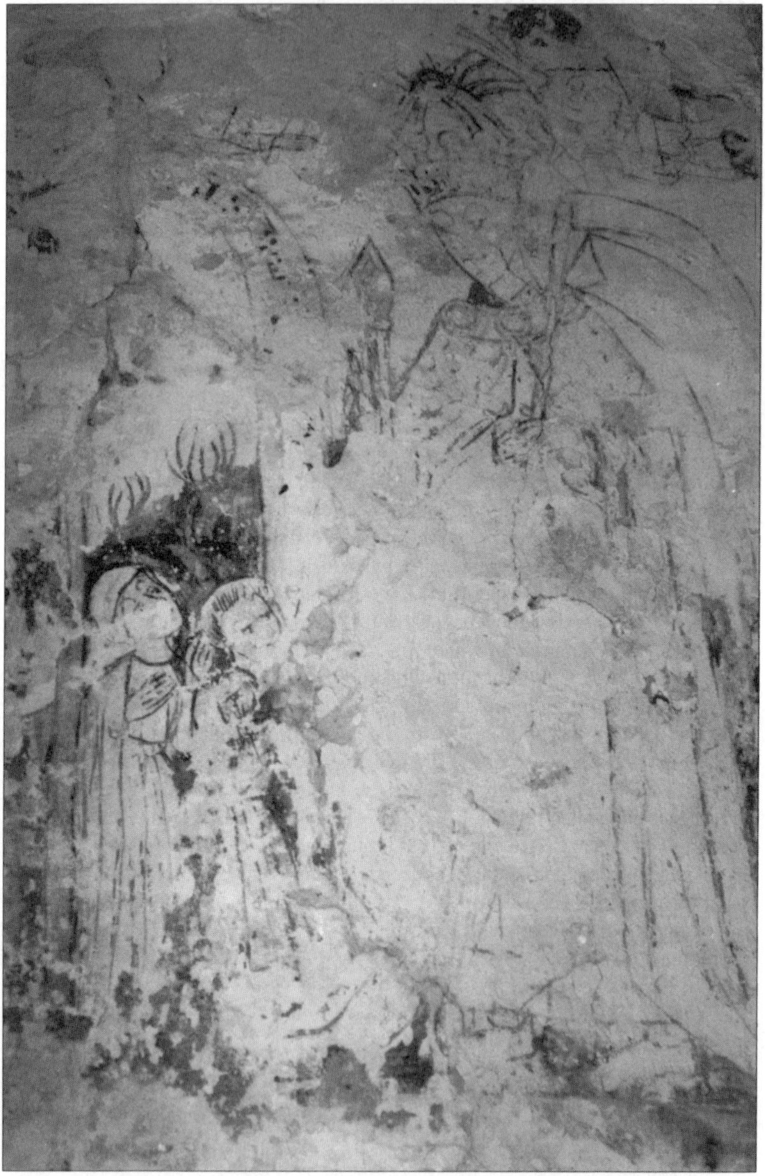

the 18th century. Although it has been dry for over 100 years, its flint lining can still be seen, with a diameter of 12 feet and a depth of 6 feet. The precise location can be found just north of the A47 between Easton and Costessey Park. Folklore insists that nearby is the point where the waggon is reputed to have crossed the Wensum, marked by wheel tracks seen on the river surface.

Not far from the Well site is a public house called The Round Well, and although it has never been properly established that it takes its name from St. Walstan's Well it is thought to do so.

Royal Norfolk Showground, COSTESSEY. St. Walstan's Hall, exhibitors' accommodation named to celebrate Walstan as Patron Saint of British Food & Farming Year, 1989.

St. Mary's, DENTON, Norfolk. One of 12 panels from an ancient rood screen, found in a damaged state in 1845, and made into a chest the following year. Walstan is depicted (indistinctly but safely) in ermine with scythe and red robe. It is defaced and measures only 12 inches x 4 inches. The panels are likely to have formed part of an original rood loft frontage.

St. Mary the Virgin, EARL STONHAM, Suffolk. This Church has a magnificent single hammer beam roof. Dated 1460, it is made of chestnut, and has 22 canopied niches, each containing a figure – one of which is St. Walstan, ninth figure on South side of Nave. All the figures are minus their heads, having been mutilated in the 1640s by the vandal William Dowsing or his agent(s). The Church is currently in need of funds for its restoration, in which cause English Heritage has recently taken a hand.

Easton College, EASTON, Norfolk. Wooden sign, carved by Harry Carter, for the Norfolk School of Agriculture (now Easton College). Walstan depicted in red robe, lying on a cart being pulled by two oxen. The sign is currently removed from site for renovation when it is hoped to make a fibreglass reproduction for outside, and display the original inside, the College (see page 162).

St. Peter and St. Paul, FOXEARTH, Essex. At present this rood screen panel is the only known representation of St. Walstan in Essex and he is seen with a crown and scythe. Although the original screen is early 16th century, the figures were much restored during the incumbency of John Foster, a high churchman in the Tractarian tradition, who was rector from 1845 until his death in 1892. On the rood screen, the male figures on the south side (left to right) are Christ, Alban, Walstan, Felix, Edmund and Augustine the Doctor.

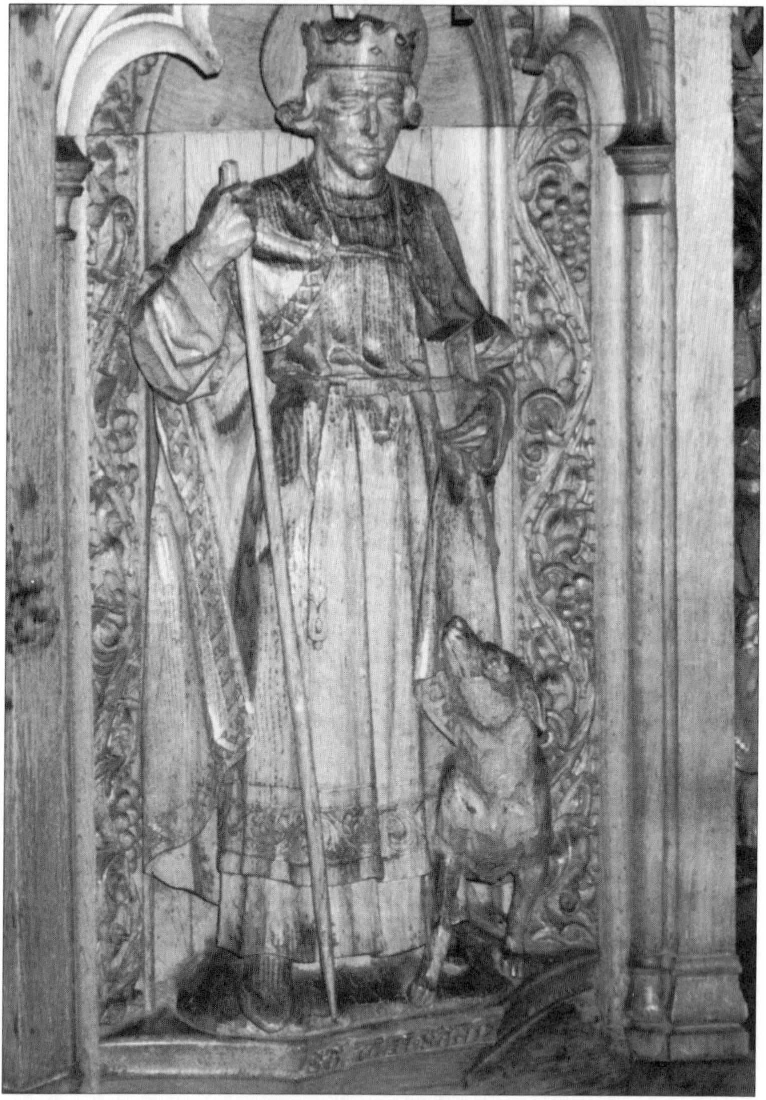

St. Edmund's, FRITTON, Norfolk (Suffolk until 1974). In the apt words of Mee, this is an '… astonishing church, (with a) blend of Roman, Saxon and Norman, and later centuries all under a thatched roof'. Here Walstan can be seen in the company of seven other East Anglian saints, Olaf, Fursey, William, Felix, Etheldreda, Ethelbert and Withburga. Walstan, with scythe and spade, is bearded and situated next to St. William, on the north side. Although the windows are 20th-century painted glass, those in the chancel were restored in 1855 by the Rev. Francis William Cubitt (1799-1882) and contain fragments of old work.

Note: Most of the windows were dedicated in 1905, and that containing Walstan given by the Misses Jane and Lucy Cubitt, in memory of their father, the Rev. Francis Cubitt. Other windows are in memory of their mother, Jane Mary Cubitt, who died in 1903, aged 97. Mr. Cubitt was the first resident Rector of Fritton and served the parish for a stated 53 years. (According to his grave stone, he died in 1882, which date appears in one of the windows in Roman numerals. However, in another of the windows, the year of his death appears as 1889. There is more confusion at the '53 years', which should presumably be 51 years, since the patronage was bought from the Old Manor by the Cubitts in 1831.) The east windows were given by Mary and Lucy's brother, Major Frank Cubitt, when he was patron of the benefice.

The shortage of facts relating to the commissioning and installation of the windows is due in part to the removal of Fritton from Suffolk to Norfolk in 1974, and in part to a disregard for bureaucracy.

St. Faith's, GAYWOOD, Norfolk. St. Walstan is depicted here in an early 20th-century wood carving with a bible and – uniquely – a dog as his specific emblems and with a staff rather than a scythe (pictured opposite). The oak pulpit, carved by Mr. N. Hitch of London in 1909, depicts St. Dunstan, St. George, the Good Shepherd, St. Walstan and St. Nicholas. It is engraved 'In Dear Memory of Thomas Edward Bagge'. There seems to be no particular reason for St. Walstan to have been chosen, but since the Church has been enlarged from the original Norman building, it is possible that the choice reflects one from an earlier period and that the dog is a mistake for a calf. There is a strong representation of East Anglian saints in the Church which incorporates the parishes of Mintlyn and Bawsey, united with Gaywood in 1937.

All Saints, GREAT MELTON, Norfolk. Stained glass window, dedicated in 1930 to Anthony and Matilda Curson. Ermined (gold) cape, with scythe and sceptre. Two white oxen at feet.

St. Andrew's, GREAT RYBURGH, Norfolk. This is the second of only two images of St. Walstan, both 20th-century, which employ the spade as a

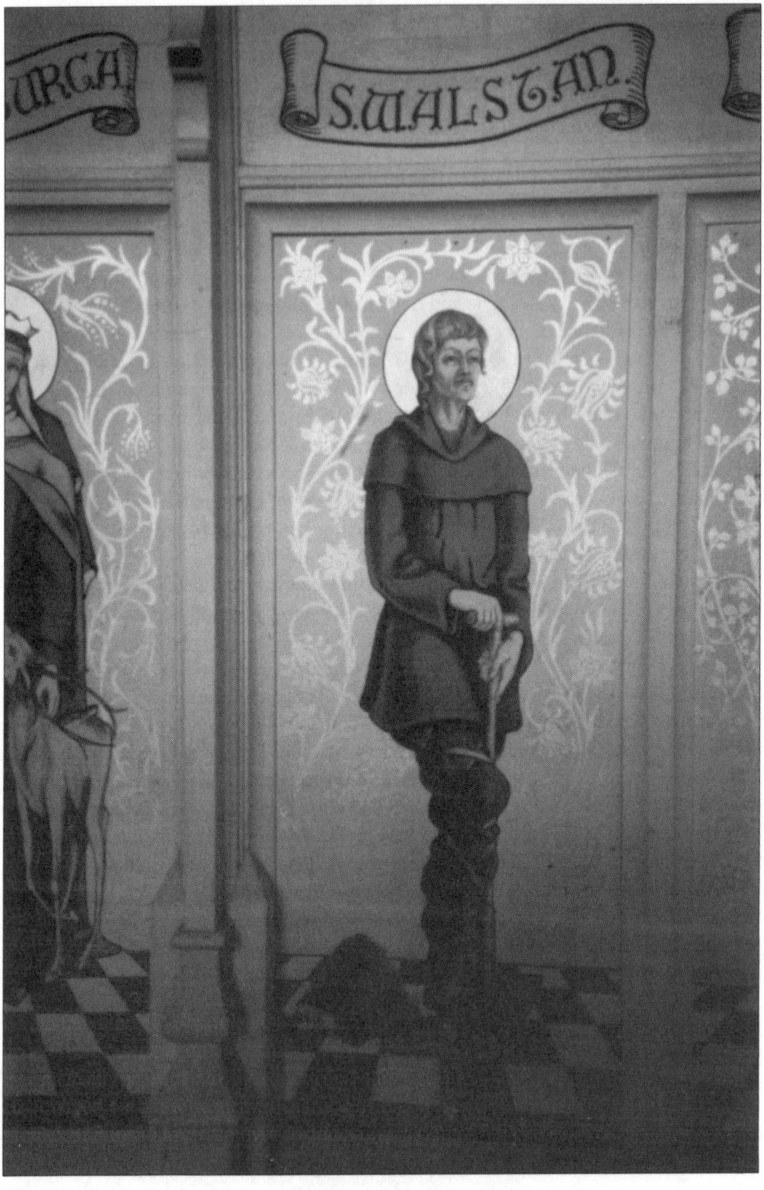
URGA
S.WALSTAN.

specific emblem. He is seen on the South Transept screen and depicted in something of an Arthurian style (see opposite). It was erected in memory of those who died in, or returned from, the First World War and has eight figures, including three other East Anglian saints – Etheldreda, Withburga and Felix.

Blessed Virgin and St. Andrew, HORSHAM ST. FAITH, Norfolk. M.R. James makes mention of Blida here, but nothing can be traced, other than a possible confusion with St. Bridget (identified on rood screen).

St. Mary's, KENNINGHALL, Norfolk. Twentieth-century stained glass window on south side of the nave, shows Walstan next to St. Felix. The window, by Kings of Norwich, was erected in memory of a local farmer, Edward Wood, of Fersfield Lodge (1906-1966). Excellent use of bold, vivid colour, with Walstan depicted, unusually, as a Medievalist (*see front cover*).

All Saints, LITCHAM, Norfolk. Once a stopping-place for pilgrims on their way to Walsingham, Walstan is depicted here on south half of 15th C screen, with crown, sceptre, and scythe; red robe with ermine.

St. Catherine's, LUDHAM, Norfolk. On the elaborately painted screen (south side) Walstan is seen with Edward the Confessor and St. Lawrence, depicted as a kingly figure with scythe and sceptre; red robe with ermine. The image is similar to that at Litcham and Denton, and is dated 1493. Said to be one of the best-preserved pre-Reformation screens in the country, SS. Gregory, Jerome, Edward and Walstan are in a different hand from that of the other eight panels.

St. Mary's, MARTHAM, Norfolk. No sign now of 'the Chapel to St. Blide of Martham' and there is only sketchy evidence that the south aisle was at one time dedicated to 'St. Blide' (Blomefield: *Reg. Alabaster Norw.* fol. 163). Mortlock and Roberts (*Norfolk Churches*) also index Walstan at Martham but give no details and mention St. Blide's south aisle dedication. *The Oxford Dictionary of Saints* says bequests to Blida's Martham Chapel were given as late as 1522 (which is, no doubt, that by Richard Fuller of Norwich quoted by Blomefield).

St. Andrew's, NORTH BURLINGHAM, Norfolk. On screen, *S. Walstanus*. Face obliterated, crowned, barefoot with scythe; ermined gold cape, over red robe, with gold purse at girdle probably to illustrate his charity to the poor. Dated 1536 this is believed to have been the last screen erected in Norfolk before the Reformation. Panel carries the word 'opifer' (succourer) or 'opifex' (worker, artisan).

St. Mary's, NORTH TUDDENHAM, Norfolk. Both M.R. James and *The Oxford Dictionary of Saints* record that an image of St. Blida forms part of the north-east chancel window. In *Suffolk and Norfolk* James says: 'Most of the nave windows have figures in the tracery lights. Nelson's book names SS. Bartholomew, Bleda, Edward Confessor, Edmund, Lawrence and James the Great'. Also, Roeder describes her as being 'venerated at North Tuddenham' and Husenbeth's *Emblems of Saints* gives '... a female with apparently the name of St. Blida ... N. Tuddenham – chancel – NE window'. However, no safe evidence of St. Blida can now be found in the Church, and Kings of Norwich discount the idea.

All Saints', NORWICH, Norfolk. See St. Julian's.

St. John the Baptist Catholic Cathedral, NORWICH. Walstan appears in one of six medallions, depicting East Anglian saints, in the North Transept or 'Queens' window. The original glass in the great triple lancet windows was destroyed in the Second World War. The centre window includes medallions containing SS. William, Sigebert, Ethelburga, Ethelbert and Godrick, and was designed by the Duke of Norfolk (as were the other two) and erected by his family in 1909.

St. James' (with Pockthorpe), NORWICH. Redundant Church (now Norwich Puppet Theatre). Original site of a 16th-century rood screen which contained, amongst others, panels of SS. Walstan and Blida. The panels were removed to St. Mary Magdalene, Silver Road (built 1901), *q.v.* when St. James' became a night shelter.

St. Julian's, NORWICH. Stone figure on the stem of the octagonal, Perpendicular font. Dated 1420, the figure appears as Wulstan in Church guide. Unusually, the saint carries a wheatsheaf instead of a scythe, said to accommodate the design. The font was originally in All Saints' Church, until 1977, when that Church became redundant. The living of St. Julian's went with All Saints' until 1930. This identification is by no means safe, but the tradition of naming the figure Wulstan/Walstan, qualifies it for consideration and is given as Walstan by Mortlock & Roberts. The font is similar to that in St. Mary Magdalene, where St. Blida has been identified as one of the stem figures, which was taken there from St. James' (with Pockthorpe).

St. Mary Magdalene, NORWICH. Two screen panels, previously at the Church of St. James (with Pockthorpe), Norwich, belonging to a set of ten. Unique example of SS. Walstan and Blida at same location and only known screen representation of Blida. Walstan wears a green robe and holds a wooden staff with a blade tied to it; Blida, also in green, holds a quill and book (probably a bible). Blida is named in the Church Guide as one of the figures on the font stem, which font was also removed from St. James'.

Note: Originally, these two panels, and the eight others at the same location, belonged to a rood screen thought to date from about 1515 (although some painting was carried out in 1479). Until this century they belonged to the now redundant Church of St. James (with Pockthorpe) in Norwich. Although the ten surviving panels are free from defacement they have suffered a degree of eccentric restoration in either the late 1800s, early 1900s, or both. It is by no means certain that Blida was originally placed next to Walstan or that the painting was, in fact, attributed to her in the first place.

The panels of Walstan and Blida are unusual on three counts: (i) in being the single example of the mother with her son; (ii) in being the only known screen imagery to be attributed to St. Blida (other than Babingley); and (iii) Walstan's scythe is unique by virtue of being a blade tied to a staff, rather than the usual scythe. (Whether or not the artist was a Norfolk man – who decided to 'dew different' – he may still be commended for his imagination.) They are also peculiar in being named Renaissance, rather than pre-Reformation.

In addition to their singular qualities, the panels have an extraordinary history. From the 16th to the middle of the 19th century, they were in St. James', though it is uncertain whether they were restored in 1515, to replace an older and pre-Reformation rood screen, or whether they originated at that time. However, they were removed from that Church sometime around 1849, presumably as part of the renovation work done to the Church fabric. In that year, Husenbeth made a drawing of the panel of St. Walstan, on which he recorded that the panels had formerly been in St. James' Church, Norwich, but were then in the possession of 'Rev. Jas. Bulwer, Aylsham, near Thetford'. He later crossed out 'Aylsham' and substituted 'Hamworth', which should more properly read 'Hunworth' since this is where the Rev. Bulwer was vicar. (This, together with a number of other Walstan drawings, mostly by Harriet Gunn, Husenbeth collected during research for his 1859 book on the life of St. Walstan although a lack of funds prevented them from being used.) The Rev. Bulwer was an antiquarian and something of an authority on the history of Pockthorpe, Hassett's House in particular. Husenbeth also stated that the panels were, at that time, 'all painted over red' and that James Bulwer removed said paint.

The exact date on which the ten panels were removed from St. James' is unclear, but obviously it was sometime around 1850. About thirty-three years later, in an 1882 edition of *Emblems of Saints*, Husenbeth was still recording that the panels were in 'private possession' at Aylsham although the Rev. Bulwer had died in 1879. By 1896, however, the panels were said by Messrs. Jessopp and James (in their joint publication on the life of St. William of Norwich) to be in the possession of Mr. J.J. and Miss Florence Colman.

During the years between 1849-1879, while in the possession of the Rev. Bulwer, or perhaps later, between 1879 and 1917 when they were returned to St. James', the panels appear to have been in receipt of some rather dubious 'restoration'. The panel depicting St. Agnes, for example, is now labelled St. Auguste (who is St. Auguste?) and what was probably a lamb is touched-up to depict a dog. The young man, or boy, with an upright sword was identified only this century (by M.R. James) as St. William, and a female saint now entitled St. Johanna is likely to have originally been St. Elizabeth of Hungary. Husenbeth identified the panel labelled 'St. Nicholas' as 'more probably St. Blaise, Bishop and Martyr'. At the same time, he identified one of the female saints – and one of those on the stem of the 14th-century font – as St. Blida.

Some of the titles might also have undergone change, while leaving the figure unaltered: Walstan, for example, now appears as 'Walston', although in Husenbeth's 1849 drawing the spelling is 'Walstan'. Similar 19th-century forms of 'restoration' (so much deplored by M.R. James, Mee, and others) seems to have been taking place at Worstead *q.v.* at about the same time. Opinions vary, however, about when the crude application of thick paint, still in evidence, was applied to the panels since there were to be opportunities later on for similar efforts to have been made.

The Rev. Sidney Long, one-time Vicar of St. James' and author of the Church's history, thought the colours reflected the 'early Renaissance origins of the panels', by which he presumably meant that the thick paint was applied in the 19th century in imitation of work done in perhaps the late 16th, or early 17th, centuries. But, whenever the work was done it was no doubt carried out ostensibly to cover flaws or defacement on the panels in line with contemporary practice. If damage to the original panels had been caused at the Reformation (likely), or during Cromwell's Rebellion (possible), it would have been better to have left them as they were – though perhaps minus the red paint – as happened at Denton, on the Norfolk-Suffolk border, where a small panel of St. Walstan was among those left unrestored but made instead into a chest for the Church of St. Mary's. Just who painted them red, and why, is mysterious indeed, and Husenbeth's statement is frustratingly brief.

However, for better or worse, the panels were at least still in existence at the end of the 19th century and known by Husenbeth to be at Aylsham, in the safe keeping of the Rev. Bulwer. Subsequently, in 1896, M.R. James knew them to be in the possession of Mr. J.J. Colman, when the panel depicting St. William was photographed for the Jessopp-James book.

Yet in 1932, Messent recorded: 'These panels are at present situated along the north wall of the chancel; they were turned out of [St. James'] at a restoration during the last century and were sold on Norwich Market for a shilling apiece. They were later purchased by the Colman family, and in 1917 were restored to the church by Mr. R.J. Colman.' Mee (in 1940) repeated the story of their having been sold for a shilling apiece on Norwich Market 'in the last century'.

How, then, had the panels been allowed to end up on Norwich market, sometime between 1882 and 1896? The Rev. Bulwer must have parted with them before his death in 1879, but by what authority were they his to dispose of? Husenbeth had written in 1859 that the panels had been taken down 'some years ago' by 'a respected archaeologist' (by which he could have meant James Bulwer) and that an antiquarian scraped off the red paint (by which he did mean Bulwer).

Fortuitously, the panels were spotted on Norwich market by an eminent member of the Colman family, Mr. J.J. Colman, Member of Parliament for Corton, who presumably paid the asking price of ten shillings for the lot of ten and thus saved them for posterity. Some time after this happy intervention the panels were passed to Mr. Russell J. Colman, who, in 1917 returned them to St. James. Was it perhaps R.J. Colman himself who saw the panels and recognised their worth? He was, after all, something of an authority on antiques. Once attention had been drawn to the panels, both he and the MP for Corton would, no doubt, have been fascinated by the two depicting Walstan and Blida. The Colman family was not without connections with Bawburgh: it was from there that the founder of the international Colman's of Norwich, Jeremiah Colman, had been married, having begun his milling career at Bawburgh Mill in 1802. It is also possible that J.J. Colman already knew something of the panels since he made acknowledgement of Bulwer's work in the Introduction to his *Norfolk Bibliography*.

The Colmans decided that the panels should be returned to their original site in St James', but nothing can be gleaned which gives any hint as to the condition of the panels at that time. Perhaps one of the Colmans had them 'restored' in 1917; they had, after all, been offered for sale on Norwich Market and might have needed some attention. Mr. R.J. Colman, Lord Lieutenant of Norfolk, was well-known for his interest in antiquities, so perhaps he, or Mr. J.J. Colman before his death, arranged for some work to be done. At the very least, he would have made sure that they were delivered safely to the Church, where they were placed on the north wall in the Sanctuary. There they remained, undisturbed, for almost thirty years.

In 1946, during the incumbency of Rev. Herbert Pitts, the ten panels were again restored, though to what extent nobody is quite sure. Could it have been then, and not in the 1850s, that the re-painting took place? If not, what could have been the nature of this further restoration? However, they were afterwards returned to St. James' and sited on the Chancel steps, five panels on each side. The work was dedicated in January, 1947, by the then Bishop of Norwich, Dr. Percy Mark Herbert, but the panels were not destined to stay in St James' for much longer.

In 1968, when St. James' was declared redundant, and the congregation moved to St. Mary Magdalene in Silver Road, it was decided to take the panels, and the ancient font, to the new Church. In 1971 the Rev. Malcolm Menin took charge of the panels and, in 1974, after again being cleaned and restored (this time 'sympathetically'), they were finally displayed in the new Church, where they can now be seen.

St. Thomas', Heigham Road, NORWICH. Drawings and plans for a stained glass window, commissioned and designed in 1960 for the Church, depicts Walstan with Bawburgh's round-towered church at foot, carrying scythe. Commission never executed but design still exists with Kings of Norwich.

St. Mary's, SPARHAM, Norfolk. On 15th C panel with St. Thomas of Canterbury. Walstan is seen here robed, with crown, sceptre (to denote royal blood), scythe, and calf-like creatures at feet. Poor example of a youthful-looking Walstan. Screen not *in situ* but framed. The scythe has a V-shaped hook at the base.

TAVERHAM, Norfolk. Village sign, carved by Harry Carter, and given by the Women's Institute in 1970: Walstan in a green robe with ermine, holding a cross in one hand. Apparel reminiscent of that at Barnham Broom and includes scythe, two calves and river in the background.

Walstanham Plantation, TAVERHAM. Site for St. Walstan's Well, in small copse below Church. Reputed to be location of Nalga's farm and Walstan's death. Norgate writes of a reference to the Well in an old lease book as '... laying between Langwongs Furlong on the part of the South and the land of Mary Branthwayt north, and abutting a way leading from Taverham to Crostwick', thus approximate to Breck Farm.

There is also a St. Walstan's Road in Taverham.

WALBERSWICK, Suffolk. See Postscript.

St. Mary's, WORSTEAD, Norfolk. Said to contain icon of Walstan and/or Blida, and given the huge importance of agriculture to Worstead, it would not be surprising to find either saint here. However, although Husenbeth (1859) states that Blida was the name of a wife who, co-jointly with her husband, gave the screen to the Church in 1512; *Blide vxoris ejus* is not now visible.

In 1917, M.R. James wrote that the name 'Blida' occurs on the screen, and in *Suffolk and Norfolk* writes that drawings of the screen, made in 1832, show a female saint without an attribute, which is taken to mean that this could be Blida. Later, however, he writes that the screen (of 1512) was the work of John Albastyr and his wife, Benedicta. The screen was ('dreadfully' he says) re-painted in 1870 when the identity of several saints was changed, a similar story to that of the St James' panels, *q.v.*

Mortlock & Roberts give the name of the 1512 donor's wife as Alice, while Cox names her as Agnes. Mee wisely refrains from naming her at all.

BEYOND EAST ANGLIA

All Saints, GRESFORD, Clwyd (formerly Denbighshire). Reference made by M.R. James (1917) to a stone figure, crowned and holding a scythe at the top of Gresford Church which is said to be Walstan. Mentioned also in Bryant's *Norfolk Churches* (1905) as being at Gresford 'crowned, holding a scythe'. Also given in Drake (*see Bibliography*) as 'Statue, Gresford Ch. Denbighshire'.

An unidentified icon of St. Walstan on an **ENGLISH CATHEDRAL** is reputed to have been the inspiration for the dedication of St. Walstan's Church in Rongai. The image of St. Walstan is said to be holding a wheatsheaf and to stand above the entrance door.

NOTE: It is apparent from part of an undated letter sent to Fr. Husenbeth that he had instigated enquiries about a dedication in Ely Cathedral, as well as one in London. The letter-writer reports back, saying '... I have made enquiries about the Church in London, and about the Chapel at Ely, but so far have ...'; the rest of the letter, and the identity of the writer, is lost.

However, new research about a dedication in Ely Cathedral has revealed that Keyser named 'Wolston' there, but the Dean and Chapter archivist thinks this is likely to refer to the wall paintings, now destroyed, which included Wulfstan, Archbishop of York (d. 1023).

So far, no Church dedication to St. Walstan has been discovered in London.

OVERSEAS

St. Walstan's, RONGAI, Kenya. Built in the early 1950s by settlers and dedicated in 1955 by Bishop Leonard Beecher and Gordon Mayo, Vicar of Nakuru. In 1986 more work took place and a vestry was added, and two years later electricity was installed.

During 1988 St. Walstan's Church Hall was dedicated by the Bishop the Rt. Rev. Stephen Mwangi. The Church is the 'headquarters' of the Parish and has nine affiliated churches.

A description of Bawburgh and a piece of stone from the Church of SS. Mary & Walstan are displayed in the tower.

CHURCHES DEDICATED TO ST. WULSTAN (WULFSTAN)

Catholic Church of St. Wulstan, GREAT HARWOOD, Blackburn. Dedicated in 1937.

Catholic Church of St. Wulstan, HIGH WYCOMBE, Buckinghamshire. To accommodate the strong Irish and English Catholic presence in the area, foundations for the new Church were laid in 1969. It was named for St. Wul(f)stan who had been Bishop of Northamptonshire in the 11th century, and had visited High Wycombe. It was consecrated in 1978 by Bishop of Northamptonshire. However, the building became unsafe only a few years later and rebuilding began in 1991. It was decided to modernise the name to Wulstan.

Parish of St. Wulstan's, WARNDON, Worcester. The Church at Warndon was dedicated in 1963. Although the Shrine of St. Wulstan in Worcester Cathedral was destroyed at the Reformation, it has not been forgotten, and plans are in hand for the Diocese to celebrate the 900th anniversary of Wulstan's death.

APPENDIX II

THE PRAYERS OF ST. WALSTAN

I. St. Walstan's prayer at the hour of his death (Nova Legenda Anglie):
Oh hope and salvation of the believers,
Oh glory and rest of those who labour,
Good Jesus, Grant your servant this mercy,
That if a labourer should have some infirmity or other bodily disablement,
Or if compelled by necessity
Anyone should reverently visit me with good will,
And in your Holy Name,
On behalf of brute animals
May he be not denied your help and, I pray Lord,
May the brute animals be restored to health.

II. Prayer reputedly used by Medieval pilgrims at the Shrine of St. Walstan. Source unknown, but it is loosely based on sentiments expressed towards the end of the Latin Life..
Oh, holy Walstan, well do you deserve praise in the Church of God!
You may be compared to the Apostles for your renunciation of
    temporal things;
You are like the martyrs by penitential mortification of the flesh;
You are the companion of Confessors for your almsgiving and pouring
    forth abundantly holy prayers.
Pray that we may so follow your steps in the way of truth and justice
    and of perfect humility;
That we may be enabled to come with you to the kingdom of light and glory,
Through our Lord Jesus Christ,
Who reigns with The Father and The Holy Ghost for endless ages of ages.
    Amen.

III. Prayer included in Item 8 and possibly, therefore, it appeared on the Medieval triptych:
You knight of Christ, Walston holy,
Your cry to hear thee meekly wee pray,
Shield us from mischeife, sorrow & folly,
Engendring and renewing from day to day,
Replenishd with misery, Job doth truly say,
& bring us to health blessed wth Jhesus right hand,
Him to love & know in everlasting land.

IV. The St. Walstan Year Prayer which was said for the first time during the Dedication Service of St. Walstan's Cell, Bowthorpe, conducted by Rt. Rev. David Bentley, Bishop of Lynn, in January, 1989. The 'St. Walstan Year' was sponsored by Norwich Diocesan Board of Social Responsibility – Norvicare – to coincide with British Food and Farming Year (1989).

Lord, our Father
Whose servant Walstan devoted his life to your service
And to the love of your land,
Bless our beloved county of Norfolk,
And grant us all a healing in our division,
A new understanding of your call to service,
And an unwavering determination
To live after the example of Jesus Christ, our Lord.
    Amen.

APPENDIX III

HYMNS TO ST WALSTAN

I. Hymn composed during 1989 and sung for the first time by the congregation of SS. Mary and Walstan, at the Patronal Service in May, 1989. The writer prefers anonymity but lives in Norfolk and was inspired by a libretto composed by Sheila Crosse for an opera about St. Walstan. One suggestion was to include a congregational procession, but this was not done. The opera, however, was performed at the Church of St. Peter Mancroft, Norwich, in 1989.

Prepare to walk the pilgrim's way
Commemorate Saint Walstan's day
And, as he turned from wealth and ease,
From wordliness come seek our peace.
    Come walk the way that Walstan trod
    To seek himself and find his God.

He saw through pride and wealth's constraint
To find the freedom of the saint
And love to glorify the least
To cure mankind and heal the beast.
    Come walk the way that Walstan trod
    To seek himself and find his God.

He saw Christ in a beggar's need
And gained in giving Christ's own creed:
By his example men believed
And he and they faith's wealth received.
    Come walk the way that Walstan trod
    To seek himself and find his God.

Tending the word of life with toil
He made himself its fruitful soil
And working with God's rain and sun
He made of prayer and labour one.
    Come walk the way that Walstan trod
    To seek himself and find his God.

His was the trust to face known death
And breathe in peace his final breath
His was the life to Christ all given
That won true wealth in earth and heaven.
    Come walk the way that Walstan trod
    With saints on high, we praise our God.

II. In *Memorials of Old Norfolk* St. Walstan is said to be included in a hymn to Labouring Saints, which contains the following verse:

Onward still the throng is moving,
There Blandin's victor palm
Phocas brings his flowers immortal
Crispin joins the gladsome psalm;
There the scythe of gentle Walstan,
There the plough of Isidore
Faithful workers for the Master
Resting now for evermore.

APPENDIX IV

VARIATIONS ON THE NAMES OF WALSTAN, BLIDA AND BAWBURGH

I. WALSTAN

De Sancto Walstano Confessore Latin title in *Nova Legenda Anglie*.

Walsham Only Walter Rye (1885) called Walstan 'St. Walsham' and entitles him 'Hermit'.

Walstan This is the modern, and most common, spelling to evolve from the other and various alternatives. It occurs in the Bawburgh, Costessey and Rongai Church dedications and was favoured by M.R. James. Blomefield uses 'Walstan' throughout, except where quoting.

Walstane (The use of the final 'e' denotes the Latin masculine vocative of a second-declension noun.) Appears in index of Nicholas Roscarrock's compendium of the English saints, compiled early in the 17th century. Same spelling occurs in Bale's account, as quoted by Blomefield. Also *Magna Britannia (Norfolk)* by Rev. Thomas Cox (MDCCXX) who copies Bale.

Walsteney See Postscript re. Walberswick.

Walston Occurs in *The History of St. Walston*, Item 8 of MS Lambeth 935. Also in *The Life of Father Ignatius* (Bertouch). Walter Rye indexes 'Walston' and 'Walstan' separately while using only the latter in the text. Used in Church Guide for Great Ryburgh. 'Saynt Walston' is named in 1503 bequest to the Chapel at Bury St. Edmunds. Mee refers to 'St. Walston of Norwich' at Sparham, although elsewhere in the same volume he uses 'Walstan' and 'Wulstun'. Also used on panel at St. Mary Magdalene.

Walstone Cited in the will of Sir Thomas Wethyr, 1528, as given in Blomefield, '... the gild of our Lady and St. Walstone at Baber'.

Walstanus Latin inscription on North Burlingham screen and given in Attwater's *Dictionary of Saints*. Also on east end window at Costessey Catholic Church.

Walstun Appears in Bryant's *Norfolk Churches* under entry for Denton.

Wlstane Invocation in a litany, ascribed to the monks of St. Alban's, dating from the second quarter of the 15th century and possibly referring to St. Walstan.

Wlstanus Abbreviation of *Wulstanus* or *Walstanus* (Latin).

NOTE: In November, 1862, workmen discovered three, late 14th-century, mural paintings in the south aisle of Norwich Cathedral, one of which was entitled 'Scs WLSTANUS'. In 1864, Husenbeth interpreted 'Scs WLSTANUS' as 'St. Wolstan, Bishop of Worcester from 1062-1095'. Although the paintings were covered up almost immediately (by a monument to the Wodehouse family) a drawing of the painting was done by Mr. F.B. Russel. It shows a figure likely to be a Bishop, rather than a farm worker, but does not explain why Husenbeth failed to use the more usual appellation of 'Wulfstan' for the Worcester Bishop (NNAS, Vol. 6.). Keyser (1883) refers to 'Wulstan' on the South wall of the Cathedral's South aisle.

Wolstane See Postscript re. Walberswick.

Wolston Used consistently in guides to St. Mary's, Bury St. Edmunds and on a brass plaque inside Church (now lost) which proclaimed the Chapel for 'Saint Wolston, Patron of East Anglian Farmers'. *Victoria History of the County of Norfolk* refers to 'St. Wolston of Bauberg' and 'St. Walstan' in the same volume.

Wulstan Appears in a framed, hand-written description of the Chapel which hangs in St. Mary's, Bury St. Edmunds. Also in the Church Guide at St. Julian's, Norwich. Although in possession of Husenbeth's *Life of St. Walstan*, Armstrong refers to 'Wulstan' in *A Norfolk Diary*. Keyser refers to 'Wulstan' at Ashby, Suffolk.

II. BLIDA

Bleda Named as 'St. Bleda, mother of St. Walsham' by Walter Rye in *A History of Norfolk* (1885). Also, M.R. James quotes Nelson as naming 'Bleda' at North Tuddenham.

Blida Named in *Nova Legenda Anglie* and Butler's *Lives*. Also in glass fragment at Cawston, and on panel at St. Mary Magdalene, Norwich. Mee refers to 'St. Blida, the mother of St. Walston'.

Blide 'St. Blide, Mother of St. Walstan' given by Walter Marsden in *Resting Places in East Anglia* (1987). Used in 1522 bequest of Richard Fuller (Blomefield). Bryant (1906) gives 'St. Blide'.

Blyth 'St. Blyth of Martham' given in *Some Early English Inscriptions in Norfolk* (Rye).

Blythe 'His father Benet, his mother Blythe by name' – Item 8. 'St. Blythe at Martham' referred to by Rev. Richard Hart in *The Shrines and Pilgrimages of the County of Norfolk*.

NOTE: Eamon Duffy (p.179 *The Stripping of the Altars*) points to Bale's use of 'Saynt Blythe' in *Comedy concernynge thre lawes*, where Bale ridicules the superstitions attached to various saints. Having requested protection from Saynt Germyne in the matter of chickens, Saynte Lenarde for the ducks, and Moses for horses, Bale writes:

'If ye cannot slepe but slumber
Geve otes unto saynt Uncumber,
And beanes in a serten number,
Unto saynt Blase and Saynt Blythe.'

Presumably this refers to a tradition or ritual to a St. Blythe involving a number of beans and links Blythe with a saint well known in Norwich, Blaise, Patron Saint of the woollen trade.

III. BAWBURGH

Baauburg (1235, Close Rolls)
Baber (Butler's *Lives*, edited by Husenbeth: 'Bawburgh, commonly called Baber')
Baberg Babor Babur (common in the early part of the 20th century)
Baburgh (one spelling in Item 8)
Banburgh (Blomefield remarked 'is called by mistake Banburgh for Bauburgh')
Barbure (Named as part of Costessey Manor in the 12th century)
Bauberg (*Victoria County History*)
Bauburc Bauburg (ll30, Index to the Charters & Rolls, British Museum)
Bauburgh (Armstrong's *History of Antiquities of the County of Norfolk* gives this under Bawburgh, as well as Bawborough, Bawburc, and Baber). Simon de Bauburgh is listed as Rector of Ashby from 1361 to 1390.
Bauburghe (1316 reference dated in Blomefield)
Bauenburc (Domesday Book)
Bawberg (Rye in *History of Norfolk*)
Bawborough
Bawburc
Bayber

NOTE: The similarity in spelling between Bawburgh and Bawdeswell gives rise to another consideration of the age and origin of the legend and there is endless amusement to be had from juggling name and place origins as sign posts to history. The Anglo Saxon 'tun' (farm or estate), for example, adds to the rural notion of 'Wals-tun', the ending being an alternative to 'Wal-stone'.

In his recent book *The Origins of Norfolk*, Tom Williamson points out that while no major Norfolk place names incorporate the Pagan words *hearg* or *wih* (meaning shrine), some incorporate *wylla* (spring or well) and suggest sites of Pagan *woeterwyllas*. Although Bawburgh has different origins, in spite of the first three letters, Bawdeswell may possibly 'refer to a spring associated with Balder, the dying and reviving god of Scandinavian and old English Mythology'. Similar derivatives can be found in Bawsey, and Bawdsey, which Norman Scarfe (*Suffolk in the Middle Ages*, The Boydell Press, 1986) points to as having evolved from 'Baldhere's islane', Baldhere's namesake being Balder.

Often, such coincidences are dismissed by experts as being just that, coincidences, although there seems no end to the conclusions being drawn from the name given to St. Walstan's mother in the English Life. While many deplore the practice of constructing history on the evidence of place name derivation, this has not prevented others from making positive links between Blythe/Blide and Blyborow/Blythburgh.

APPENDIX V

MISCELLANEOUS DATA

Feast Day The 30th May is given in both the Latin and English Life and is generally accepted to be the date of Walstan's death, and therefore his feast day. Husenbeth, however, stated that in some old English Calendars it is taken to be 28th December (*Catholic Almanack*, 1687; *Manual*, editions of 1706 and 1728; *Paradise of the Soul*, 1720).
NOTE: M.R. James gives the *Manual* edition as 1708.

Blomefield writes '… he is said to die in 1016, on the third of the calends of June', taking it literally from the account by Bishop Bale, who in turn probably took it from the Latin Life (1516). The NLA gives: '*Migrauit ergo ad dominum egregius iste sanctus Walstanus anno ab incarnatione domini millesimo sexto decimo, tertio kal Junii*' (This distinguished St. Walstan migrated to the Lord in the year of the Incarnation of Our Lord 1016, on 30 May). This June reference occasionally leads to confusion.

However, the Roman Calendar was arranged around the Ides, Kalends and Nones. The Kalends of a month was the first of the month, but they counted backwards, beginning on what is now regarded as the previous month. Thus, counting back from the third Kalends of June, we arrive at 30th May (Source: Rollason). There have been several civil and religious Calendars and thus as many changes and variations in their content.

Other saints, including Felix I, Pope and Martyr; Hubert of Maastricht; Ferdinand III, and Joan of Arc share 30th May (in one or other Calendar), which often accounts for the omission of Walstan from shortened or edited lists. (The Ramsgate Monks, in *The Book of Saints*, list 23 – including Walstan – for 30th May.)

The May and June dates can be significant in distinguishing Walstan of Bawburgh from Bishop Wulfstan (c.1008-1095), whose Feast Day is 19th January.

Although there is no known Feast Day for St. Blida, Roeder credits St. Blida with the Patronage of Mothers.

Patron of Agriculture Other saints credited with patronage of agriculture or farm workers include Isidore the Farmer (c. 1070-1130), honoured as Patron Saint of Farm Labourers in Spain, Canada and Mexico, whose feast date is 10th May. No iconography exists in East Anglia for St. Isidore, other than a road in Kesgrave's Grange Farm, near Ipswich. The name 'St. Isidores'

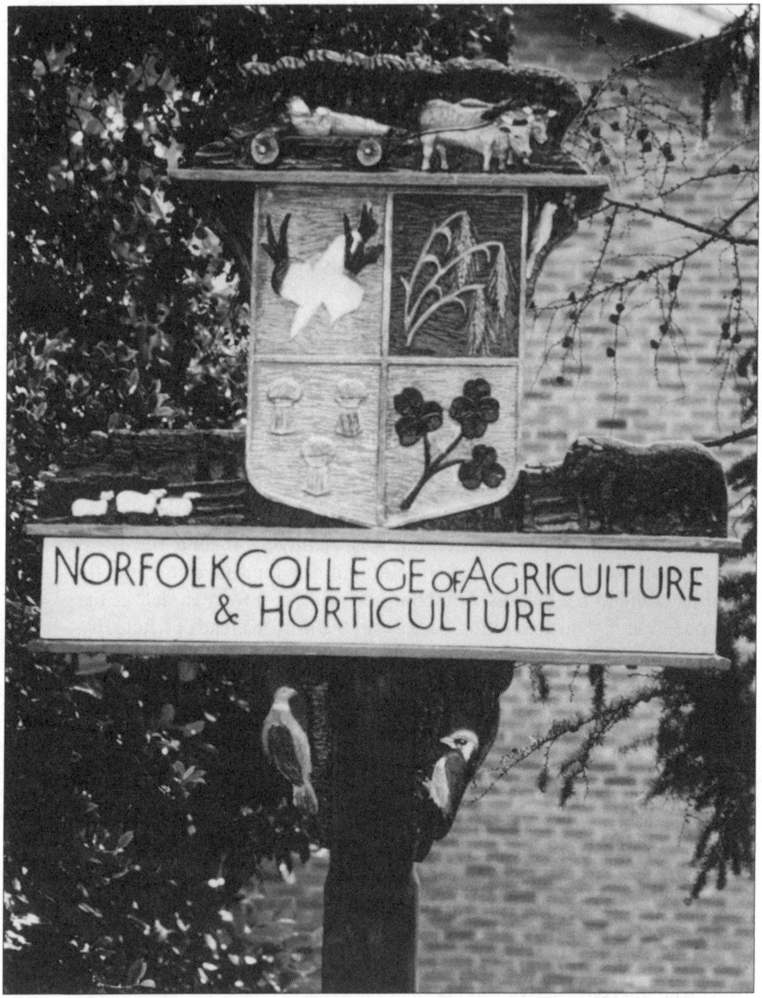
NORFOLK COLLEGE OF AGRICULTURE
& HORTICULTURE

came from one of the owners of the land on which the Grange Farm homes were built in the l990s. (Source: Jill Palmer)

Abbot Benedict (c.480-c.550 AD), is Patron of Italian Farmers and author of the Rule which bears his name.

The Oxford Dictionary of Saints gives Phocas of Sinope as Patron of Agricultural Workers, but most versions of this 4th-century martyr name him as Phocas the Gardener.

Roeder lists Abden and Sennen, Gratus of Aosta, Judocus, Ulrich, and Abbess Walpura under the Patronage of Farming. She credits the Patronage of Peasantry to Bishop Wulfstan.

Cattle are said to have been taken to the Italian shrine of St. Antony of Padua to be blessed or cured of disease, and St. Francis of Assisi is popularly regarded as Patron of Animals and Birds.

In *The Book of Saints*, the Ramsgate Monks give 'Albert the Farmer' as an alternative name for Blessed Albert of Bergamo (or Ogna), a peasant farmer who was persecuted by his wife for his generosity to the poor and destitute.

Attwater, in *The Penguin Dictionary of Saints*, gives Notburga (d. l3l3) as the Patron Saint of Hired Hands in Tirol and Bavaria, in celebration of her work on a farm and the legend of the sickle that suspended itself out of reach in the air when Notburga refused to reap corn on a Sunday.

Emblem Generic emblems include a crown and/or sceptre, to denote royal blood. Specific emblems are a scythe (emblem shared by St. Sidwell) and two calves. (St. Sidwell can also be seen with a well, but, although Walstan is associated with three wells, it is not a specific emblem.) SS. Walstan and Sidwell can be distinguished from one another as Sidwell is usually carrying her head (severed from her shoulders by reapers at her stepmother's behest) and is a female saint.

In *The Oxford Dictionary of Saints*, Juthwara (sister of St. Sidwell) is also credited with the scythe as her emblem.

Husenbeth credits the Martyr, Valentius, with the scythe emblem, as does Vince in *Discovering Saints in Britain*, while Roeder lists Albert of Bergamo and Sidwell.

Although the sickle, as distinct from the scythe, is mentioned in Item 8, there is no known representation of Walstan with a sickle. It is more often attributed to St. Notburga, and sometimes to Isidore the Farmer (occasionally called Isidore the Farm Servant, or Isidore the Labourer). Roeder attributes the sickle to Serapion, Hermit of Arsinoe.

Ears of wheat or a wheatsheaf are more usually attributed to St. Fara (or Burgundofara) who died circa. 660, or St. Walburge (d. 779), but at St. Julian's, Norwich, Walstan is seen holding the stalks and ears of corn.

Roeder attributes corn to SS. Hilda, Walpurga (Walburge/a), and Walther of Pontoise.

At North Burlingham, Walstan is depicted with a purse, to illustrate his charity.

Williamson (NNAS, 1957) describes Walstan at Barnham Broom as holding a shepherd's crook.

Christopher Woodforde (*The Norwich School of Glass-Painting in the Fifteenth Century*, OUP, 1950) points out that the scythe held by St. Walstan at Sparham is one of particular ornateness and is taken to be a good example of the 'Norwich' form of scythe, which shows the snatch with a double end, held by a pin and, apparently, hinged. (See also *English Medieval Painting*, T. Borenius & E.W. Tristram, 1927, pl 81.)

In this century, two representations of St. Walstan (Fritton and Great Ryburgh) have included a spade, although the spade is more usually attributed to St. Fiacre or the aforementioned St. Phocas.

Uniquely, Walstan is depicted at Gaywood with a dog by his side and holding a staff in one hand and a bible in the other hand. The representation is modern and captioned.

Merle Tidey, in her *Walberswick Guide*, refers to 'St. Wulstan, the Ploughman's Saint'.

APPENDIX VI

CHRONOLOGICAL REVIEW
(NATIONAL OR SIGNIFICANT EVENTS IN BOLD)

A.D. 55-450   **Roman Britain**

450-613   **The Coming of the English**

613-1017   **Division into Kingdoms**

975   Walstan born in Bawburgh

988   He leaves home to work as farmworker in Taverham

1016   **Death of Ethelred II and his son, Edmund Ironside**
Walstan died at Taverham on 30th May
Bishop Aelfgar of Elmham attends the burial site at
    Bawburgh and allows Walstan's remains to be venerated
    as the relics of a saint

1017-1066   **Danish Rule**

1047   Bishop Aethelmar of Elmham dedicates the Bawburgh
    Church to SS. Mary and Walstan, and a Shrine Chapel
    to St. Walstan

1066   **The Norman Invasion**

1235   Eudo, Abbot of Bon Repos, gave patronage of Bawburgh
    to monks of Holy Trinity, Norwich

1240   Rectory of Bawburgh appropriated by Bishop William
    de Ralegh of Norwich Cathedral Priory

1260   **Publication of *The Golden Legend* by James of Voragine**

1272   Rioters pillage and burn Norwich Priory

1278   Messuage built on the north side of Bawburgh Church
    to house priests and visiting pilgrims

1320   Extensive re-building of the Chancel in Bawburgh Church

1326   Thomas de la Mare serves his probation at Wymondham
    Abbey, then a cell of the Order of St. Benedict

1340   John of Tynemouth begins work on the *Sanctilogium*

1348-9   **Black Death**

1349	Death of John of Tynemouth Thomas de la Mare elected Abbot of St. Alban's
1433	Completion of the Chapel of St. Wolston in St. Mary's, Bury St. Edmunds
1445	Richard Wright of Bawburgh claims the Dunmow Flitch
1456?	Capgrave at work adapting the *Sanctilogium* and re-naming the collection *Capgrave's Legends*
1460	Further re-building of the Bawburgh Shrine Chapel
1476	**William Caxton sets up the first English printing press**
1516	Wynkyne de Worde publishes the full version of *Nova Legenda Anglie*. Includes fifteen New Lives, one of which is Walstan Richarde Pynson publishes the same Collection in English
1538	Destruction of the Shrine Chapel at Bawburgh Norwich Cathedral Priory abolished; Rectory of Bawburgh transferred to Dean and Chapter of Norwich
1546	Bale writes *The Actes of Englyshe Votaryes*
1553	**Death of Edward VI, accession of Mary I** Grant of Costessey Manor given to Sir Henry Jernegan
1558	**Death of Queen Mary, accession of Elizabeth I**
1633	Bawburgh Church repaired and tiled at the Revision
1637-38	Matthew Wren, Bishop of Norwich, orders further restoration of Bawburgh Church
1648	Property of Sir Henry Jerningham under protection of Oliver Cromwell
1649	**Charles I beheaded** **Commonwealth Government begins**
1658	**Death of Oliver Cromwell** Anonymous scribe makes a copy of 'an ancient triptych', extant as *The History of St. Walston*, (MS Lambeth 935, Item 8)
1660	**Restoration of the English Monarchy** Philip Tenison, Archdeacon of Norfolk, dies and a shroud brass laid in his memory in Bawburgh church
1696	Dr. Thomas Smith catalogues the Cottonian Collection, which contains John of Tynemouth's *Sanctilogium*

1731	Fire destroys much of the Cottonian Collection, including the *Sanctilogium*
1756-59	Publication of Butler's *Lives of the Saints*
1761	Publication of Bishop Challoner's *Memorial of Ancient British Piety*
1763	*The Gentleman's Magazine* carries news of the miraculous water at St. Walstan's Well
1805	Blomefield records the Walstan legend in *History of Norfolk*
1819	The Miracle of Mr. Francis Bunn
1820	Fr. F.C. Husenbeth appointed Chaplain at Costessey Hall
1833	**The Hadleigh Conference/Establishment of the Oxford Movement**
1841	St. Walstan's Chapel, Costessey, opened by Fr. Husenbeth
1859	Fr. Husenbeth publishes his *Life of St. Walstan, Confessor*
1864	Pilgrimage of Fr. Ignatius to St. Walstan's Well
1872	Death of Fr. Husenbeth
1892	Rev. Gabriel Young installed as Vicar of SS Mary & Walstan
1901	*Nova Legenda Anglie* re-published (in Latin)
1909	Duke of Norfolk windows dedicated in St. John's Catholic Cathedral in Norwich; contains a medallion of St. Walstan
1912	Third National Catholic Congress pilgrimage to Bawburgh, to be recorded the following year in Picton's *A Great Gothic Fane*
1913	Thanksgiving Pilgrimage of Norfolk Catholics to Bawburgh
1917	M.R. James publishes *Lives of St. Walstan* Mr. R.J. Colman restores screen panels of SS. Walstan and Blida to St. James (with Pockthorpe), Norwich
1920	Faculty for tablet in St. Wolstan's Chapel, St. Mary's Church, Bury St. Edmunds, in memory of those members of the Suffolk Yeomanry who died in the First World War
1931	**Walsingham Shrine re-opened** Anglo-Catholic Pilgrimage to Bawburgh led by Rev. W.E. Duxson, rector of St. John Maddermarket. Nuns from St. Augustine's Lodge, and the Rev. A. Hope Patten, Vicar of Walsingham, walked in procession

1934	Second Anglo-Catholic Pilgrimage
1935	Third Anglo-Catholic Pilgrimage
1951	Pilgrims Service at Bawburgh, led by Rev. A.A.C. Barwood, Rector of St. Edmund's, Taverham
1952	Water from St. Walstan's Well, Bawburgh, declared unfit to drink
1955	Dedication of St. Walstan's Church in Rongai, Kenya
1967	Medieval wall painting discovered at Cavenham: later found to depict St. Walstan
1976	Anglo-Catholic pilgrimage from Taverham to Bawburgh
1982	Members of Bawburgh Methodist Chapel join in the St. Walstan's Day Service at Church
1989	**St. Walstan Patron Saint of British Food & Farming Year** Inter-denominational pilgrimage from Taverham to Bawburgh, followed by an Open Air Service conducted by The Bishop of Norwich Dedication of St. Walstan's Prayer Cell, Bowthorpe
1992	St .Walstan instanced by Eamon Duffy in *The Stripping of the Altars*

APPENDIX VII

DE SANCTO WALSTANUS CONFESSORE

(CONCERNING ST. WALSTAN THE CONFESSOR)

The following is the first published translation of the entry in the 1901 *Nova Legenda Anglie*, and appears by courtesy of Dr. D.W. Rollason, of the Department of History, Durham University. (Editor of the 1901 NLA, Carl Hortmann, had corrected the 1516 text where there seemed to be errors, but none could carry a significantly different meaning from his own version.)

SAINT Walstan, a man acceptable to God, was born in the southern part of Great Britain in the vill of Bawburgh. He derived his parentage of distinguished royal stock, his father being called Benedict, his mother Blida. From his earliest childhood, he showed himself in the true intention of his mind to be obedient to the divine will in all things. He showed himself full of the grace of humility towards the greatest and the least, deviod of all pride and arrogance, striving with all his mind and in all honesty to be humble and virtuous with dove-like simplicity.

When he reached the age of twelve, imbued in the spirit by divine inspiration and by the evangelical teaching, 'He who will not renounce all that he has, cannot be my disciple', and having received general permission from his parents, St. Walstan renounced against their will all right of royal succession which he was entitled to thereafter. And so that he might be at leisure to devote himself more freely to prayer and other acts of contemplation without the pomp of the world, he left his birthplace, and did not delay to reach northern parts as quickly as he could.

In the name of Christ St. Walstan bound himself in servitude and as it were in the strictness of obedience to a certain inhabitant of the vill of Taverham so that he should humbly serve him in all things. To such an extent was he inspired with the grace of divine virtue, that not only did he give to the poor the victuals supplied for his own sustenance, but he also distributed his clothes and shoes to needy and sick people, exposing himself bare-foot to various sufferings.

When one day a certain pauper asked alms of St. Walstan and he was moved with great piety, he gave his own footwear to the pauper, on condition that the pauper should not reveal the gift to anyone. But as it has often been said, no pestilence is worse than the familiar enemy, it happened that the evil and most pernicious wife of the man whom St. Walstan was serving found out about this gift. Astutely inventing some plausible necessity, she sent without delay the most holy confessor Walstan barefoot to the wood in order to load thorns and thistles on to a cart. But since Almighty God defends his faithful in all dangers, he miraculously visited St. Walstan, so that he sat and boldly stood with the bare soles of his feet on the sharpest points of the thorns and thistles without suffering any harm from their punctures, as if they were roses redolent with the sweetest fragrance. In proper order, with the Lord's help, he gathered them together into the cart as that opprobrious woman had ordered. When the woman saw this miracle, she recognized the guilt of her iniquity and, throwing herself in floods of tears at St. Walstan's feet, she begged forgiveness. The man of God benignly raised her to her feet and forgave her all the injury she had done to him.

When his master saw the signs and miracles which St. Walstan performed with God's permission, he came to love him devoutly, and publicly declared that he would make him his heir, since he had neither natural nor legitimate offspring. St. Walstan rejected this promise with all his heart, and he asked for his labour nothing more than the offspring to be born to a certain cow, which he asserted would be sufficient reward. His master agreed at once to this request. When the time came, the aforesaid cow gave birth to two male calves, which St. Walstan tended and fed as well as he was able, not out of human greed, but so that God's will might be fulfilled through them, as he had been divinely informed through an angel of God, that is that through them he should be miraculously led to the place where his body would be buried.

When one Friday, St. Walstan was scything with a companion in a certain meadow, the angel of God appeared to him and said, 'Brother Walstan, on the third day from today you will enter paradise', and at once vanished from his sight. Walstan thanked God for this divine revelation of his destiny, and without delay he respectfully asked and most devoutly received confession and with great contrition of heart the sacrament of the precious body and blood of Our Lord Jesus Christ and extreme unction from his priest.

On the next day, the Saturday, at the ninth hour, St. Walstan threw his scythe from him and asserted that he was in no way permitted to work from that hour until the morning of the following Monday, because he could hear at that moment emanating from the celestial realms the sound of heavenly bells and the ineffable notes of trumpets. He said to his companion, 'If you are willing to believe, and to approach me and to place your foot devoutly on my foot, you will see with me the gate of heaven open and angels of God ringing the bells to the glory and praise of the holy and undivided Trinity'.

When the time of St. Walstan's death came, that is the Monday of the following week, he went out as usual to work in the meadow with his companion. There he called together his master and certain other honest persons, he fulfilled his last wish and commended his soul to God, the blessed Virgin Mary, and all the saints. He added in addition that his body should be decently placed in a cart, and that his two bulls should be yoked to it and, without any driver, should take it wherever God should ordain. At once he prostrated himself, and prayed to God, saying, 'O hope and salvation of the believers, O glory and rest of those who labour, good Jesus, grant your servant this mercy, that if a labourer should have any infirmity or other bodily disablement, or if compelled by necessity anyone should reverently visit me with good will and in your holy name on behalf of brute animals, may he not be denied your help and, I pray Lord, may the brute animals be restored to health'. When he had finished speaking, a voice from heaven said: 'O holy Walstan, what you have asked has been granted. Come from your labours to rest, come from your misery to salvation'. And at once in the aforesaid meadow he rendered his spirit to Almighty God. Those who were present with St. Walstan when he went up to heaven and left this world are most veracious witnesses to the fact that it was as if a dove whiter than snow came out of the mouth of the saint and flew up to heaven, disappearing on high in a shining cloud.

Honest persons who were there put the holy body of Walstan on his cart as he had ordained, and the bulls took the road directly towards the wood of Costessey. On that journey the following miracle occurred. When the bulls with the holy body entered a pool of very deep water in the aforesaid wood, God granted this miracle for love and honour of St. Walstan, that the wheels of the cart passed over the yielding and naturally liquid surface of the water as if over land or some other firm and consolidated material without sinking at all. The marks of those wheels are said even today to appear on the surface of the aforesaid water.

Another miracle also happened. When in the aforesaid wood, the bulls stood for a while with the body of St. Walstan on top of a steep hill, a spring of water as a sign of grace for love of St. Walstan appeared against the nature of the place (for until that time no water had been found there) and through divine mercy is still there today.

The bulls went down from that place with the precious body towards the vill of Bawburgh. When they had come almost to the place where the body now lies buried, they made another stop in a certain place, where for love of St. Walstan the divine piety made another spring of wonderful power against fevers and many other infirmities, which is still there today.

The body of the holy man Walstan was placed in the church of Bawburgh, which is dedicated in his name, and for love of him God performs diverse miracles. For there the paralysed are cured, the blind receive sight, the deaf can hear, the mute speak, the lame walk, those with fever are relieved, the possessed are freed from demons, those deprived of their eyes or their genitals are found worthy to receive new members through the merits of St. Walstan. Not only are catholic people freed from various ailments by this saint, but also brute animals suffering from whatever complaints are restored to pristine health.

Dearly beloved, let us commend therefore this solemn day of St. Walstan, who that he might gain everlasting life, left transitory things; that he might live chastely, frequently afflicted his flesh with fasting and gave his victuals to the poor; and that he might remain in constant virtue and humility rejected the royal succession of his parents and bound himself to the service of simple rural persons. O St. Walstan, justly are you to be praised in the church of God. Through the abdication of temporal things you can be compared to the apostles; through the penitential mortification of your flesh you are similar to the martyrs; through the giving of alms and the effusion of holy prayers you are a companion of the confessors.

That excellent man St. Walstan migrated to the Lord in the year of the Incarnation of Our Lord 1016, on 30 May. Sighing after him, dearest brothers, let us follow in his footsteps along the paths of truth and justice and of perfect humility, that we may be worthy to come with him to the realm of light and glory, in which God reigns, world without end, Amen.

APPENDIX VIII

EXTRACT FROM 'THE HISTORY OF ST. WALSTON'

The following is an account of the eleven miracles of Item 8, MS Lambeth 935, as copied by Fr. F.C. Husenbeth on 30th December, 1858, from a transcript of the manuscript executed by Canon J.C. Morris in the same year. The extract appears by kind permission of the Rt. Rev. Leo McCartie, Bishop of Northampton.

Fr. Husenbeth made small and modernising adjustment to several words but did not alter the basic sense of the verse. His most significant change was the substitution of 'Bowthorpe' for 'Crowthorpe'.

In the 1658 copy 'the' appeared as 'ye' and 'them' as 'ym', etc., and are here modernised, as are many of the words which included a double or final 'e' (the 'e' being omitted). This updated extract appears for information only, and anyone wishing to study the text for academic purposes is advised to consult the Lambeth manuscript.

Those extracts from Item 8 which appear in the main body of the book are taken from the version published in 1917 by M.R. James, which were in turn checked against a facsimile copy of Item 8 provided by the Bodleian Library (Oxford University), and are included by permission of Lambeth Library.

(MIRACLE 1)

A lunatic man, mad as any hare,
Brought by his friends to Walston's shrine,
Manacled, in his shirt, and feet bare.
They entered the church at the hour of nine,
A priest to Mass should go that time.
As soon as they prayed St. Walston to
The frenzy and madness was all gone.

(MIRACLE 2)

A woman who dwelled in Bawburgh towne,
When men were shoting in the street,
She moved walking up and down.
A sharpe arrow with her body did meet,
Such time as the sun gave his great heat.
The arrow taken out, she had such grievance
She could neither laugh, sing, nor dance.

Brought she was, as God would it have,
By her friends to Saint Walston,
And laid on the ground next to his grave
She took strength to her anon.
And when all this thing was done
She eat cockles, which was truth,
Out at the wound they came to her friends ruth.

On Walston she prayed and cried fast
To have succour and ready remedy,
Holy Walston hear her in haste
Summoned and healed the woman needy.
A marvellous work of God and speedy
She made a vow when she was here,
To seek St. Walston once in the year.

(MIRACLE 3)

A priest who was born in Honyngham
Thirty and six year of age and more
A wen on his body by growing came
To ride or go it grieved him sore:
In his mind made a vow and God before
To visit St. Walston a remedy to have
Of God and St. Walston devoutly did crave.

As he sat at the tomb with great devotion
Took the water which lay thereupon
In faith anointed his wen to his salvation
Trusting to God and Holy St. Walston
To have remedy, though it be not anon.
Said mass, and prayed to the day's end
God and St. Walston remedy, me send.

That day and the next praying, at the grave,
With water evermore anointing his wen,
Departed weeping remedy could not have.
When he had walked a little from then
He felt a moisture in his hose, broken was the wen.
To the place he looked, the guts appeared out
'I shall turn to holy Walston, and cast no more doubt'.

He came to holy Walston long ere he did dine,
Took the water of the tomb and washed his wound.
It began to dry up, and close well and fine,
Devoutly prayed holy Walston in that stound,
And would not depart from that ground.
God saw his faith and his good intent;
And sent to him health ere thence he went.

(MIRACLE 4)

A woman of [Bowthorpe] Crowthorpe, a town here beside,
Grievously diseased with sickness in her back,
To St. Walston goeth, God be her guide.
She came home again right a great shake.
The great pain in her bones would not slack;
Braiding Walston, said, 'As I am true wife,
I shall never seek thee while that I have life'.

The next day to the field she goeth, for to share
A sickle she takes in her right hand,
With her left wrought to her many an ear.
Divers folk beholding there as she stond,
Marvellous God, what is that sond?
Sickle neither wheat could cast away,
Till she came to Walston the next day.

(MIRACLE 5)

A man in Bawburgh which a shapter [thaxter?] was,
Down fell backwards in a deep pond.
Two days lay there; a marvellous case,
In depthness of the fit upon the sond,
Up take fast knit in death's bond,
To church borne buried to be,
His neighbours following that for to see.

Before Walston's tomb the bier was set,
Soon after men prayed he made moving,
Up they him take anon without letting
To God and St. Walston they made loovyng.
This holy Walston's name doth spring,
In divers and many mo countries than this,
For these and many mo miracles I wys.

(MIRACLE 6)

A knight Sir Gregory Lovell called,
With great sickness and great bone ache,
You shall hear what him befalled,
He was cast down in his bed, nake,
No man to heal durst him take,
Neither in city, burgh nor towne,
Full of pains from foot to the crown.

When he had spent both silver and gold,
Nothing ensued of amendment,
Moveable and unmoveable, he would have sold,
For ease and health had to his intent,
If God to him it would have sent,
Wife and children if he had not had,
And lived in poverty as God bad.

It happened by means of Walston and God's grace,
To muse in mind upon a night,
A meane make to holy Walston in that case,
For water to his well he sent as tyte,
Therewith him washed and also dyte
And remedy readily should have anon,
By the grace of God and holy Walston.

These things done as it is aforesaid,
Within ten days consumed the sickness
To visit St. Walston he made abraid
Felt in his members life and quickness.
Not perfectly recovered, but found faintness
A little while continuing after in great wealth
And found in himself sure and perfect health.

(MIRACLE 7)

A blind man, called Swanton by name,
Had a son might neither stop nor goon,
But in all his after limbs was lame.
One might creep on earth or stand
They prayed to God and St. Walston,
With water of his well did him bathe,
Now goeth right up, and his health hath.

(MIRACLE 8)

In Canterbury a crafty man dwelled full right
A weaver and lived by his occupation
Sore vexed with bone ache both day and night.
Specially of his leg, and judged by estimation
That never to be restored to his operation,
Supported by crutches goeth, Holy Thomas to pray
And so continueth long and many a day.

This pain continued, and would not cease.
It hap'd a pilgrim of this country
St. Thomas to visit his vow to release.
This lame man doth behold: to him goeth he,
'Man' he saith, 'God comfort thee',
And asketh the cause of his grievance.
'I am visited' he saith, 'after God's pleasure.'

The cause briefly declared, the pilgrim said
'To holy Walston labour with all they might,
'Though shalt in that place of God by him have aid,
'And thy lame leg shall be made full right
'Go thou forward on this night
'A leg of wax offer thou also,
'Though shalt have health ere thou go'.

This man in his heart avowed anon
To come to that place wheresoever it is,
Where the body lieth of holy Walston,
He had not gone far from thence I wys
But the pain did slack out of his limbs,
His staves he laid aside then,
To the city of Norwich the way he went.

A leg of wax he did make there
According to his counsel aforesaid,
In his arm he it did bear
To the town Bawburgh and there it laid
Before St. Walston, and heartily prayed
Many foks being when he did depart
Both leg and body hale and quarter.

(MIRACLE 9)

John Pygoot a husband(man) of Carleton town
Here beside dwelling many a day
Visit with God's hand and cast down
Upon the bed in the which he lay
Thirty one weeks his joints aching aye,
He promised to God and to St. Walston also
Him for to visit the first thing that he should do.

To Bawburgh the way he took full right
With great pain upon his crutches did creep
His wife upholding and helping with all her myght
For pain and anguish often moved to weep
Before St. Walston kneeling ere he should sleep,
Praying for health if it should God please,
Soon after in himself he felt great ease.

His crutches laid down, he doth uprise,
The pain greatly slacked, he was full glad,
He talked with the priest, and asked his advice,
With sober countenance, wise words and sad
The priest gave him counsel and also him bad
To pray a season and abide what God would send
He offered there his crutches, and was well amended.

(MIRACLE 10)

St. Walston a petitioner for labourers he was
To God, from whom all succour and health come,
Showed upon a man a marvellous case
In Flegge under a shod cart was nome,
Laden with wheat to all man's dome,
Impossible a man thereunder to abide,
Alive St. Walston saved that tyde.

In harvest time truly this case befel
He laboured to Bawburgh to St. Walston.
When he came there as I you tell
The night was come, the day was gone.
The church key he caught anon
To a neighbour in the town he showed the thing
That by God and St. Walston he was living.

A cart of wax he would have had made
To show the story as it was done.
He might not tarry, for the haste he had
But needs must home, as he was borne
And should turn again hastily and soon
St. Walston to visit. He took the way
Into Flegg to his labour the next day.

(MIRACLE 11)

Katherine, a maid in Bawburgh towne,
Recklessly a pin in her mouth took
From thence into her throat it fell down.
There sorely festered and fast it stook.
She waxed faint, her friends to her did look
She rolled, she coughed, it would not out gone.
They brought her to church to St. Walston.

The time of the day was near the prime,
A priest to Mass should go that tyde.
The maid lay still all that time
St. Walston's help for to abide.
Her friends sait by, and mouth opened wide,
To pray heartily God and Saint Walston
The pin sturt out, the maid went home.

APPENDIX IX

SELECTIVE BIOGRAPHIES

BALE, John (1495-1563). Born at Cove, near Dunwich in Suffolk, he was sent to the Carmelite convent in Norwich at the age of twelve where he learned to be a zealous Roman Catholic. After Cambridge he embarked on a controversial career, first by converting to Protestantism then putting aside his monastic habit in order to take a wife. Prior to becoming Bishop of Ossory, he held livings in Suffolk and Norfolk; his controversial preaching led to his once being arrested on a charge of high treason. Among his prolific writings is *English Votaries*, in which he indulges his tendency to the erotic by comparing Walstan to Priapus, a Greek God represented in a caricature of the human form, grotesquely misshapen, with an enormous phallus.

BENEDICTINES, The Religious Order of (est. early in the 6th century by St. Benedict). The Rule of St. Benedict was brought to Britain by St. Augustine in 597 and grew to become the richest and most famous of all the religious orders. Augustine had been sent by Pope Gregory, who is most famously remembered for having seen Anglo Saxon slaves in a Roman market and determined upon their conversion to Christianity. Commonly called the Black Monks, because of their black robes, the Benedictines had abbeys and cells all over Britain, and the cathedral churches of Bury, Norwich, Westminster and Glastonbury belonged to the Order. Two cells existed in Norfolk, at Wymondham and Binham. The Benedictines appear to have championed St. Walstan, possibly because of their involvement in agriculture and the pioneering work done by the early monks in clearing land for farming.

BLOMEFIELD, Francis (1705-1752). Topographer and writer, he set up a private press in 1736 and began to issue his *History of Norfolk*. The story of Walstan appears under his entry for Bawburgh, (Vol. II). It is one of the most accessible, and therefore oft-quoted, versions of the legend. Blomefield included Bale's reference to Walstan as appearing like the Greek God, Priapus, thereby re-committing this unfortunate comparison to posterity. Three volumes of Blomefield's were published posthumously by the Rev. Charles Parkin. The bulk of material came from work by the Norfolk antiquary, Peter Le Neve (1661-1729); John Kirkpatrick (1686-1728); and Thomas Tanner (*q.v.*). Drawings by the botanist and antiquary, Dawson Turner (1775-1858) were added to Blomefield's *Norfolk* in 1841.

BOLLANDISTS, The. Founded by John Bolland (d. 1665) on the precedent of Fr. Herbert Rosweyde (d. 1629), who attempted to meet Protestant criticism of the Catholic veneration of saints. This society of Jesuit scholars devoted their scholarship to the scientific study of the lives of the saints. Based in Brussels, the first two volumes of their *Acta Sanctorum* was published in 1643. Their sceptical approach to time-honoured legends led both to respect and resentment. The best known of the Bollandists was Hippolyte Delehay (1859-1941); anyone wishing to indulge their scepticism of the lives of the saints should refer to Delehaye's *The Legends of the Saints*.

BUTLER, Alban (1710-1773). Born in Northamptonshire, but educated in France. Ordained priest in 1734. From 1745 to 1756 he was priest and tutor to the Duke of Norfolk's family and resided for a time at Norwich as Missionary Apostolic. Author of *The Lives of the Fathers, Martyrs and Other Principal Saints*, first published in London during 1756-59, he records the sources for the Walstan entry as (i) Capgrave fol. 285; (ii) his old manuscript life; (iii) Blomefield, *History of Norfolk*. Nothing in his account relies on the Lambeth Life and, if he in fact saw Item 8 for himself, did not take Blythburgh as Walstan's birthplace (assuming that (ii) was, in fact, Item 8 and not any other).

CAPGRAVE, John (1393-1464). Augustinian friar, theologian, and historian, he was born in Norfolk, where he lived for most of his life. When an inmate of the Austin Friary at Lynn he wrote several theological and devotional works, the most important being his revision of John of Tynemouth's *Sanctilogium*, which he later published under his own name. His main contribution to the Collection was to change the order of names from that of the calendar to that of the alphabet. Capgrave's *Legends* formed one influence for the 1901 *Nova Legenda Anglie*, but the entry for Walstan in the original 1516 NLA is still, but wrongly, attributed to Capgrave as primary.

DE LA MARE, Thomas (1308-1396). A Benedictine monk, who in 1341 became Prior of Tynemouth, and was elected Abbot of St. Alban's in 1349. He served his probation in the cell of Wymondham during 1335, and was a close friend and fellow scholar of John of Tynemouth. After John's death in 1349, Thomas took responsibility for his friend's manuscripts and it is thought that by this route, a copy of the legend of St. Walstan was eventually deposited in the Benedictine library of Westminster Abbey, where it was found by William Caxton or his foreman, Wynkyne de Worde.

GIBSON, Edmund (1669-1748). One-time Bishop of London, he was domestic chaplain to Archbishop Tenison in 1698. Later, as librarian at Lambeth, he arranged a collection of manuscripts left by the Archbishop which included papers which probably belonged to the Archbishop's close relative, Philip Tenison, Archdeacon of Norfolk. The documents are extant as part of MS Lambeth 935, Item 8 of which is the 1658 copy of *The History of St. Walston.*

HUSENBETH: Frederick Charles, D.D. (1796 - 1872). Ordained Catholic priest in 1820, and in July of that year went to Costessey Hall, near Norwich, as Chaplain to Sir George Stafford Jerningham, who became Baron Stafford in 1824. He lived in Costessey for fifty-two years and opened St. Walstan's Chapel there in 1841. He was appointed Grand Vicar of Norfolk and Suffolk in 1827, and in 1850, Pope Pius IX conferred on him the honorary title of Doctor of Divinity. A scholar and writer of some stature, he championed St. Walstan in much of his work and, when editing Butler's *Lives of the Saints*, did not omit Walstan. In 1859, when Provost of Northampton, he wrote *The Life of Saint Walstan, Confessor.* He died in the presbytery adjoining St. Walstan's and is buried at Costessey. [Note: The Catholic Diocese of East Anglia was not formed until 1976, when Norfolk, Suffolk and Cambridgeshire were removed from the Diocese of Northampton.]

IGNATIUS, Father (1837-1908). Born Joseph Leycester Lyne, at Barking in Essex, he embarked in childhood on a life-long mission of monastic revivalism in the Church of England. After spending some time as an assistant clergyman he moved to Suffolk, where he took his 'vows' under direction of the Rev. George Drury (Vicar of Claydon and Akenham), who gave him the name Ignatius. In 1864 he moved to Norwich and established Elm Hill House as a monastery for his Third Order, where his High Church ideas and eccentric behaviour caused open riots. A revivalist and fundamentalist, his pilgrimage to St. Walstan's Well in 1864 sparked off anti-Catholic riots in Norwich, although he was in fact still a member of the Protestant Church. His host at Claydon, the Rev. Drury, later became a leading figure in what became known as the Akenham Burial Case, brought about principally by a Bapist minister, the Rev. Wickham Tozer. George Drury refused to allow Mr. Tozer to conduct a burial service in Akenham Churchyard and the ensuing proceedings eventually led to the Burial Reform Act of 1880. Part of the interrogation in a libel case brought by Drury against the *East Anglian Daily Times* concerned his association with Ignatius, which by then was badly soured.

JAMES, M.R. (1862-1936). Born the son of a clergyman, near Bury St. Edmunds, he became an eminent linguist, medievalist, palaeographer, and biblical scholar. He also wrote ghost stories, now published as classics. In 1917, while Provost of Eton College, he wrote *Lives of St. Walstan*, for the Norfolk & Norwich Archaeological Society, with a transcript of the English

Life being published for the first time. While he always remained sceptical about the legend of St. Walstan, he included it in *Suffolk and Norfolk* but never really explored its origins in any detail. After more discoveries in the nation's archives, he collaborated with Augustus Jessopp in writing the *Life of St. William of Norwich.*

LELAND, (or LEYLAND) John (l506?-l552). After taking Holy Orders in l525, he became tutor to the younger son of Thomas Howard, Duke of Norfolk. In l533 he was commissioned to search English libraries, abbeys and priories for records, writings and legends and in doing so became the earliest of the English antiquaries and was able to save some of the Medieval legacy fated for destruction by Henry VIII. Bale used much of Leland's work in his own and as a basis for *English Votaries.*

TANNER, Thomas (l674-1735). An antiquarian of lasting importance, he became private chaplain to the Bishop of Norwich in l698, and later collated to the chancellorship of Norwich diocese. In l703 he became Commissary in the Archdeaconry of Norfolk, and three years later Commissary of the Archdeaconry of Sudbury and the town of Bury St. Edmunds, Suffolk. His brother, John, was Vicar of Lowestoft. Tanner wrote prolifically and collected a huge number of manuscripts, though some of inestimable value were badly damaged during a move from Norwich to Oxford when the barge carrying them sank. Although on one occasion material sent to Tanner by Blomefield was lost, it is reasonably certain that at least two of Tanner's folio volumes (in Latin) were used by Blomefield for the *History of Norfolk*, which was dedicated to Tanner.

TENISON, Philip (1612-l660). Born in the Isle of Ely, he later went to Trinity College, Cambridge. In l642 he was instituted to Wethersfield in Essex, afterwards Rector of Hethersett and Foulsham, and later Archdeacon of Norfolk. He is thought to have commissioned the 1658 copy of the triptych, known as Item 8 of MS Lambeth 935. Although he was ejected from vicarship during Cromwell's Rebellion, he lived to be restored to Foulsham and had Grant of Arms in l660, the year of his death. He was related to Edward Tenison of Norwich (1673-1735) and to Archbishop Tenison (*q.v.*) who crowned Queen Anne. The Archdeacon has a shroud brass memorial in Bawburgh Church.

TENISON, Thomas (l636-1715). Grandson of Philip Tenison, he became Archbishop of Canterbury in 1695, having served as Upper Minister at St. Peter Mancroft, Norwich. When Rector of St Martin-in-the-Fields, Tenison founded the first public library. During his lifetime he acquired a valuable library of his own, which was later collated by Edmund Gibson when he was librarian at Lambeth. Item 8, the 1658 English Life, bears his inscription and formed part of the Archbishop's manuscription collection which he passed to Gibson. His son, John Tenison, became Rector of Mundesley, Norfolk. Thomas Tenison is best remembered for having crowned Queen Anne in 1702; for being an anti-Roman controversialist; and as a founder member of the Religious Societies (now SPCK).

TYNEMOUTH, John of (?1290-1349). Historian and Benedictine monk, his *Sanctilogium* formed the basis for the 1516 *Nova Legenda Anglie*. Although the Collection was later edited by Capgrave, and has become known by that name, the authorship was John of Tynemouth's and represents one of the earliest attempts at a compendium of lives for English saints. One time vicar of Tynemouth Priory, he joined the Benedictine Order of St. Alban's and sometime during the 1340s returned to the Hertfordshire Mother House when he began writing. He toured England in search of material for his collection of 157 saints' lives. It was previously thought that the *De Sancto Walstano Confessore* of the *Nova Legenda Anglie* was taken from a MS by John of Tynemouth but this has now been found to be unsubstantiated.

WREN, Matthew (1585-1667). Ordained deacon and priest in 1611, he was translated by Archbishop Laud to Norwich in November, 1635, where he succeeded in raising the temperature of the East Anglian puritans. He married Elizabeth Cutler of Ringshall, Suffolk, and had nine children, though several of them died in infancy. The architect, Sir Christopher Wren, was his nephew. In 1637 Wren ordered that Bawburgh Church be restored and in 1639 attempted to get Bowthorpe Church re-built. Wren's own determined antagonism towards the Puritan ideal resulted in his rousing puritanism in East Anglia to a dangerous pitch of rebellious fury at a very critical time.

YOUNG, Rev. Gabriel (1845-1934). Born in Ceylon, his family returned to England in the 1860s and Gabriel was ordained at Ripon in 1869. After holding curacies at Acle, Coddenham, and Acle again, he and his (by then) wife and children arrived in Bawburgh to take the Vicarship of St. Mary & St. Walstan in 1892. (The Rev. Hicks Thomas Deacle had died in 1891, after 31 years as Vicar.) The Rev. Young caused extensive renovations to be made to the Church, which he found in a deplorable state of repair. His wife, Caroline, died in 1904, and youngest daughter, Agnes, the following year. He served the church and village of Bawburgh for almost forty years, until his retirement in 1931. His remaining two daughters, Helena and Margaret (known as Marjorie) followed their father in becoming village stalwarts. In 1971 parishioners commissioned the statue of St. Walstan in memory of Margaret; it now stands in front of the window which replaces the entrance to the old Shrine Chapel. Gabriel's son Annesley went to America eventually becoming Priest in Charge of the Church of the Divine Love in Montrose.

BIBLIOGRAPHY

ATTWATER, Donald *Father Ignatius of Llanthony* (Cassell & Company Ltd., 1931)

ATTWATER, Donald *A Dictionary of Saints* (Burns Oates & Washbourne Ltd., 1938)

ATTWATER, Donald *The Penguin Dictionary of Saints* (Penguin, 1965)

BALE, Bishop *English Votaries* (1546)

BARRETT, W.H., and GARROD, R.P. *East Anglian Folklore and Other Tales* (Routledge & Kegan Paul, 1976)

BAUD, Dom J., O.S.B. *Dictionnaire d'Hagiographie* (Paris, 1925)

BENEDICTINE Monks of St. Augustine's Abbey, Ramsgate *The Book of Saints* (Adam & Charles Black, 1947)

BERTOUCH, the Baroness de *The Life of Fr. Ignatius, OSB, The Monk of Llanthony* (Methuen, 1904)

BLOMEFIELD, Francis *History of Norfolk* (1805)

BOND, Francis *Dedications & Patron Saints of English Churches* (OUP, 1914)

BORD, Janet & Colin *Sacred Waters* (Granada Publishing, 1985)

BRYANT, T. Hugh *The Churches of Norfolk* (1898-1915)

BUTLER, Rev. Alban *The Lives of the Fathers, Martyrs, and Other Principal Saints* (Various Editions)

BUTLER, Rev. Alban *The Lives of the Fathers, Martyrs, and Other Principal Saints* (D. & J. Sadlier, New York. 1853)

Butler's Lives of the Saints, Ed. H. Thurston & D. Attwater (1956)

Butler's Lives of the Saints, Ed. Michael Walsh (Burns & Oates, 1991)

Butler's Lives of Patron Saints Ed. Michael Walsh (Burns & Oates, 1987)

BUTLER, N.V. Pierce *A Book of British Saints* (The Faith Press Ltd., 1957)

CHALLONER, Bishop *A Memorial of Ancient British Piety* (1761)

COOK, G.H. *Medieval Chantries & Chantry Chapels* (Phoenix House, 1963)

COX, Charles J. *County Churches of Norfolk Vols. 1 & 2* (George Allen & Co. Ltd., 1911)

DELEHAYE, Hippolyte *The Legends of the Saints* (Translation by Donald Attwater, Geoffrey Chapman, 1962)

DIXON, G.M. *Folktales and Legends of Norfolk* (Minimax Books, 1980)

DRAKE, Maurice and Wilfred *Saints and Their Emblems* (Warner Laurie, 1916)

DUFFY, Eamon *The Stripping of the Altars* (Yale UP, 1992)

DUKINFIELD, Astley, H.J. *Memorials of Old Norfolk* (Bemrose & Son, 1908)

DUTT, William A. *Norfolk* (Methuen, 7th Edition, 1929 & Various Editions)

DUTT, William A. *Highways and Byways in East Anglia* (Macmillan, 1923)

FARMER, David Hugh *The Oxford Dictionary of Saints, 2nd Ed.* (OUP, 1987)

GARDNER, Thomas *An Historical Account of Dunwich, Blithburgh, Southwold with remarks on some places contiguous thereto* (1754)

HOLWECK, Rt. Rev. F.G. *A Biographical Dictionary of the Saints* (B. Herder Book Co., 1924)

HORSTMAN, Carl Ph.D. *Nova Legenda Anglie* (Clarendon Press, Oxford, 1901)

HUSENBETH, F.C. *The Life of Saint Walstan, Confessor* (Thomas Jones, 1859)

HUSENBETH, F.C. (Ed) *Butler's Lives of the Saints* (1857-60)

HUSENBETH, F.C. *Emblems of Saints by which they are distinguished in works of Art* (Burns & Lambert, 1850)

KETTON-CREMER, R.W. *Norfolk in the Civil War* (Faber & Faber, 1969)

KEYSER, C.E. *List of Buildings in Great Britain having Mural and Other Painted Decorations* (1883)

JAMES, M.R. *Suffolk and Norfolk* (J.M. Dent & Sons Ltd., 1930)

JESSOPP, Augustus, D.D. *One Generation of a Norfolk House* (Burns & Oats, 1878)

LONG, Rev. Sidney *The History of the Church and Parish of St. James with Pockthorpe, Norwich* (Graham Cummings, c. 1961)

MARSDEN, Walter *The Resting Places of East Anglia* (Ian Henry Publications, 1987)

MARSHALL, Arthur Calder *The Enthusiast* (Faber & Faber, 1962)

MEE, Arthur *Norfolk, Suffolk, Essex* and other volumes of *The King's England* series (Hodder & Stoughton, c. 1940s)

MESSENT, Claude J.W. *The City Churches of Norwich* (H.W. Hunt, 1932)

MILBURN, R.L.P. *Saints and Their Emblems in English Churches* (Oxford University Press, 1949)

MORTLOCK, D.P. *The Popular Guide to Suffolk Churches* (3 Vols) (Acorn Editions, 1988)

MORTLOCK, D.P. & ROBERTS, C.V. *The Popular Guide to Norfolk Churches* (3 Vols) (Acorn Edition, 1985)

NORGATE, T.B. *An Illustrated History of Taverham* (1969)

NORGATE, T.B. *The History of Costessey* (1972)

OLLARD, S.L. and CROSSE, Gordon *A Dictionary of English Church History* (A.R. Mowbray, 1912)

PAINE, Clive *St. Mary's, Bury St. Edmunds* (1986)

PAINTER George D. *William Caxton* (Chatto & Windus, 1976)

PICTON *A Great Gothic Fane* (W.T. Pike & Co., Brighton, 1913)

PYNSON, Richarde *The Kalendre of the newe Legende of Englande* (1516)

ROEDER, Helen *Saints and their Attributes* (Longmans, 1955)

ROLLASON, David *Saints and Relics in Anglo-Saxon England* (Basil Blackwell, 1989)

RYE, Walter *Some Early English Inscriptions in Norfolk* (Various Editions)

SHORTT, L.M. *Lives & Legends of English Saints* (Methuen, 1914)

STANTON, Richard *A Menology of England and Wales* (1892)

STEER, Francis W. *The History of the Dunmow Flitch Ceremony* (Essex Record Office Publications, 1951)

TAYLOR, Richard *Index Monasticus* (1821)

TWINCH, Carol *A Village Guide* (1981)

TWINCH, Carol *A Brief Guide to the History of St. Mary & St. Walstan, Bawburgh, Norfolk* (1982 and 1987)

TWINCH, Carol (Ed) *Walstan of Bawburgh* (Media Associates, 1989)

TYMMS, Samuel *St. Mary's Church, Bury St. Edmunds* (1854)

TYMMS, Samuel *Handbook of Bury St. Edmunds* (Various Editions)

WESTWOOD, Jennifer *Gothick Norfolk* (Shire Publications, 1989)

WILLIAMSON, Tom *The Origins of Norfolk* (Manchester University Press, 1993)

WYNKYNE de Worde *Nova Legenda Anglie* (1516)

Victoria History of the Counties of Norfolk, Suffolk and Essex (c. 1906)

VINCE, John *Discovering Saints in Britain* (Shire Publications, 1990)

VORAGINE, Jacobus de *The Golden Legend* (Translated by William Granger Ryan, Princeton UP, 1993)

Also:

MS 3041: Nicholas Roscarrock

Catalogue of the Manuscripts in the Cottonian Library (extract), Thomas Smith, 1696

MS Lambeth 935, Item 8

MS (Bodleian) Lat. Liturg. g. 8 (litany fol. 3v)

The Will of Sir Wm. Gardiner, Priest (Bury Record Office, Pye/J545/5)

Extracts from The Proceedings of the Norfolk & Norwich Archaeological Society include:

Lives of St. Walstan, M.R. James (Vol. 19, 1917)
A Prehistoric Site in the Yare Valley Henry de Caux (Vol. XXVIII)
Bowthorpe Hall Rev. Augustus Jessopp (Vol. 8, 1877)
Bawburgh Old Hall (Vol. 23)
The Shrines & Pilgrimages of the County of Norfolk Rev. Richard Hart (Vol. 6, 1864)
Mural Paintings in Norwich Cathedral Rev. F.C. Husenbeth, CC (Vol. 6, 1864)
Saints on Norfolk Rood Screens and Pulpits W.W. Williamson (Vol. XXXI, 1957)
Medieval Roodscreens in Norfolk and *The Roodscreens of Norfolk Churches* Dr. Simon Cotton (Vol. 40)

Extracts from the Eastern Daily Press include:

New Role for Norfolk's Gentle Giant, Charles Roberts (23rd January, 1989)
A Farming Saint Mavis Scarles (14th May, 1983)
A Norfolk Lourdes (September 1913)
Pilgrimage to Holy Well of St. Walstan (August, 1931)

Miscellaneous articles and extracts (not in alphabetical or date order):

Bawburgh News, Nos. 1 – 96 (Editor Carol Twinch)

Bawburgh News, Nos. 97 to date (Editor Betty Martins)

A.M.D.G. *St. Walstan and the Miraculous Well at Babur* (Edition undated but attributed as reprint from *Norwich Mercury*, Saturday, 19th November, 1898)
Note: The original was by Husenbeth probably in leaflet form, a copy of which was used by the *Norwich Mercury* (A.M.D.G., *ad majorem Dei gloriam*, to the greater glory of God).

The Gentleman's Magazine & Historical Chronicle, July-September, 1763

The Gentleman's Magazine Library, 1896 (Classified Collection, 1731-1868)

History of Antiquities of the County of Norfolk (Armstrong) Vol. IV

A Cell of Healing Eldred Willey (*The Tablet*, December, 1991)

A Head Office Outing (*The Norwich Union*, Midsummer, 1903)

The Little Known Saint Carol Twinch (*Town & Country*, May, 1979)

Farmworkers' Own Saint Carol Twinch (*Farming News*, June, 1984)

St. Walstan of Bawburgh, B.H. Pettitt (*Norfolk Fair*, December, 1978)

Bawburgh and St. Walstan H. de Caux (*East Anglian Magazine*, 1948)

Saints of East Anglia N.V. Pierce Butler (*East Anglian Magazine*, May, 1952)

St. Walstan of Bawburgh, An Intriguing Local Saint of the Soil Ian Martin (*East Anglian Magazine*, July, 1978)

A History of Church Farmhouse Geoffrey Kelly (Privately Published, 1988)

Story of St. Walstan Walter J. Piper (*Northamptonshire Diocesan Magazine*, 1915)

In Memoriam, Fr. F.C. Husenbeth (*Northampton Catholic Magazine*, Vol. 14, November, 1872)

St. Walstan R.C. Fiske (*The Norfolk Ancestor*, Vol. 2, September, 1981)

A Norfolk Holy Well Peter Fitzjohn (*East Anglian Magazine*, July, 1934)

A Norfolk Miscellany, St. Walstan of Bawburgh S.G. Thicknesse (*Eastern Daily Press*, Undated)

Norfolk Village's Forgotten Saints (*East Anglian Post*, June, 1988)

The Pride of Norfolk Paul Johnson (*East Anglian Magazine*, July, 1958)

A Forgotten Shrine in Norfolk Leslie Nicolson (*Church Times*, 1956)

Norfolk Fair Album Philip Hepworth (*Norfolk Fair*, Undated)

Something About Foxearth Church Kenneth Nice (1993)

Some Notes on the Rood Screens of Norfolk John T. Varden (*East Anglian Handbook*, 1890)

The Saint with a Scythe Miriam Gill (Submitted for publication in *The Suffolk Institute of Archaeological Proceedings*)

Stonham Earl Meeting and Excursion 1871 (*Suffolk Institute of Archaeological Proceedings*, Vol. V)

Will of Theodred, Bishop of London (*Suffolk Institute of Archaeological Proceedings*, Vol. VII). *Note:* In the will of Theodred (who was also Bishop of Hoxne) at Bury St Edmunds, he says: 'And I give Wolston the land at Wortham as it stands.'

A Thousand Years of Village History, Ashby, Suffolk Rev. Dr. Edward C. Brooks (Ash Trust, 1990)

Taking the Waters in Norfolk Mary Manning (Norfolk Industrial Archaeological Society, 1993)

Rumburgh Remembered Caroline Cardwell (1977)

In and Around the Village of Walberswick Merle Tidey (1987)

St. Andrew's, Walberswick, History of the Church (1988)

St. Walstan of Bawburgh Robert Halliday (Journal of the Norfolk Archaeological and Historical Research Group, No.13, 1994)

Plus numerous articles, letters, histories and anthologies, too numerous to mention – and many of them anonymously written – but each important in their contribution to this search for the legend of St. Walstan.

INDEX